Understanding Conflict and the Science of Peace

Walter Isard

BLACKWELL
Cambridge MA & Oxford UK

First published 1992

Blackwell Publishers
Three Cambridge Center
Cambridge, Massachusetts 02142
USA

108 Cowley Road
Oxford OX4 1JF
UK

Library of Congress Cataloging-in-Publication Data

Isard, Walter.
    Understanding conflict and the science of peace / Walter Isard.
        p.   cm.
    Includes bibliographical references and index.
    ISBN 1-55786-310-5 (alk. paper).—ISBN 1-55786-311-3 (pbk. alk. paper)
    1. Peace—Research. 2. International relations—Research.
3. Conflict management—Research. I. Title.
JX1952.I775   1992
327.1'72'072—dc20   91-35772
                                                                               CIP

British Library Cataloguing in Publication Data

A CIP catalogue record for this book is available from the British Library.

Typeset in 10½ on 13 pt. Baskerville by ST Associates, Wakefield, MA
Printed in the USA

This book is printed on acid free paper.

Contents

Preface

I was born shortly after the end of World War I. Throughout the 1920s (middle and late) and 1930s, I heard a great deal about that war. Associated with my memories of this and the diverse theories of the war's causes are vivid recollections of the stock market crash and all the subsequent hypotheses about why it happened. I went through the dismal 1930s, and upon high school graduation joined the numberless jobless, frustrated in the search for work. I was a conscientious objector during World War II, unable to see any rationality in war itself. Later, I saw and wrote about the Vietnam War, and for four decades pondered over the USA–USSR confrontation and the many years of the Cold War – witnessing at the end the unbelievable and unpredictable political breakdown of the Soviet system and the unification of the East and West Germanies.

As one trained in economics, I try to understand what is going on in Eastern Europe and note the virtual inability of many distinguished colleagues to steer this area's economies through major transitions necessitated by the collapse of Soviet authoritarianism. For some years, I have had to admit that we economists (including some highly abstract mathematical scholars, whose writings I, fortunately also trained in mathematics, can digest) have little understanding of the ups and downs of the stock market and, more important, of economic activity, and have limited ability to prescribe desirable economic policy.

Finally, as I write this book, I am witnessing the Iraq–U.S. confrontation, the conduct of another war, and the subsequent efforts to control the inflammable Middle East conflict.

My memories and my thinking over six decades lead me, as many others have been led, to the conclusion that those struggling for arms control, prevention of war, and maintenance of peace must deal with extremely complex phenomena. No one – and I do mean no one – can fully understand these phenomena. (Frequently major economic forces are involved, and economists certainly do not fully grasp the interplay of these.) It is quite possible that a little knowledge of a problem may result in policies that lead to worse outcomes than policies based on no knowledge at all. (I myself am guilty of contributing a little knowledge to a complex problem, which I think has probably helped to generate a worse outcome than would otherwise have come about.) Nevertheless, I am inclined to go along with my colleagues in believing that in general some knowledge is better than none, and more is better than less, and that some of our efforts may do some good. Thus, I write this book. It is my hope that the limited knowledge herein may lead to better policy and better outcomes.

Recently, I had occasion to read John Maynard Keynes's classic treatise, "The Economic Consequences of the Peace," written in his youth in 1919 while the Big Four were writing the World War I peace treaty. He stated vehemently, "If the European Civil War is to end with France and Italy abusing their momentary victorious power to destroy Germany and Austria–Hungary now prostrate, they invite their own destruction also, being so deeply and inextricably intertwined with their victims by hidden psychic and economic bonds" (p. 5). He went on to deride Britain and the United States as passive, unconcerned, and/or *knowledgeless* onlookers. He was opposed to the severe reparations imposed on Germany. Now, with World War II behind us, we may well ask: did not these reparation burdens intensify Germany's economic plight, especially during the 1930s, and generate long-lasting resentment which made possible the rise of Hitler and a still more devastating world war?

Keynes lamented the Big Four's limited perspective which he attributed by and large to limited knowledge. (Of course, we must acknowledge that had the Big Four constructed a peace treaty along the lines Keynes recommended, we cannot state incontrovertibly that the outcome would have been better.) His was an appeal for political leadership with greater vision based in large part on greater knowledge.

During the Cold War era, I too was impressed by political leaders' limited knowledge concerning arms escalation and control and the back-and-forth effects of forces that can lead to war. In the Preface to *Arms Races, Arms Control and Conflict Analysis* (1988) I wrote: "After all no one knows all there is to know about the *interplay* of forces governing a major conflict, say, the U.S.–Soviet arms control conflict. For example, consider two of the major figures deeply involved in the U.S.–Soviet negotiations on arms control (1986–7) while this book was being written: U.S. Secretary of State George Shultz, whom I came to know when both of us taught elementary economics at MIT using the Samuelson textbook in its first mimeographed form, and Ambassador

Max Kampleman (Head, U.S. Delegation to Negotiations on Nuclear and Space Arms), with whom I engaged in extensive discussions when we were fellow conscientious objectors at the Big Flats campsite during World War II. Both have brilliant minds, tremendous intellectual capacities, and enormous stocks of knowledge. Yet each could learn much about the U.S.–Soviet arms control problem from writings of scholars reported upon in this book" (writings from many different disciplines).

This present book, too, is motivated by a desire to bring together in one place knowledge obtainable from a number of disciplines—to provide a multidisciplinary background for understanding conflicts and the peace-making process. Unlike the *Arms Races* book, which was written for scholars and designed to present rigorous analysis with no hesitancy at using mathematics, this book aims to present materials in an elementary textbook fashion so that anyone who can add, subtract, multiply, and divide can read what scholars from several different disciplines have said. The sections requiring somewhat more involved multiplication and some ninth-grade algebra are marked OPTIONAL and may be skipped without interfering with the flow of the argument. Readers who want more information on particular points or who seek deeper analysis of certain relationships may refer to the *Arms Races* book, from which practically all the materials and analysis in this book are drawn.

Besides exposing readers lacking training in mathematics to basic knowledge from several disciplines, this book has another purpose. Like many political leaders and laypersons who are "culture blind"– who fail to know about or understand the ways and behavior patterns of cultures other than their own – scholars, too, are culture blind. A well-trained economist typically knows relatively little about political, sociological, psychological, geographic/regional science, and anthropological factors affecting behavior and tends to explain everything in terms of the economic culture. Similarly, the political scientist, the psychologist, and the anthropologist each has a limited mind-set. In essence, each discipline has developed its own culture. All too often, in studying behavior, scholars fail to give adequate weight to factors outside their own disciplines, and to appreciate the methods and understand the mathematics used in other fields. Scholars interested in my *Arms Races* book may have found it useful to read the chapters dealing with materials from their own and closely allied disciplines, but may have stopped short of reading materials from distant disciplines with whose tools, methods, and theories they were unfamiliar.

This book, however, in restricting itself to an elementary textbook presentation of materials, should make it easy for scholars to broaden their range of knowledge concerning relevant factors from other fields. Of course, readers may find the material relating to their own field much oversimplified. I apologize for this, but it is unavoidable in a short book. I hope these same readers will find rewarding other materials, especially the analysis of the interplay of factors.

One caveat. This book aims at a multidisciplinary approach. Obviously all the relevant knowledge cannot be covered. There is much too much to know and understand. Nor have I, being trained in economics and mathematics, been able to avoid bias in the materials and analysis I have chosen to present. Nevertheless, I believe that the coverage is sufficiently extensive and objective to provide most readers–scholars, political leaders, and informed laypersons – with new, useful knowledge and analytical insights beyond their own disciplines and specializations.

This book has one additional, perhaps more important aim. It has been designed to provide basic materials for college courses at the undergraduate level. It aims to deepen understanding of conflict situations, how they arise, escalate, and de-escalate, and how they can be managed and resolved, partially if not wholly.

It can serve as a textbook for courses in peace studies and peace science. Those teaching undergraduates may wish to use this book as core reading, with or without the more analytical sections. In doing so, they will need to assign supplementary readings – especially from areas that have not been properly addressed or touched upon in this book (theology, history, game theory). Other teachers may wish to use this book as supplementary reading in areas not covered in core materials assigned in their courses. Those teaching peace economics courses, for example, might want to do this. This book may also be assigned as reading in general education courses, particularly those that attempt to deepen their students' analytical thinking on social problems.

My motivation to write this book stems from the way traditional disciplines have discouraged a balanced presentation of conflict analysis materials to college undergraduates. It has often been said that with our youth lies the future of civilization, and it is incumbent upon us to furnish them with a much more balanced stock of knowledge relating to civilization-threatening conflicts.

Walter Isard
Cornell University
July 1991

Acknowledgments

In writing this book, I have had tremendous help from my wife, Cary. She has provided support and encouragement, has gracefully put up with the inconveniences that go with writing still another book, and has provided many hours of invaluable editorial assistance.

I am also indebted to a host of scholars from various disciplines who presented ideas at conferences of the Peace Science Society (International) and ECAAR (Economists Against the Arms Race). This book is primarily a restatement of their thinking, hopefully ordered in a systematic fashion that leads to analytical fusion. Many of their ideas are contained in the 29 volumes of *Papers* published by the Peace Science Society (International), later replaced by the *Journal of Peace Science*, now renamed *Conflict Management and Peace Science*.

At the risk of failing to mention the many scholars whose analyses and suggestions have influenced my thought and my writing, let me nevertheless mention some: Norman Alcock, Heyward Alker, Charles Anderton, Kenneth Boulding, Steven Brams, Stuart Bremer, Stanley Brunn, Nazli Choucri, Claudio Cioffi-Revilla, Karl Deutsch, Roger Fisher, Bruce Fitzgerald, Thomas Fogarty, Stephen Gale, Michael Intriligator, Douglas Johnson, Herbert Kelman, Lawrence Klein, Robert Kuenne, Harold Lasswell, Wassily Leontief, Nancy Meiners, Richard Merritt, Robert North, Anatole Rapoport, Bruce Russett, Thomas Saaty, Thomas Schelling, David Singer, Christine Smith, Jan Tinbergen, Murray Wolfson, Julian Wolpert, and Dina Zinnes.

Teresa Thresher has provided patient and outstanding assistance in the preparation of the manuscript and figures. Helena Wood was also exceedingly helpful.

Cambridge University Press has kindly permitted me to use materials contained in my book *Arms Races, Arms Control and Conflict Analysis: Contributions from Peace Science and Peace Economics*. The Peace Science Society (International) has permitted me to use materials from my article "Progress in Global Modelling for World Policy on Arms Control and Environmental Management," *Conflict Management and Peace Science*, 11:1, 1990, pp. 57–94.

Finally, in writing this book and others, I wish to acknowledge the valuable direct and indirect assistance provided by the very helpful staff of the Reference Department at Cornell University's Olin Library. Caroline T. Spicer, the department head, in my opinion has built up – from the standpoint of information friendliness, accessibility, and coverage – one of the best, if not *the* best reference facility in all the university, city, and national libraries at which I have searched for knowledge during almost three-score years.

1 *Introduction and Overview*

The history of humankind and the rise and fall of civilizations is unquestionably a story of conflict. Conflict is inherent in human activities. It is omnipresent and foreordained.

These are strong statements. Yet they are indisputable. Pick any point in history. Hone in on a fight between primitive man[1] and a carnivorous beast. This is a zero-sum game. To survive, each needs to devour the other. The payoff to the victor is +1, to the loser, –1. The sum is zero.

The simple zero-sum game became more involved. Nature endowed modern humans with superior brains. Homo sapiens acquired a much greater capacity than other species to think through problems and to learn. The species discovered, for example, that a team of two could increase the probability of victory. But then the spoils had to be divided. Should there be an equal division, with payoffs +1/2, +1/2, and -1 (still zero sum), or should the stronger be entitled to a larger share? If so, how much larger? Had a simple conflict led to a more involved conflict?

Human learning took another direction: tools were discovered and hence weapons could be fashioned. Traps were set. Thus, each individual could have a prey, and conflict over division could be avoided.

However, the problem did not remain and was perhaps never this simple. What happened when the stock of prey was depleted? Who had the right to hunt the remaining beasts? What happened when humans multiplied and there were more mouths to feed than food to go around. Resources became scarce. Is this not the problem today with billions of people living on earth and millions starving? Is not the current confrontation between Arab and urban-industrialized countries a conflict over control and use of resources–oil now being the key one? Assuming the world survives chemical, biological, and/or nuclear warfare, are major conflicts impending over use of limited environmental resources, and the limited capability of the environment to absorb CO_2 and other emissions caused by human activity?

Unhappily, the answer to these questions is yes! This stems from the interplay of numerous social, political, and economic forces–such as cultural traits which affect birth and death rates and population size and insatiable wants of people–forces that press societies and their leaders to seek more resource inputs for more production of more goods. Trade is a civilized means for societies to obtain more resource inputs–say, when each of two societies has a resource surplus the other needs. Military venture, however, is also a frequently used means of grabbing resources–either directly from another society, such as Iraq's recent seizure of Kuwait, and/or indirectly through control of other populations and their activities, such as Britain and its colonies in former times.

In the following chapters we shall examine some of the basic forces and behavior leading to military ventures or the threat of such–or to the buildup and build-down of military capabilities.

1.1 Some underlying drives

To have reached the present level of civilization (if one can characterize our state of affairs as civilized), man must have been simultaneously: (1) competitive; (2) curious and inventive; (3) cooperative; and (4) self-propagating.

1. *Competitive* In the game of survival, given two men equal in physical strength and brains, the more aggressive and determined man, the one more inclined to fight, was more likely to survive a battle against a beast. The more complacent, lazy, indifferent, non-aggressive man was less likely to come out alive.

2. *Curious and inventive* Having a good brain and being curious per se, coupled with needing to do battle for food, led early man to fashion tools, to figure out new ways of doing things–in short, to develop technology. Over the long run, both military and non-military technology has moved forward, not necessarily continuously and not without steps backward. And it can be expected to do so indefinitely. Space exploration, the desire to answer the question, how did the universe come about? will lead to more and more development–perhaps to technology beyond our control?

3. *Cooperative* Given a need for food to survive and for shelter to protect against a harsh environment, early man faced challenges beyond the capacity of a single being. To move a boulder blocking the opening of an ideal cave, to overcome a mammoth, and to perform other difficult tasks required more than one person. Moreover, the mating and the need to nurture offspring led to speciali-

zation of tasks between the sexes. (Cooperation and specialization, of course, were not confined to Homo sapiens; other animal societies exploited their advantages.) All the while, man's aggressive nature and propensity to fight has caused clashes between groups (cooperation and competition being internal to each)–between clans, then tribes, then larger communities–nowadays between countries with populations in the millions, between alliances of nations with hundreds of millions, and probably in the near future between whole cultures spanning the globe. At the same time, cooperation and specialization within groups has led to further technological development (tools, machines). Tremendous advances in communication have led to new forms of social, economic, and political organization (for example, multinational enterprises and world institutions aiming to manage conflicts). Within groups, of course, a very limited number of saintly and altruistic units emerged to foster cooperation among the aggressive units, thereby deriving self-esteem, peace of mind, gratification, and other positive returns (praise, respect). But their impact has not been able to brake man's competitive, aggressive drives.

4. *Self-propagating* For humans to continue to exist, self-propagation was necessary. And since at any time aggressive and determined individuals were more likely to survive, their genes (the source of their aggressiveness and determination) were the ones most likely to be passed on. Over time, genes embodying complacent and nonaggressive traits were likely to be eliminated in a species. Furthermore, the more vigorous pursuit by aggressive personalities of scale economies and advantages from specialization within cooperative organizations of ever increasing size has tended to increase the power of weapons and the probability of mass destruction.

These are broad generalizations, involving major simplification, and ignoring socialization processes, education, environmental shocks, and other important forces. Attention to these can lead and has led others to different, equally valid interpretations of human evolution.

Given our simplified depiction of the evolution of civilization as being unavoidably subject to conflict, even massive conflict (and this will be true for many other interpretations), one may well ask, has there been progress?–at least during the last half of the 20th century? Can we even define progress? Old and experienced men, even the wisest among them, often have given up after decades of struggling for "ideals." If they cannot see progress–if they can only point to ever-widening aggression and warfare–and if some, in their disillusion-ment, conclude that there is no use in struggling to resolve conflicts–should others concur?

Indeed no! The desire to survive and experience life's sensual, emotional, and other gratifications is too strong. Let youth pay no attention to such wise old men–and cling to their own ideals.

So on with the book–in essence a book on understanding conflict, on effective conflict management, and hence a challenge to those with "desire-to-survive" genes who want to exercise some control over life-threatening conflicts among societies to enhance their enjoyment of life and reap its rewards.

The next chapter examines some of the most basic underlying forces leading to conflict. These are cultural or culture-oriented. Religious differences, nationalism, contrasts in ideologies, and the propensity of groups to adopt "US" and "THEM" categories are dis-cussed as conflictual factors; so also is culture as a constraint on individual behavior–all as seen by cultural anthropologists, social organization scholars, and some psychiatrists.

To the cultural perspective of individual behavior, chapter 3 adds the analytical thinking of economists and game theorists. It considers the key attitude variable, strategy in an internation conflict situation (as in a Prisoner's Dilemma game), and arms escalation and de-escalation and their control.

The economist's and game theorist's perspective of what governs behavior (within a given environment) is inadequate for a cognitive scientist, psychologist, and sociologist. As developed in chapter 4, these scholars attach critical importance to: the role of scripts, schemas, lessons of history, and other mental representations; learn-ing from experience and from search and problem solving; political subculture influences; and the impact of psychological stress on behavior in crises and the play of behavioral pathologies.

But central to all internation conflict is politics, the arena of the political scientist. Chapter 5 examines the crucial behavior of political leaders–their drive to maximize power or voter support; their sensi-tivity to interest group pressures; their competition and need to form coalitions; and their concentration on the short run. It also takes up the impact of geography and resources on behavior and nation power.

To set forth an effective policy, foreign or domestic, advocates often must present data to support their claims. Chapter 6 deals with data-generating methods and models–for example, projection of impacts of arms expenditures on economic welfare (national and local income, industrial output, and employment)–all also helpful for evaluating different policies.

But as so often happens, two (or more) political leaders set forth contrasting policies, each based on an argument appealing to a leader's constituency. Chapters 7 and 8 look at ways to manage or settle conflicts that may result–paying attention to key characteristics of conflict situations, principles of negotiation and mediation, and qualitative and quantitative conflict management procedures with properties to match the key characteristics–and with some reference to ongoing conflicts.

The last chapter attempts to synthesize all the material presented earlier. One must recognize that most analysts, negotiators, mediators, and other third parties have been trained in a particular discipline, profession, or business, be it political science, sociology, economics, regional science, geography, anthropology, law, engineering, diplomacy, theology, finance, or some other. As a consequence, each one approaches a conflict wearing the blinders of that discipline, often reinforced by life experiences and the principle of cognitive consistency (which we shall discuss). It is hoped that this synthesis will help these individuals to understand some of the factors they may knowingly or unknowingly have ignored or played down, and to gain much deeper insight into the interplay of all factors; and provide students interested in conflict analysis and peace studies with a balanced background for their life's work. The interdisciplinary field of peace science will some day blossom so that training in conflict analysis and management can be obtained in a much more balanced fashion and be more effective than at present.

Notes

1 For ease of reading, by "man," "he," and "his," I mean "man/woman," "he/she," and "his/her," respectively.

2 Cultural Background: Anthropological and Social Organization Approaches

2.1   Introduction

We start this text by looking at culture. We know that there are striking differences among cultures and that these differences are a major factor in generating conflicts and causing wars. If we can know what lies behind the differences–say, between the Arabs and the industrialized Western societies–perhaps we can better control the intense conflicts they generate. Moreover, we need to understand cultural differences in order to investigate how they can be preserved when desirable–and preserved without giving rise to major, violent conflict. To begin, we must define culture.

2.2   Definitions of culture

Culture is a very complex concept. Many definitions have been offered. The anthropologist, the sociologist, the psychologist and other specialists each defines it differently in accordance with the core of his own discipline. Each discipline is concerned with how culture influences action and how in turn action influences culture. Because peace scientists are also concerned with action, it helps to examine these different definitions and to come to our own understanding of the concept. The actions peace scientists are concerned with pertain to managing conflicts, coping with them, and, we hope, resolving them in order to achieve a more peaceful world. Such actions include decision making, policy formation, legislation, instinctive behavior, and even inaction (do nothing).

Webster (1986) provides several useful definitions of culture. One is "that complex whole that includes knowledge, belief, morals, law, customs, opinions, religion, superstition and art" (p. 552). Other words may be inserted, such as traits, traditions, folkways, institutions, government, ideas, values, standards, sentiments, language, tools, material devices, artifacts, religious places, buildings, machines, communication devices, technology, and social, economic, and political institutions and organizations. But this definition is very general. It fails to suggest major differences among cultures. A second definition by Webster which does so is "the body of customary beliefs, social forms, and material traits constituting a distinct complex of tradition of a racial, religious, or social group" (p. 552). Many racial, religious, and social groups exist in this world, and since typically each has a *distinct* body of customary beliefs, social forms, and material traits, it is not surprising to find differences among their cultures–major as well as minor. These differences often pertain to beliefs and behavior that give rise to and perpetuate conflict. To illustrate, let us look at religious differences.

2.3   Conflicts arising from religious differences

Throughout history major conflicts have been generated by religious differences. This is so because religion is often the core element around which many societies have organized themselves. One can point to major conflicts associated with the Crusades (1095–1270). The first Crusades were Christian military expeditions called for by Roman Catholic popes and directed against Muslim control of Jerusalem and the Christian shrine of the Holy Sepulchre. Of course, power and profit motives were involved as well. For example, merchants in Genoa, Venice, and other Italian cities joined up, motivated by a search for new markets, especially in the later Crusades.

Or one can cite the Thirty Years' War which ravaged the Germanic states several centuries later. Three religious doctrines were vying for dominance: Catholicism, Protestantism, and Calvinism. War spread throughout Europe and came to involve the Germanic states, Denmark, Sweden, Poland, Russia, France, Austria, Spain, and the Netherlands. Eventually the struggle became purely political.

Down to the present day, we find religious differences playing a major role in generating conflict and violence. Witness (March, 1992):

1. *The protracted Northern Ireland conflict*   Often characterized as Catholics versus Protestants (an overly simplistic view, to be sure), this conflict dates back at least to the 16th century when Henry VIII of England declared himself king of Ireland and tried to introduce Protestantism into that predominantly Roman Catholic

country. Many uprisings and revolts ensued; an independent Republic of Ireland finally emerged in the 20th century, along with the State of Northern Ireland, the latter under British jurisdiction. Notwithstanding major efforts at reconciliation, Northern Ireland remains the scene of intense conflict–centered around Catholic claims (and Protestant counterclaims) of denial of civil rights, discrimination in employment and housing, and other inequities and injustices. Pessimists view this religion-oriented conflict as having caused such deep divisions as to make any satisfactory resolution virtually impossible within the next several generations.

2. *The Arab–Israeli conflicts* At issue here, on the one hand, is the strong desire of Jews to reclaim Palestine, their spiritual birthplace and home for thousands of years. On the other hand, Arabs, who also trace their ancestry back to Abraham, claim the land of Palestine because over time it had become chiefly Arab, where Arabs have lived ever since they conquered it in the 600s A.D. In 1947 the United Nations divided Palestine into an Arab state and a Jewish state. The Jewish state took the name of Israel in 1948. Neither side was satisfied with this division and wars erupted–in 1948, 1967, and 1973. Today, Arab–Israeli hostility is as deep-seated as ever.

3. *Other Mid-East conflicts* Along with the Arab–Israeli struggle, conflicts among other religion-oriented groups in the Middle East have surfaced and intensified: Christian–Muslim fighting in Lebanon, violence between Sunnite and the Shi'ite Muslims, Islamic Fundamentalist determination to unsettle the Egyptian regime, bitter emotional fighting in Israel between two religious orders, Ashkenazis and Sephardics. The Middle East continues to be a hotbed of disquiet and disputes–home to Northern Ireland–type protracted conflicts that may never be resolved.

As we glance back through history, we cannot help but note the glaring gap between religious doctrine and actual practice. Almost all religions set peace and harmonious relations among groups (nations, races, ethnic societies) and individuals as basic goals, and yet so many wars have sprung from religion-oriented conflict. Major rifts (although nonviolent) have developed even within historical peace churches–Mennonites, Brethren, and Quakers. Within the Quaker fold in the United States, for example, Gurneyites and Hicksites had a serious falling out during the 19th century. Is conflict endemic and absolutely essential for human survival? This is a question the reader may struggle to answer after finishing this book.

Differences in political institutions, social forms, economic organization, and ideology also can generate conflict, violence, and war. Differences between left and right leading to the Spanish Civil War of the 1930s; the struggle of non-Fascists against Nazis in World War II; the current confrontation between communist North and noncommunist South Korea; tension between Mainland China and Taiwan; all find their roots in ideology. Nor must we fail to note the deep-seated cultural differences in ideology and political and economic institutions long existent between communist Soviet Union and democratic United States, which during the Cold War era gave rise to tremendous military arsenals of both conventional and nuclear weapons, with potential for complete destruction of the human race.

2.4   Cultural complexes

There is more to cultural differences than variations in single traits or other elements. The second Webster definition refers to cultural complexes. A cultural complex may be defined as a group of interrelated cultural traits dominated by one essential trait. (In this definition, a trait should be viewed as any material element [such as wearing shoes or playing soccer] or nonmaterial element [such as a belief in spirits] that is significant for a culture and that is one of its simplest identifiable characteristics.) Nationalism is a cultural complex. It is an attitude, feeling, or belief associated with national consciousness. For the individual, it involves a sense of identifying with or belonging to a large group of people having a number of traits in common–traditions (history), religious practices, language, idioms, ethnic customs and folkways. Nationalism means loyalty and a duty to the nation–state, whose welfare is considered of paramount importance. Often it leads to a feeling of national superiority, to glorification of national virtues, to concern for one's own national interests to the exclusion of the rights of other nations and groups. It can generate a sharp division between "US" and "THEM" (to be discussed at length below), which can lead to international conflict.

There are other cultural complexes besides nationalism. The rice complex is typical of many Oriental societies where rice growing is the key activity for sustaining life and thus a core trait around which are clustered a multitude of other traits (harvest rituals, pressure for a male offspring). Or we can point to the cultural complex of nomads, centered around the core trait of directed, noncyclic migration; for example, the Bedouins, a proud and independent Arab people, roam the deserts seeking fresh water and pastureland for their camels, goats, and sheep, living in tents and wearing clothing made from animal skin and hair.

A society (social system) usually is comprised of a number of cultural complexes (dominant themes), sometimes not fully consistent with one another. In the United States, the nationalism complex exists alongside the sports complex, associated with love of the game (baseball, football, basketball, and hockey) and the excitement generated by team competition. Add to these the democratic–equal opportunity–free enterprise–laissez faire ideological complex; the industrial–military complex (reflecting close ties between the military and big industry) oriented to national security objectives; regional complexes (the South, the Midwest, New England [Yankee], California); the "Establishment"; diverse complexes associated with different ethnic and religious groups; and so forth. Together they form what has been designated the cultural pattern of the United States.

2.5 Adaptation to physical environment versus the dominance of social organization

We need to examine some major differences in the views of anthropologists and sociologists. On the one hand, there are *cultural ecologists*. These scholars view human society and culture as products of *adaptation* to given environmental conditions; differences among cultures to a large extent can be explained by the influence of different environments. Theirs is a materialist explanation and often they cite archeological evidence. They would point to the Bedouins as a clear-cut illustration of environmental adaptation. How else could people survive in the desert than by migrating and living as they do? Extremists among these ecologists appear to profess an ecological determinism and a vulgar cultural materialism. They speak of an environment's *carrying capacity*, the potential population density given the state of the technology. When population mounts and exceeds this capacity, change must take place–change that can lead to intense conflicts among societies, and to war.

In contrast, some cultural anthropologists and sociologists (sometimes called *structuralists*) recognize the relation between population and environment, but argue that societies can and do take steps to alter environmental influence. A society can develop new technology (recall the saying "necessity is the mother of invention"); it can change its social, political, and economic organizations and institutions; it can change the landscape (blasting tunnels to permit communication, constructing dams and irrigation ditches to turn barren land into productive soil, and so forth). Physical environment thus becomes relatively passive in the hands of a determined, vigorous, and creative society. These scholars may consider the Mormons a case in point. A zealous religious group fleeing from repression transformed an arid valley land, a sagebrush wasteland, into hundreds of permanent, thriving communities–in their words, a green and wholesome "Kingdom of God." They were the first in America to build community irrigation projects. Consider also the Pilgrims in New England, who overcame the rocky soil and harsh, niggardly environment of Plymouth. Or note a more recent phenomenon, namely, transformation by the Israelis of the semi-arid, formerly desolate Negev region–a tremendous achievement. On the other hand, there have been times when people were unable to adapt to or alter environments that had become harsh and unwelcome. In recent years, the inability to adapt to the encroaching Sahara desert, whether periodic or not, in the sub-Sahara Sahel area of Africa is a case in point.

Weighing objectively the evidence presented by cultural ecologists on the one hand and structuralists on the other, one can only be eclectic. Clearly, both environmental and social forces are at play; at times physical environment factors dominate; at other times, social factors are more influential. Figure 2.1 is one way to illustrate this. This figure depicts the relationship between forms of social organization, forms of technology, the natural environment, and human groups. The cultural ecologist traces what happens in the development of a culture by starting with Natural Environment and following the arrows around. The structuralist starts with Forms of Social Organization and follows the arrows around to explain how a society exploits the environment to attain its goals. We may therefore argue that one cannot reach any definitive and general conclusion as to which is the dominant force in cultural development and survival, but we must recognize that in any specific situation either environment or social organization may dominate, or perhaps neither; some intricate mix of the two may prevail.

Before leaving this issue, we should point out how such views can be exploited to justify war. A striking example relates to the most

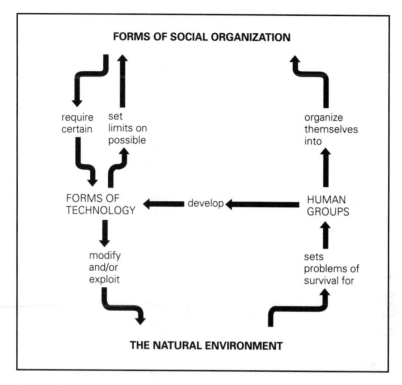

FORMS OF SOCIAL ORGANIZATION

require certain   set limits on possible

organize themselves into

FORMS OF TECHNOLOGY ◄ develop ◄ HUMAN GROUPS

modify and/or exploit

sets problems of survival for

THE NATURAL ENVIRONMENT

Hunter, D.E. and P. Whitten (eds.) 1976, p.99

Figure 2.1 *Relations Between Social Organization, Technology and Environment*

destructive war yet experienced by humanity, namely, World War II. Underlying this armed conflict was the cultural ecological concept of *Lebensraum* (living space)–the asserted need for enough territory to assure the economic self-sufficiency of a state–territory needed to relieve population pressure. In *Mein Kampf* (the bible of Nazism, the National Socialist movement in Germany before and during World War II), Adolph Hitler proclaimed the supremacy of the Aryan races, holding the Germanic to be the purest of these, and propounded an extreme nationalism calling for unification of all German-speaking people. To achieve this unification, new "living space" for the Germanic peoples was required, he claimed, and was to be wrested from the Slavs east of Germany, whom he considered degenerate. Consistent with his belief, Hitler, having become dictator in 1934, built up Germany's military might, annexed Austria (March, 1938), forced Czechoslovakia (with the acquiescence of France and England) to cede the Sudetenland (September, 1938), sent troops into Prague to take over the rest of Czechoslovakia (March, 1939), and shortly thereafter invaded Poland (September, 1939) and later other areas of Eastern Europe.

2.6   The uniqueness, yet common elements of cultures

Other issues divide anthropologists. *Cultural relativists* maintain that every culture is unique. Each possesses its own set of customs, beliefs, values, and traits, which lead to organizations and institutions that are linked and interact in their own particular ways. Each is a closed, self-contained system, judged in terms of its own values and moral codes. There is no objective basis for determining whether one is superior to another–whether the Polynesians' or the Aborigines' or French Canadian society, or any other, is the best.

On the other hand, *structuralists* are highly critical of this particu-larist approach which denies any common cultural features or general forces at play as cultures and societies evolve. These anthro-pologists look for principles that apply to most if not all cultures; they search for regularities or laws of structure or of historical process in social systems. For example, in almost all cultures, one finds initiation ceremonies (passage at puberty into adulthood) and marriage cere-monies, and in many cultures one finds witchcraft beliefs. Consider the Third World countries. Is there not a culture complex of "Third World" poverty (interrelated traits of poverty, inequity, and discrimi-nation) common to many areas, varying in minor aspects but *universal* nonetheless? Today tremendous conflicts arise between these coun-tries, and between those already developed. Even greater conflicts are likely to arise as poverty-stricken populations vigorously demand civil rights, equal opportunity, more political power and a more equitable division of world resources.

Again, we must be eclectic. Each culture has its particular values, religious practices, moral codes of behavior, customs, laws, and so forth. Yet among cultures there are common traits and complexes. Most cultures, if not all, need effective organization (social, political, and economic) to promote growth and well-being and to restrict excessive competition and minimize physical violence. Viewed from this standpoint, world security depends on harnessing the cooperative practices of different cultures and modifying their competitive drives in ways that curb their divisive tendencies, in order to achieve harmony but without destroying cultural diversity. There will always be diversity among cultures, of course. The world's vastly different physical environments and geographic features require different adaptations so that people can survive and achieve efficiency.

2.7   Evolutionary processes in cultural development

Returning to the meaning of the word *culture*, neither of Webster's first two definitions speaks to the important historical fact that culture relates to a process of accommodation and change over time. Fortunately Webster gives us a third definition which does so: [culture is] "the total pattern of human behavior and its products embodied in thought, speech, action and artifacts and dependent upon man's capacity for learning and transmitting knowledge to succeeding generations through the use of tools, language and systems of abstract things" (p. 552). Here "learning and transmitting knowledge to succeeding generations" is the central concept. This definition encompasses the dynamics of cultural evolution and points to the relevance of the study of cultural history. Such history provides insight into the role of conflict, competition, and cooperation in social development.

First, there is the factor of cultural selection. Species and societies with strong adaptive traits are better able to survive and increase in a given environment. Among such traits are behavior patterns of individuals and groups. Species and societies whose individuals and groups are more aggressive, stronger, more vigorous, and more enterprising tend to survive. Part of being more enterprising involves exploiting gains from cooperation and specialization that team efforts permit–such efforts as moving boulders, building dams, and changing the course of a stream.

At the same time, when two or more species or societies seek to live in, and thus compete for, the same physical environment (niche), the society with the more aggressive, vigorous, and enterprising individuals and groups will win out and supplant the others. Their potential success in conflictual situations and their greater ability to survive (which may call for considerable cooperation among their own individuals and groups) tend to lead them to use violence and even wage war when problems with other societies arise.

Thus have cooperation and competition (with the tendency to engage in violence) existed side by side as cultures have developed.

Cultural history also records the diffusion of ideas, technology, and other elements and complexes–their spread over time from point of origin to other areas. This leads to the existence of common elements such as language (English has become the international means of communication), technology, and know-how (for example, ways of fighting disease, constructing irrigation systems). Presence among cultures of such common elements (cultural convergence) facilitates cooperation; in general, the more societies have in common the better their understanding of one another.

Alongside this cultural diffusion doctrine is a belief held by some anthropologists that cultural development basically follows a given path. One early view supported *unilinear* development, the notion that most, if not all, cultures follow similar developmental stages (a time path): invention of tools, domestication of plants and animals, development of urban civilization, and, lastly, industrial revolution. Other anthropologists who put forth a *multilinear* theory of evolution concede this tendency for cultures to follow a time path of development but recognize that each culture develops unique traits in the process of both adapting to and altering its physical environment. Moreover, over time, the developmental paths of these cultures may diverge (cultural divergence), leading them to become less and less alike. Despite diffusion processes tending toward more common elements (cultural convergence), increasing differences–for example, in views on how to exploit, manage, or conserve the environment–can overcome peaceful forces generated by more common elements, and give rise to sharp conflict.

2.8   Personality and behavior: effect on cultural development

To further our understanding of culture, we should consider one more definition. Two distinguished anthropologists, Alfred Kroeber and Clyde Kluckhohn after listing more than 150 definitions of culture, presented an omnibus of their own:

> Culture consists of patterns, explicit and implicit, of and for behaviour, acquired and transmitted by symbols, constituting the distinctive achievement of human groups, including their embodiment in

artifacts; the essential core of culture consists of traditional (i.e. historically derived and selected) ideas, and especially their attached values; culture systems may, on the one hand, be considered as *products of action, and on the other hand as conditioning elements of further action.* (1952, p. 180; italics my own)

The statement in italics emphasizes the role of individual and group behavior as well as the underlying motivation, attitudes, frustrations, hang-ups, perceptions and misperceptions, cognition, and so forth. But at the same time it makes clear that all these behavioral aspects are strongly influenced by culture itself.

Let us spell this out. In the past, anthropologists took the position that a typical personality prevails among people living in a society because of the culture they share. Child rearing and other familial social experiences, kinship relationships, subsistence techniques (such as hunting and agricultural practices), religious practices, and customs and folkways prevalent in a culture give rise to a common basic personality structure. (For example, a person living in a society dependent upon nomadic hunting for survival tends to be more independent than one who grows up in a society engaged in sedentary agriculture.) Some anthropologists claimed that many folkways become habits, become automatic and stereotyped through repetition, and that often they are nonrational in that no intelligent personal judgment gave rise to them. In this sense folkways lead to common behavioral patterns and typical individual personalities. These earlier anthropologists attributed differences in personalities to differences in culture. With each national culture they associated a national style and character. In today's world they would have pointed to differences in national style in recent arms control negotiations: United States negotiators tended to favor a series of small steps to reach agreement; the Soviets tended to make high demands initially, favoring large steps, willing to make rapid concessions later on.

More recently, anthropologists have come to recognize that factors other than culture influence individual and interpersonal as well as group and intergroup behavior, factors intertwined with cultural elements in intricate ways. Biological processes (for example, an individual's glandular secretions) have an important influence on formation of personality (aggressiveness, emotional stability, ability to comprehend). Individuals within a culture are exposed to different life situations, and so internalize different cultural aspects. As a consequence of these and other influences, a diversity of personalities, of concepts of right and wrong, of proper societal policies or goals, can develop within a well-organized and stable culture. The modern view is that a diversity of personality types characterizes a well-structured society, and that any given culture, while constantly affecting its people's personality development, is itself modified (usually very slowly) by ongoing individual, interpersonal, group, and intergroup behavior (conscious and unconscious). We thus see how leaders with very different personalities and behavioral patterns, with different cognitions, values, and ideals, and with antithetical mental representations of the world can arise in the same society–a Roosevelt and an Eisenhower in the United States, a Bismarck and a Hitler in Germany, a Chamberlain and a Churchill in Britain, a Stalin and a Gorbachev in the Soviet Union. We recognize that societies must have leaders; they play a very significant role. Their personalities and their values critically affect society's well-being and its interactions with other societies.

2.9   The US and THEM in conflict and war

Before closing this chapter, we turn to the fields of social psychology and psychiatry in order to understand the US and THEM dichotomy which so dominates people's thinking in times of crisis and war. Social psychologists and psychiatrists, of course, differ from one another in their views as much as anthropologists and other social scientists. Many scholars are skeptical of the theories and hypotheses of psychiatrists. I present them here because they bring out most point-edly the US and THEM distinction so very important for under-standing conflict.

According to the Committee on International Relations of the Group for the Advancement of Psychiatary, at the moment of birth, a baby's physical union with its mother is severed. It is thrust into a world in which it must distinguish between *self* and *other*. From this stage on, its growth depends on this distinction, mother being the prototypical *other*. At the same time, the baby depends on the mother for nurturing. This reunion with the mother introduces a contra-diction; for the baby it creates an ambivalent relationship. Later, parents shape and redirect the child's ambivalence, finding "good" within the family and "bad" outside. Still later the child typically joins one or more groups–a play group, school group, or neighborhood group. As an adolescent a young man may join a gang or a social group (party); influenced by his parents, he becomes an increasingly conscious member of a religious, ethnic, or political group, especially when other contrasting groups exist. This is most likely to occur in a community where many families share a common history, ancestry, language, religion, race, legends, and ethnic heroes, and have similar customs and notions of class and economic status, manner of dress, and ideas of right and wrong. These shared traits serve as a common denominator for members of a group.

When he is old enough to participate in increasingly complex groups, perhaps involving specialized roles, group membership provides a source of strength. Group members are drawn together by the sense of weakness that each one has. They depend on one another, and especially on their leader (who in turn depends on general support from members), to defend them against others, to survive in a competition, and for help in confronting an unfriendly world. Having similar customs, ideas, and background, an individual is comfortable with other members of the group. However, with strangers, outsiders with other heritages who believe and think in unfamiliar ways, individuals feel less comfortable. Thus, an individual comes to differentiate between US (members of our group) and THEM (outsiders).

According to psychiatric doctrine, there is more to it than this. Some schools of psychiatry maintain that a common need to set up an enemy evolves from the early distinction between self and other. The Arabs have a saying, "My brother and I against our cousins, we and our cousins against the world" (Committee on International Relations, 1987, p. 115). The individual (and in turn the group) needs to cast off undesirable aspects of his own personality and project them onto others. He identifies an enemy to embody these undesirable aspects, differentiating between US and THEM. Members of a group having similar background and mores tend to interact intensively, to agree on who is US and who is THEM. We see this happening in children's play groups, adolescent gangs, and adult religious and ethnic groups, for example, Protestants and Catholics in Northern Ireland. US and THEM categorization permits the denial of in-group hostility, and the association of all "bads" with THEM. During World War I, for example, people in the United States (as part of the group of nations called the "Allies") denigrated the people of Germany and Austria–Hungary (the "Axis" nations) as *Huns* and *barbarians.*

It is important to bear in mind that the tendency for an individual to project onto outsiders some of the character weaknesses that he does not wish to acknowledge in himself goes along with an inclination (1) to consider his own group (the US group) the center of everything, and very special; (2) to take pride in and boast of the US group; and (3) to undervalue THEM. More important, members of the US group, thinking and behaving in this way, are unaware that members of the THEM group are engaging in this same kind of evaluation for the very same reasons. Members of each group are culturally blind, and see the world in terms of objects and relationships they have grown up with, unaware of objects and relationships significant to other cultures (largely because of an individual's limited ability to process and store knowledge).

In international relations and conflict management, the US and THEM dichotomy is omnipresent. Since the end of World War II, we have had until recently a bipolar world: the United States versus the Soviet Union, or NATO (an organization of "Western" countries with the United States as leader) and the Warsaw Pact (an organization of "Eastern" countries with the Soviet Union as leader). This phenomenon of nations or alliances of nations pitted against each other–as during the Cold War period lasting until the end of the 1980s–has been called *ethnonationalism*. The term refers to psychological processes common to ethnic groups (discussed above) and to nationalism (viewed as a combination of patriotism and consciousness of nationality). Ethnonationalism has been at the root of most, if not all, major wars and is likely to underlie any major war that may occur in the future.

2.10 Summary and questions

There are many differences among cultures, and these can give rise to serious conflict. For centuries religious and ideological differences have generated major conflicts and large-scale physical violence, and continue to do so, even though both sides may claim they are fighting "the war to end all wars"–to establish peace and the Kingdom of God on Earth.

We examined the concept of a cultural complex–a complex centered around a core trait. Nationalism is such a complex; and although it may serve as an effective force for attaining an efficient economic organization and enhancing social welfare, all too often it has led to major conflict and war. It does so when two or more nations in conflict all harbor feelings of national superiority, glorify national virtues, and are overly concerned for their own national interest to the exclusion of the rights of other nations.

Typically, cultural complexes interconnect to form society's cultural pattern. To understand how the culture pattern of a society interacts with other forces to generate a cooperative or a competitive society, we must pay attention to constraints imposed by physical environment as well as to drive exhibited by a vigorous, well-organized people. Resource limitations often spur a culture to engage in warlike activity in order to acquire territory and resources to support its people. On the other hand, some societies, through ingenuity and sheer determination, have surmounted obstacles posed by exceedingly harsh physical environments without resorting to violence. We need to examine behavioral and organizational processes underlying cooperation and competition to understand the history of peace and war, and to be ready to serve as effective third parties to disputes when we are asked to propose conciliating arrangements.

We discussed the uniqueness of cultures, as well as universal relationships which tend to make them similar. Is the search for peace via cooperative processes a universal trait? Or is a propensity for competition and aggression common to all cultures? Or is a like combination of these traits present in all cultures? Or does each culture possess its own unique combination of these traits–so that it becomes impossible to generalize about how these traits affect individual and group behavior? And is there not a poverty culture common to Third World countries which must be squarely faced as we seek solutions to world problems?

Further insight into the role of competition and cooperation comes from recognizing that cultures evolve over time. Species and societies whose individuals and groups have been more aggressive, more vigorous, and more competitive than others have tended to survive (survival of the fittest), other things being equal. But other things generally have not been equal. The better organized species and societies, in particular those that are internally cooperative, have also tended to survive.

Diffusion of ideas tends to make cultures more alike. At the same time, as each culture moves along its particular developmental path–each path having its unique aspects–cultures become more diverse and less alike.

Some anthropologists claim that most, if not all cultures experience the same stages of development. This raises the question: are we at a point where cultures that have reached the advanced urbanized–industrialized stage are moving into a *world region stage* where national drives and sovereignty give way to cooperative organization on a world-region level? Are Western European nations at this stage? Or are Western and Eastern European nations together moving into a stage where a world region is the European continent?

We discussed the role of personality in cultural development as manifested in individual and group behavior. Existing societal traits influence all individuals in a given community and so tend to generate a common personality, both individual and group. At the same time, different biological processes and different life experiences can generate a variety of personalities–a Gorbachev and a Stalin, for example. A society's cultural development and its foreign and internal policies are greatly influenced by the personalities of its leaders and of its diverse groups.

Concern with the effect of personality on social development and national behavior leads us to consider some hypotheses and theories in psychiatry and basic insights from the field of social psychology. According to some psychiatrists, distinction in early life between *self* and *other* gradually develops into US and THEM categorizing. In any case, belonging to a group is a source of strength; an individual comes to rely upon help from other members of the group in facing an unfriendly world.

By and large, individuals have more interaction and become more familiar with members of their own group than with "outsiders." As a consequence, they typically fail to appreciate the desires and goals of those in other groups and the relationships that govern their behavior. They do not realize that members of other groups consider themselves special and tend also to be culturally blind.

Some psychiatrists maintain that each individual, group, and culture has a need for an enemy onto which to project its own undesirable traits. When a conflict among nations arises, each projects onto the other its unwanted characteristics and other negative elements. This projection intensifies in times of crisis and war. History is replete with examples of this process–all major wars have been characterized by US and THEM phenomena.

We close this summary with a basic question this chapter raises. Culture evolves; its development is the result of a steady, continuing interaction over time among individuals, groups, cultural folkways, and institutions–a *dynamic* process. Two instances of a dynamic may be cited: (1) Growth of the Nazi culture from insignificance to overwhelming dominance in the early 1940s was in large part a consequence of a grossly deficient World War I Versailles treaty which left the German population deeply resentful of its humiliating stipulations. There followed inflation in the 1920s, impoverishment of Germany's middle classes, widespread unemployment during the Great Depression of the early 1930s, and subsequently the extremely skillful political maneuvers of a fanatical demagogue. (2) Disappearance of the Cold War syndrome in the late 1980s and early 1990s was a result of steadily increasing impoverishment of the Soviet economy during the 1980s, stemming from the mounting arms race against a persistent enemy (United States and the NATO bloc). This situation compelled the emergence of a leader (Gorbachev) innovative enough in interacting with a deadweight political organization and other national institutions to change drastically the course of the Soviet economy.

Awareness of cultural dynamics raises a basic question. Can a dynamic arise that takes away the occasion for war?

References

Committee on International Relations, Group for the Advancement of Psychiatry (1987) *US and THEM: The Psychology of Ethnonationalism.* New York: Brunner/Mazel.

Fairchild, H. P. (ed.) (1970) *Dictionary of Sociology.* Westport, CT: Greenwood Press.

Hunter, D. E. and P. Whitten (eds.) (1976) *Encyclopaedia of Anthropology.* New York: Harper and Row.

Kroeber, A. L. and C. Kluckhohn (1952) "Culture: A Critical Review of Concepts and Definitions," *Papers of the Peabody Museum of American Archaeology and Ethnology,* Vol. 47, no. 1.

Lindzey, G. and E. Aronson (eds.) (1985) *The Handbook of Social Psychology.* New York: Random House.

Mitchell, G. D. (ed.) (1979) *A New Dictionary of the Social Sciences.* Hawthorne, NY: Aldine.

Price-Williams, D. R. (1985) "Cultural Psychology," in Lindzey, G. and E. Aronson (eds.), *The Handbook of Social Psychology.* New York: Random House.

Seymour-Smith, C. (1986) *Dictionary of Anthropology.* Boston: G. K. Hall.

Tetlock, P. E., J. L. Husbands, et al. (1989) *Behavior, Society and Nuclear War.* New York: Oxford.

Webster's Third New International Dictionary. (1986) Springfield, MA: Merriam-Webster.

3   Individual and Group Behavior: Economic and Game Theory Approaches

3.1   Introduction

In this chapter we examine the behavior of individuals and groups. Why do they take specific actions, make particular decisions, issue certain commands and orders, propose specific policies? We are especially interested in decisions or proposals regarding the level of military expenditures, and the use and nonuse of physical violence. To answer these questions, we use concepts from economics and game theory such as payoff, profits, gains and losses, and expected values.

3.2   Attitude as a factor in simple decision making

Start with an extremely simple situation. There is a dictator (or very strong political leader). He has a problem. Certain groups of dissenters and underprivileged people are demonstrating and pressing for reform. The dictator sees three possible actions he might take. The first, which we call a_1, is *to crush the movement with physical force*. The second, a_2, is *to do nothing*. The third, a_3, is *to negotiate a settlement of the issues involved*. If the dictator selects action a_1, he figures there will be negative effects, for example, lingering, bitter resentment among his constituents. He may assign to these effects a value of -10. If he does nothing, (a_2), the negative effects, he estimates, will be smaller, say -5. For he anticipates that the groups will disagree on which specific reforms should be given priority and that the resulting infighting will exhaust their energies and resources; they will fail to agree on an unambiguous program for reform.

When he considers the third action, he knows that negotiating a settlement will necessitate meeting some of the groups' demands; he assigns to this action a -30. Accordingly, we can set up a simple payoff table (Table 3.1). If the dictator is rational and behaves as an economic person, he will naturally choose action a_2, the one that minimizes his perceived loss. By minimizing loss, he maximizes the power he retains.

Change the situation somewhat. A strong leader of the dissidents and underprivileged emerges. If this were to happen, reasons the dictator, and if he were to crush the revolt (action a_1) and nip this leader's efforts in the bud, his loss would be 30, since he anticipates more lingering resentment among his constituents. On the other hand, if he does nothing in this situation (action a_2), he can assume that the dissident leader may well unify the various groups around a specific reform program, organize their energies effectively, and be successful in forcing it through. The dictator calculates his loss, were this to happen, as 90. Finally, if he chooses to negotiate, the dictator could prevent a reform movement from snowballing by working out a compromise, for which he assumes the loss to be 40.

Thus, our dictator has two *sets* of estimated losses: *one* where a strong leader is assumed not to emerge, as recorded in table 3.1, and reproduced as column 1 in table 3.2; and a *second*, if such a leader were to emerge, as recorded in column 2 of table 3.2. We can call table 3.2 a table of losses, or a payoff table (payoffs here all being negative), or a payoff matrix, to use the terminology of economists. (A payoff matrix is an ordered, rectangular set of numbers, where each number has been assigned a specific row and a specific column.)

Table 3.1

Action	Payoff
a_1	−20
a_2	− 5
a_3	−30

Table 3.2

Action	No leader emerges	Strong leader emerges
a_1	−20	−30
a_2	− 5	−90
a_3	−30	−40

Examine table 3.2. Which action will the dictator choose? The answer to this question is not simple. A great deal will depend on his attitude (recall from chapter 2 that attitude can reflect influences of the culture from which a person comes). If he is a pessimist and assumes that the worst will always take place, he will see -30 as the worst that could happen from choosing action a_1. He sees -90 as the worst possible outcome if he chooses a_2. And he sees -40 as the worst possible outcome of choosing a_3. Thus, to minimize his loss, given this pessimistic attitude, he chooses action a_1. Note that a leader who is conservative and prefers to deal with sure things only also will choose action a_1. By doing so, he satisfies himself that his loss will not exceed 30–that his power will not be reduced by more than 30. Typically, any leader at the helm of a Big Power, or a first-rank organization, or an old established firm in a major industry, will tend to be conservative. He may have little to gain in a conflict situation and much to lose. Stalin's actions in crushing reform movements within the Soviet bloc during his dictatorship reflected a conservative attitude. So did many actions of her prime ministers when the British Empire dominated the world. Likewise, some of President Bush's conservative "wait-and-see" policies may be regarded as "risk-averse."

A leader may have a different attitude. He may be an optimist. Everything will go his way. "God is with him." If he chooses action a_1, the best that can happen to him is a loss of 20. If he chooses action a_2, the best that can happen is a loss of only 5. And if he chooses action a_3, the best that can happen is a loss of 30. He will select action a_2, the action that gives him the best of the best. When the fanatical religious leader Ayatollah Khomeini chose to continue Iran's war with Iraq when Iraq offered to engage in peace negotiations, he was behaving, some might claim, as a "God-is-on-my-side" optimist. In the context of table 3.2, he would have judged that at most the loss to his country would be 5 if he did nothing (that is, did not engage in peace negotiations).

There is still another attitude, namely, that of a careful, calculating behaving unit. The dictator may attach a probability to the emergence of a strong leader from among the dissidents and underprivileged. Suppose he assigns a probability of 50 percent to this possibility and thus also a 50 percent probability to the possibility that such a leader will not emerge. Accordingly, in valuing action a_1, he argues that there is a 50 percent chance of receiving outcome -20 (an expected value of -10) and a 50 percent chance of receiving outcome -30 (an expected value of -15). All told, the expected value for a_1 is $(.50 \times -20) + (.50 \times -30) = -25$. Similarly, he derives an expected value of $(.50 \times -5) + (.50 \times -90) = -47.5$ for action a_2; and an expected value $(.50 \times -30) + (.50 \times -40) = -35$ for action a_3. He will choose a_1 for which the expected loss is smallest.

On the other hand, suppose the dictator considers the rise of a strong leader very unlikely. Suppose he estimates this possibility at only 10 percent, and conversely the absence of a strong leader at 90 percent. He will calculate his expected payoffs for each action as follows:

$$a_1 = (.90 \times -20) + (.10 \times -30) = -21$$
$$a_2 = (.90 \times -5) + (.10 \times -90) = -5.4$$
$$a_3 = (.90 \times -30) + (.10 \times -40) = -31$$

Clearly, he will choose action a_2, and do nothing.

The above are oversimplified examples of most real-life situations. Many factors other than attitude are involved in any decision-making process. These illustrations merely help us formulate a rather precise method of analyzing the effect of the attitude variable on choice of action.

We have discussed the choice of action by a specific behaving unit, namely, a dictator. This simple analysis pertains also to choice of action and behavior of most individuals or groups. Attitude is one of a number of basic variables that must be taken into account to understand decision making and policy formulation.

3.3   OPTIONAL: The attitude variable in more complex decision making

A simple two-column payoff matrix may reflect the limited ability of some decision makers (some claim that ex-President Reagan's capabilities were confined to strategies that could be covered by a two-column payoff matrix), but it cannot represent the strategizing of a skillful, highly insightful political figure such as Gorbachev.

Consider a more complex situation than that depicted by table 3.2. Let there be a third state of affairs where a political leader is sensitive to world opinion, and may be subject to significant negative sanctions from other nations. A third column in a payoff table or matrix then is needed to cover the possibility that the outside world comes to support the reform movement.

The three possible scenarios, then, are:

1. No leadership and organization develop among dissidents and underprivileged and they receive no support (political, material, or other) from the outside world (represented by column 1 of a new payoff matrix, table 3.3).
2. Strong leadership and organization develop among groups demanding reform but no support is received from the outside world (represented by column 2 in table 3.3).
3. Strong leadership and organization develop and strong support is received from the outside world (represented by column 3 in table 3.3).

Losses in the first two columns of the new payoff matrix are the same as in table 3.2, since table 3.2 is based on the implicit assumption that there is no involvement (interaction) with the outside world. In column 3 of table 3.3, the leader estimates a loss of 35 were he to adopt action a_1. This loss is greater than the loss in column 2 for the same action a_1 since negative sanctions from the outside world are deemed likely if troops are sent in to crush the revolt. Were the dictator to take action a_2, he estimates an outcome of -100 in column 3, a greater loss than the outcome of -90 in column 2 from action a_2, since he foresees some negative sanctions from other nations for his doing nothing. However, were the dictator to adopt action a_3 (seek a compromise via negotiations with the dissidents and impoverished), will not the response from the outside world be favorable? This favorable response, he reasons, would considerably offset any loss of power from compromising; he thus estimates the outcome here to be only -10.

Table 3.3

Action	No leader emerges, no outside support	Strong leader emerges, no outside support	Strong leader emerges, outside support
a_1	−20	−30	− 35
a_2	− 5	−90	−100
a_3	−30	−40	− 10

Once again, if the dictator is a pessimist, or highly conservative and wanting to be sure that his loss will not exceed 35, he will choose a_1. If he is an extreme optimist, he will once again choose a_2. However, if he assigns probabilities to the three possible states of affairs and acts as an economic man, he may well choose action a_3. He will do so, for example, were he to judge all three scenarios equally likely, or the probability of support from the outside world (column 3) to be 50 percent, with 25 percent assigned to each of the other two situations.

Suppose the problem of assigning probabilities is too complicated for the dictator; it may be beyond his capabilities. He then may adopt a simple approach that reflects a middle-of-the-road attitude–based on a mix of pessimism and optimism. He may identify for each action the best possible outcome and the worst, and simply average the two to derive a value for that action. Accordingly, the value of a_1 would be -27.5; of a_2 -52.5, and that of a_3 -25. He will choose a_3 to minimize his expected loss.

Many other specific attitudes prevail. Moreover, as already implied, the behaving unit's objective may vary. He may wish to minimize his losses, maximize his gains, minimize his expected losses, or maximize his expected gains. Or he may want to minimize his regret. A behaving unit may be motivated to do this when he knows that he is a regretter and will always criticize himself for not having chosen the action corresponding to the best outcome that would have been possible had he foreseen the state of affairs that actually materialized. Or he may simply want to find an action that leads to a satisfactory outcome (sometime called a satisficing action). Or in situations where his satisfaction or utility is not a simple function of his payoff, he may want to maximize his expected utility–a concept too technical to be discussed herein.

To sum up, many specific attitudes can prevail in a given decision situation, and a decision maker can have one of many different objectives. Corresponding to each combination of attitude and objective is a best action. There is no one action that is best for all combinations.

3.4   Interdependence and behavior: the Prisoner's Dilemma game

In the above examples we assumed a static situation, that is, that the leader of the dissidents and impoverished does not react to the action chosen by the dictator. This can be the case. But in most situations, two behaving units involved in a conflict react to and/or take into account each other's possible actions. Take the classic Prisoner's Dilemma game, for example. This game derives its name from a situation in which two suspects are questioned separately by the district attorney. They are each guilty of the crime of which they are suspected, but the district attorney does not have sufficient evidence to convict either. The state, however, does have sufficient evidence to convict each prisoner of a lesser offense. The alternatives open to the suspects, whom we shall call John and Mary, are to confess or not to confess to the serious crime. They are separated and cannot communicate. If both confess, both will receive severe sentences, which, however, will be reduced, say, to five years in prison because of the confession. If only one confesses, the other will have the book thrown at him, namely, a longer prison term, say, eight years, and the informer will go scot-free. If neither confesses, they cannot be convicted of the serious crime, but will surely be tried and convicted for the lesser offense, for which each will receive, say, a one-year prison term.

This situation is depicted in table 3.4. John's two actions, "do not confess" and "confess," are indicated along the rows, Mary's down the columns. Each cell contains two numbers. The first is John's payoff (his prison sentence) if he takes the action corresponding to the row containing that cell, and if at the same time Mary takes the action corresponding to that cell's column. The second number in that cell is Mary's payoff (her prison sentence) when the same actions are taken. For example, the numbers 8,0 in the upper right cell of the table indicate an eight-year prison sentence for John and no years for Mary, if Mary confesses and John does not. And the numbers in the lower right cell indicate that each will receive a five-year sentence if both confess.

Table 3.4. *A prisoner's dilemma game (outcomes are: years in prison)*

John's action	Mary's Actions	
	Do not confess	Confess
Do not confess	1,1	8,0
Confess	0,8	5,5

In this game situation, payoff (outcome) to each participant (player) depends not only on the action he/she chooses but also on the action chosen by the other. John knows that his outcome depends on the action Mary will choose (which John cannot know). Aware that he and Mary are hostile toward each other, he may well reason that Mary is going to be solely interested in her own welfare and that therefore she will confess. And, if I do not confess, John tells himself, she will go scot-free, which is better for her than a one-year sentence were she also not to confess and be sentenced for the lesser crime. Also, if we both confess, reasons John, Mary knows that she will receive a five-year prison term which is better than the eight years she will receive if she does not confess and I do. So John concludes that Mary will choose to confess.

Using the same logic, Mary concludes that John will confess. Reasoning in this way, each concludes that it is best to confess.

Now, instead of heading the rows and columns "Do not confess" and "Confess," we could designate them "Cooperate" and "Do not cooperate." This would be more appropriate for a Sam and Olga who have been good friends, or who had studied the Prisoner's Dilemma game together in college so that each knows that the other also understands the game. Accordingly, each may be quite certain that the other will choose a "cooperative" strategy, cooperation being the result not of direct interaction but simply of understanding the problem. In this way, each will spend one year in prison rather than five.

We dwell at length on the Prisoner's Dilemma game because many scholars and political analysts have viewed the arms race between the United States (or NATO countries) and the Soviet Union (or Warsaw Pact countries) during the Cold War as such a game. We set up table 3.5 accordingly, assigning arbitrary payoff values.

Table 3.5. *The U.S. - Soviet Union Prisoner's Dilemma game*

	Soviet Union Actions	
U.S. action	*Cooperate*	*Do not cooperate (defect)*
Cooperate	3,3	–13,9
Do not cooperate (defect)	9,–13	–6,–6

According to this game, at any point in time, the Soviet Union and the United States can choose to develop (presumably in absolute secrecy) or not to develop a new advanced weapons system. If both choose not to do so, each would gain 3, since the billions of rubles and dollars which would be spent on weapons can instead support desirable social welfare programs or be used in other productive ways. If both nations choose to develop new weapons, each would become less secure; the probability of overall destructive warfare, either from accidental war or terrorist operation, would increase–the payoff would be -6. If one country chooses to cooperate, and the other chooses to develop the new system, the former's security would decrease (-13 payoff), while the other's security from having a superior military capability would increase (payoff +9).

In actuality, both proceeded to develop an advanced weapons system; like John and Mary, neither trusted the other and neither attributed to the other a friendly, cooperative attitude which could have led to higher payoffs for each.

3.5　OPTIONAL: The Chicken game

Another two-person game frequently discussed is *Chicken*. This game takes the form of table 3.6.

Table 3.6. *The game of Chicken*

John's action	Mary's Actions	
	b_1	b_2
a_1	3,3	2,4
a_2	4,2	1,1

The rows again indicate two possible actions by John, a_1 and a_2. The columns indicate two actions by Mary, b_1 and b_2. Payoffs to each player for each given joint action are specified within cells. For example, if John takes action a_1 and Mary action b_2, John's payoff is 2 and Mary's 4.

In this game there are two stable equilibrium outcomes (4,2) and (2,4). To see this, suppose the players are initially at (3,3), because

John has chosen a_1 and Mary b_1. John could change his action from a_1 to a_2, thereby increasing his payoff to 4. Mary could do the same, that is, change her action from b_1 to b_2, thereby increasing her payoff to 4. However, if they were to make these changes simultaneously they would both receive their worst outcome, namely, 1, since the set of payoffs in cell $a_2 b_2$ is (1,1). Whoever is the more aggressive, and changes his/her action first, obtains his/her most preferred outcome (4) (in the outcome set [2,4] in cell $a_1 b_2$ if Mary is the more aggressive, or in the outcome set [4,2] in cell $a_2 b_1$ if John is the more aggressive). The other must then accept a lower payoff (2). For once the outcome set (2,4) or (4,2) is reached, neither John nor Mary has any incentive to change his/her action. For if John were the less aggressive, and were to change from a_1 to a_2 when Mary has already chosen b_2, his outcome would drop to 1 because the new set of outcomes (1,1) corresponding to $a_2 b_2$ would result. John in effect is the "chicken." Although at the start he could have increased his payoff by changing his action from a_1 to a_2 provided he did so before Mary, he hesitated to do this for fear that Mary would simultaneously change her action from b_1 to b_2 and that as a result they would end up in an $a_2 b_2$ situation with a set of outcomes (1,1).

This Chicken game has sometimes been used to describe the behavior of two nations in conflict.

Of course if at this point in the game John changed his objective (and thus the game itself) and was no longer 100 percent concerned with maximizing his own payoff, he might *out of spite* choose a_2, since by doing so he would lose only 1 and Mary would lose 3. Since in real life players' objectives and game characteristics can and do change as plays are made, the relevance of simple games like Chicken and Prisoner's Dilemma for understanding and describing the behavior of two nations in conflict is open to question. These games, however, do provide insights into strategic behavior, and often are so employed by analysts. For example, mutual cooperation (obtaining the outcome [3.3]) can result from changing the rules to allow for more moves and countermoves.

3.6   The escalation process

The Prisoner's Dilemma game as just presented for the United States and the Soviet Union, which many claim was indeed the situation in which these two military powers found themselves for many years until

Gorbachev rose to power, is static. It relates to a decision at one point in time, and to a climate where there is no cooperation or communication, or where communication is poor and distrust prevails. However, the development of weapons arsenals in both the United States and the Soviet Union took place over a period of time, and involved actions and reactions by each party not depicted by the payoff matrices presented thus far. To portray the process of action and reaction over time which leads to mounting levels of military expenditures, we construct figure 3.1. Measured along the vertical axis are military expenditures of the Soviet Union (expenditures in rubles are converted into equivalent U.S. dollars); along the horizontal, military expenditures of the United States (in U.S. dollars). Suppose at a given point in time the Soviet expenditures are 200 billion as indicated by point A on the vertical axis, and that U.S. expenditures are also $200 billion as indicated by point B on the horizontal. Point N can then represent these two levels of expenditures.

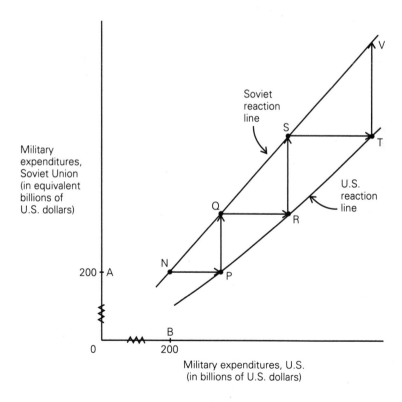

Figure 3.1 *An Escalating Arms Race*

Suppose a conservative government comes into office in the United States and contends that the previous administration allowed the U.S. military arsenal to fall well behind the Soviets. Accordingly, it increases the U.S. military budget by, say, $30 billion, corresponding to the line stretch **NP** in figure 3.1. Now, nations engaged in weapons development naturally try to keep their operations secret from their opponents (and even allies). However, the Soviet leaders get wind of this increase and are thus put under pressure to increase their nation's military budget. They might respond with a corresponding $30 billion increase, but since they probably have incomplete information about this new U.S. weapon development which may represent a qualitative advance in attack capability, to make certain the Soviet is not surpassed in military prowess, they are more likely to increase their budget by more, say, $35 billion, corresponding to line stretch **PQ**. Point Q represents the new set of military expenditures.

Sooner or later the U.S. learns of this increase in Soviet military expenditures and, to maintain its own national security, responds with a second increase in the next time period, not $35 billion to match the Soviet increase, but more, say, $40 billion (corresponding to the line stretch **QR**), since it, too, has only limited information on steps the Soviet is taking, and since it, too, fears falling behind in the arms race. Thus we arrive at point R.

The Soviet learns of this second increase. It enlarges its military budget a second time, again by somewhat more than is needed to reach parity with the U.S., say, by $45 billion (corresponding to stretch **RS**). Once again the U.S. responds, say, by $50 billion (corresponding to **ST**). And so the arms race escalates. In a sense this is what happened during the Cold War period following World War II up until the time Gorbachev assumed power in the Soviet Union. The last set of increases in military expenditures was associated with the Strategic Defense Initiative, or Star Wars, a development President Reagan initiated and to which the Soviet Union began to respond.

It is clear that if an arms race were to go on and on without constraint, with military expenditures growing ever larger and larger, eventually a nation's total production (Gross National Product, or GNP) would be used to build weapons. However, as we shall see, well before this point is reached, escalation necessarily will have stopped because of economic exhaustion.

The above description of the arms race can be generalized to depict the escalation of hostilities in many different conflict situations–in divorce cases between individuals; in conflicts between two ethnic groups; between two religious groups, or two subgroups of the same religion; in conflicts between labor and management; between one region and another within a nation; and so on. To illustrate better this escalation process, we present figure 3.2. Let the level of hostility of party #1 toward party #2 be measured along the vertical axis, and the hostility level of party #2 toward party #1 along the horizontal. Suppose the two parties are at point D where their hostility levels are low, these levels being measured from origin 0 representing zero hostility. Suppose party #2 directs an unkind remark at party #1, perhaps because of some seemingly minor conflict, such as, who is to get out of a warm bed to fondle a crying baby. Party #1 may respond with a withering comment, and party #2 in turn retaliates with very biting language. Party #1's next remark is nastier still, and provokes an even more hostile response from party #2. And so on.

Unlike figure 3.1, where the reaction lines appear to be straight, although they have some curvature, the hostility process like the one

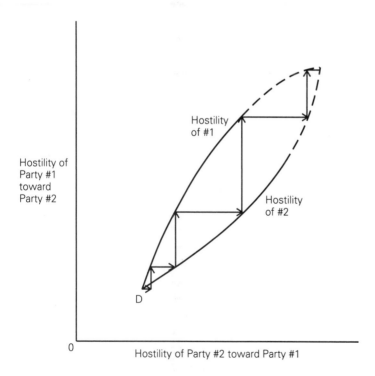

Figure 3.2 *Hostility Escalation*

described might follow paths with significant curvature, as in figure 3.2. There the hostility process from point D on is of an explosive character for a while. However, after a point, as so often occurs in reality, reactions can reach a limit, assuming outright physical violence or the equivalent has not taken place. No individual can direct hostile statements at another more than 24 hours a day. A group cannot continue indefinitely issuing increasingly hostile statements. It runs out of resources–financial, time, and so on. So also a nation can run out of resources in an arms race where warfare has not already broken out. When resource limits are approached the reaction curves start turning downward, as indicated by the dashed part of the curves in figure 3.2. No such limits were approached prior to the outbreak of World War I. However, before Gorbachev assumed power in 1985, the Soviet economy was approaching these limits. It is clear that President Reagan's buildup of the U.S. weapons arsenal during the 1980s (at the expense of programs to mitigate severe domestic social and economic problems) forced a retaliating response by the Soviet. There followed a series of alternating reactions by both countries, and by the end of the decade, the Soviet was using such a large portion of its resources for military preparedness that not enough was left to meet its civilian needs and to maintain productive capability. Reagan, whether he knew it or not, *initiated economic warfare*, forcing the Soviet Union into such high military expenditures as to lead it to the brink of economic bankruptcy. (See the discussion in the appendix to this chapter.)

3.7   The de-escalation process

Because the Soviet economy was in such dire straits when Gorbachev rose to power, he was able to persuade his political colleagues to accept his proposed policies of glasnost and perestroika. The Soviet people were extremely dissatisfied with their level of income and the kinds and amounts of goods available for purchase. Gorbachev had to reduce military expenditures to free up resources for the production of civilian goods. It was auspicious for him to initiate unilaterally a de-escalation (disarmament) process whose mechanism we now examine.

In figure 3.3 the upper portion of figure 3.1 and the U.S. reaction line in that figure are reproduced. A new Soviet reaction line is drawn. According to the Soviet's old reaction line, its response to the last increase in the U.S. military budget of $50 billion (represented by line stretch **ST**) should be an increase of $55 billion, corresponding to the dashed stretch **TV**. But such an increase would have bankrupted the Soviet economy, as Gorbachev must have recognized. A far-sighted Soviet leader like Gorbachev, realizing that the USSR can no longer afford the arms race, yet fully aware of the short-run need to maintain as strong a position as possible vis-à-vis the U.S., might decide that the Soviet cease aiming for parity, particularly in light of the "overkill" capacities of both nations. (Each possesses sufficient weapons to wipe out the other many times over.) Such a leader might strongly recommend that the Soviet shift its behavior (reaction curve), and that the Soviet response be more friendly. He is now about to move along a new reaction curve, such as the dashed curve in figure 3.3. He might suggest a unilateral action, a small decrease, say, **TW**, of Soviet's military expenditures for nonstrategic weapons in the hope that the U.S. will follow suit and reduce its own military expenditures by an amount **WX**. If he is successful and if the U.S. does react as hoped for, he might then call for a second reduction of **XY** in the Soviet budget, which he hopes will lead to a further reduction of **YZ** in the U.S. budget. And so on. In short, a de-escalation process will have begun. We may say that this process more or less characterized the pattern of Soviet and U.S. actions and reactions during the late 1980s and early 1990s. As we have witnessed, the process led to decreasing hostility and increasing friendship between the two Big Powers.

Like the escalation phenomena, this discussion of de-escalation is greatly oversimplified. Nonetheless, it is instructive.

We should note that any unilateral initiative aimed at de-escalation should have certain built-in features. First, it must not significantly affect a nation's ability to retaliate should it be attacked. Second, the initiative should be one whose extent (for example, the amount of reduction in military expenditure) will increase, the greater the opponent's degree of reciprocation. Third, the initiative should be designed and communicated to the opponent to emphasize a sincere intent to reduce tension and build trust. Fourth, it should be announced publicly and identified as part of a deliberate policy of reducing tensions. And fifth, this announcement should include an explicit invitation to the opponent to follow suit–all of this not only to convince the opponent of one's good intentions, but also to enlist world support for continuing the de-escalation process. Sixth, if its opponent does not respond to the first overture, the initiating party should persist with unilateral actions, as long as they do not affect its ability to retaliate. Finally, the initiative must be as unambiguous and

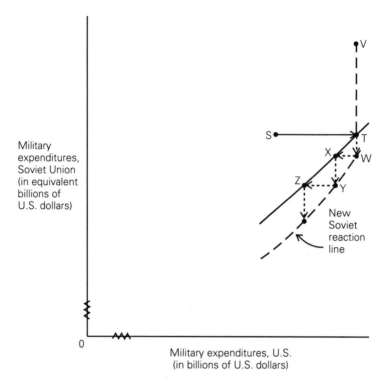

Military expenditures, Soviet Union (in equivalent billions of U.S. dollars)

Military expenditures, U.S. (in billions of U.S. dollars)

Figure 3.3 *Deescalation of Arms Expenditures*

as susceptible to verification as possible. If it is designed to be flexible, that is, if it contains several different plans for reducing military expenditures, each should be stated as unambiguously as possible and be as susceptible as possible to verification.

3.8   Summary

In this chapter, we have begun to examine individual and group behavior, borrowing from economics such concepts as payoff matrix and expected gains and losses. We first considered the attitude variable, and how specific attitudes such as that of the 100 percent conservative and the mixed pessimist-optimist determine which of several actions (options) will be chosen. We next looked at a behaving unit acting in a game-type situation where the outcome for him from any action he selects depends on which action a second behaving unit (often his opponent) adopts. Here we illustrated different outcomes from several possible combinations of actions by two protagonists in a Prisoner's Dilemma game and a Chicken game–two games often taken to represent the situation of two nations in conflict, the first being associated with an arms race and the inability to reach a disarmament treaty or other form of cooperative agreement.

Next, we examined the conflict escalation process in general, paying special attention to the arms race between the U.S. and the Soviet during the Cold War period. Finally, in the last section, we saw how exhaustion of resources, production capability, time, and other basics can lead to a de-escalation process. In particular, we examined how potential exhaustion and bankruptcy of the Soviet economy was initially responsible for generating a de-escalation process, starting in the late 1980s.

Appendix to Chapter 3: Economic Warfare

Why was the Soviet Union on the brink of economic bankruptcy when Gorbachev ascended to power in 1985? This can best be explained using the classic guns-and-butter illustration of the economist. At any point in time, a nation has a given stock of resources–land, minerals, labor (skilled and unskilled), production know-how, industrial plant and equipment, transportation facilities, liquid capital available for investment in new plant and equipment and development of human resources, and other assets. These can be used to produce either military goods (tanks, aircraft, nuclear weapons), designated *guns*, or civilian goods (food, clothing, housing, automobiles, TV sets), designated *butter*, or both. In figure 3.4, where output of guns is measured along the horizontal axis and output of butter along the vertical, the nation may be producing the combination of **OA** (=**BS**) amount of guns and **OB** (=**AS**) amount of butter as represented by point S. Given the same set of total resources it could have produced the combination **OC** (=**DR**) of guns and **OD** (=**CR**) of butter as represented by point R. Or it could have produced any combination of guns and butter represented by points along the curve **PRSP′**. Accordingly, **PRSP′** has been rightly termed a *production possibility curve*–on the assumption that the nation's economy is operating efficiently.[1] Note that this curve shows the trade-off or substitution possibilities of butter for guns, and guns for butter. For example, a nation producing a

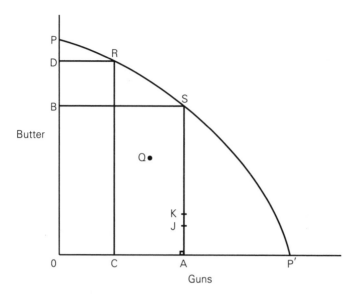

Figure 3.4 *The Resource Allocation Problem*

combination of guns and butter represented by point S may wish to increase its output of butter from **OB** to **OD** (an increase of **BD**). If it does this it can produce only **OC** of guns (a decrease of **CA**). **BD** amount of butter substitutes (trades) for **CA** of guns. Conversely, increasing guns (moving) to the right of point S and down the curve mean a decrease in butter.

The line **AS** which represents output of civilian goods can be divided into three segments. **AJ** represents output which must be devoted to replacing worn-out or obsolete equipment and industrial plant–designated replacement investment. **JK** represents the quantity of goods used primarily for construction of new plant and equipment (and also for development of human skills and R and D [research and development]). **KS** represents the civilian output (food, clothing, electricity) directly consumed by the population. Because there has been **JK** new investment in plant and equipment, the production capability (resources) of the nation is increased. For any given amount of butter the economy can now produce more guns than before. Or for any given amount of guns, it can produce more butter than before. In effect, the production possibility curve has been pushed out to become the dashed curve **TS'T'** of figure 3.5. Now the nation can produce **OA'** (=**B'S'**) of guns and **OB'** (=**A'S'**) of butter— that is more of each—as represented by point S' on the new production possibility curve.

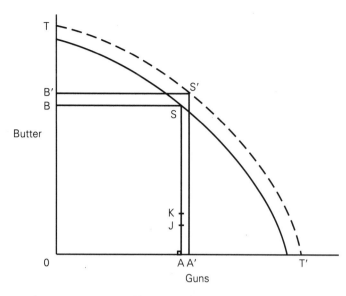

Figure 3.5 *Resource Allocation With Increased Production Capability*

However, suppose the nation (such as the USSR during the 1980s) decides it needs to produce more than **OA'** of guns, say, **OA''** of guns, because of a major arms buildup by its opponent (the U.S. during the Reagan regime). Clearly, it no longer will be able to realize the increase in butter output that was possible when only **OA'** guns were produced. This is brought out in figure 3.6, where both the old and the new (dashed) production possibility curves of figure 3.5 are reproduced. If a nation produces **OA''** of guns, it can produce only **A''U** of butter. If approximately the same amount of civilian output **A''J'** (=**AJ**) as before is required to replace worn-out industrial plant and equipment, and if the nation insists on maintaining the same level of civilian output **J'U**(=**KS**) for direct consumption, there is nothing left over for producing new industrial plant and equipment. Hence, the production possibility frontier **TUT'** remains unchanged.

Next, assume that the opponent builds up its military strength still further–as the U.S. continued to do during the 1980s, particularly with the initiation of its Star Wars program. The nation (USSR) will want to match this by increasing its guns output even more, say, to **OA'''**. This is shown in figure 3.7 where the new production possibility curve **TUT'** of figure 3.6 is reproduced. Now the civilian output must be further decreased to **A'''V**, and either the amount of civilian goods distributed for direct consumption must be reduced, or the replacement of some obsolete and worn-out industrial plant and equipment

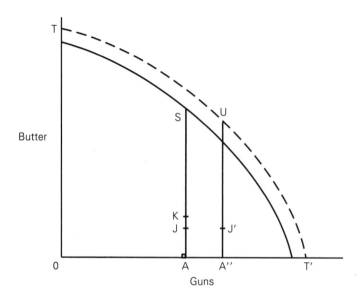

Figure 3.6 *Resource Allocation With Increased Arms Production*

must be foregone. A nation (USSR) engaged in a Cold War and greatly concerned with security may decide to reduce the amount of civilian goods distributed to its population–but ultimately as the arms race escalates, this policy will lead to popular resistance and civil unrest. Sooner or later, perhaps even at the very start in order to avoid unrest, the nation will begin to reduce the amount of goods allocated for the replacement of obsolete and worn-out industrial plant and equipment. Say this replacement segment is reduced to the level **A'''J''**. (Goods distributed to the population is **J''V**.) But this means that productive capacity (resources for production) will decrease in the following time period. As a consequence, all possible combinations of military and civilian goods that can be produced efficiently will lie on a lower production possibility curve, such as the lower dashed curve in figure 3.7. The production possibility curve has contracted. It is no longer possible to produce **A'''V** of civilian goods if the nation insisted previously on producing **OA'''** of guns. It can only produce **A'''W** of civilian goods. This means fewer civilian goods distributed to the population and fewer goods allocated for replacement. But fewer goods for replacement leads to further con-traction of the production possibility curve. And so forth, round by round, until ultimately the nation's economy breaks down (economic bankruptcy). In essence, the opponent has succeeded in waging effective economic warfare.

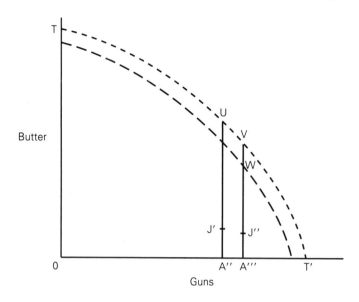

Figure 3.7 *Resource Allocation: Decreased Civilian Production from Major Increase in Arms Production*

Note

1 If the economy is not operating efficiently, the nation could be producing a combination of goods represented by point Q, clearly less desirable since point S corresponds to a greater production of both guns and butter. For every combination represented by a point within the area bounded by the production possibility curve and the axes, there is always a point on the curve itself that represents the greater production of both types of goods.

   Note that the production possibility curve is concave to the origin, rather than being a straight line. This is because an economy typically does not possess resources in the exact proportion that is best for the production of either military goods or civilian goods. For example, if the economy has four times as many units of labor as land, and if for the production of civilian goods the most productive combination is three units of labor per unit of land, then after some designated point (say, S), as the economy devotes more and more of its resources to producing civilian goods, it will run into diminishing returns (this often occurs in agriculture). The ratio of labor to land will exceed three, the most productive ratio. Similarly, after a point there will be diminishing returns in the production of military goods as the economy concentrates more and more on this.

References

Brams, Steven (1985) *Rational Politics, Decisions, Games and Strategy.* New York: Academic Press.

Isard, Walter (1988) *Arms Races, Arms Control and Conflict Analysis: Contributions from Peace Science and Peace Economics.* New York: Cambridge University Press, Chaps. 2 and 3.

4 Individual and Group Behavior: Cognitive Science Psychological and Sociological Approaches

4.1 Introduction

Thus far we have assumed that individuals and groups behave as economists and game theorists say they do. These scientists tend to emphasize the more objective features of a situation–such as payoffs, actions that involve precise dollar reductions in military expenditures, and well-defined reaction lines and curves. They assume that individuals and groups are highly rational. Obviously, they are not describing the real world. Individuals and groups are subjective and emotional in their behavior and can be highly so. In fact, according to some cognitive scientists, psychologists, political scientists, sociologists, and others, the analysis of behavior set forth heretofore has little relevance for understanding behavior. What do they consider important?

4.2 The mental representations of behaving units

First, take the cognitive scientist. He is interested in information processing–how the mind receives information, stores it, retrieves it, transforms and transmits it. He emphasizes one's representations of the world and everything in it. There are different kinds of *mental representations*. One is a *mental image*–a representation of something not physically present or which one has never seen, such as an elephant, or an Iraqi village, or an event that is purely imaginary such as a witch riding a broom. Cartoonists have represented the Soviet Union as a huge, lumbering, ugly bear. A mental image also may be a map–a map of things in space, a map of one's city or campus, or the Arabian desert. It may be detailed and fairly accurate, or a rough sketch with little correspondence to reality.

A mental representation may also be a *script*–a chain of events that fit together–things a person expects will happen after a first event occurs. This is often termed a *causal scenario*. It may be a *story* in which one event causes another, moving from an original situation to an end point. The domino theory was a widely held script during the 1960's which influenced the United States' decision to send troops to Vietnam. Against the background of civil unrest in Southeast Asia at that time was the belief that once a nation falls to Communism, its neighbors will fall as well, like dominoes in a standing set when one is knocked over.

Another type of mental representation is a *schema* (often considered a script). A schema is a cluster of knowledge about a situation involving one or more objects, one or more events, one or more relationships, or some of each of these. One may have a schema about bombing a city based on a study of World War II experiences. He may visualize a set of buildings—multistory offices at the center, homes around the center, an industrial area off to one side fed by several rail lines, with airplanes dropping bombs on the industrial area, already partially destroyed and ravaged by rapidly spreading fires. If he now thinks about bombing the area of a city that harbors terrorists, as some political leaders might advocate, he can use this schema instantly to project (forecast) the destructive effects. It provides a skeleton structure of a bombing attack; it represents a collection of facts, events, and relations having to do with bombing, which is in memory. It leads to certain expectations of the outcome of an attack. The schema provides also a structure within which any new knowledge or data on bombing can easily be recorded (or, to use a more technical word, *encoded*) in memory. Such new data may in turn lead to a change in the schema. A schema is a way of organizing information, of absorbing, encoding, and storing new facts and new relationships that may alter the schema itself. It enhances one's understanding of a situation or sequence of events, or episode. It indexes and stores information in the mind for ready access when needed. It can be very useful in assessing a situation and in planning for contingencies. Napoleon and Hitler had schemas in mind when they invaded Russia. In both cases, their schemas fell short; snowstorms foiled their efforts and led to defeat. It may be assumed that each assigned too low a probability to the emergence of Russian resistance which would slow down their advance and thus subject them to the hardships of winter weather. Being "risk-averse," or imbued with unfounded and unbounded optimism, each decided to invade.

One set of scripts of major importance in decisions regarding the use of military force in international conflicts has been *lessons of history*. Recall the series of events subsequent to the 1938 Munich meeting where British and French leaders reached a compromise with Hitler. The British and French allowed the Germans to take over the Sudetenland, that area of Czechoslovakia closest to Germany. Soon the rest of Czechoslovakia fell to Hitler, then Poland, then in time Yugoslavia, and so forth. This domino script, starting with the appeasement of Hitler at Munich, impressed John F. Kennedy during his formative college years. With this script in mind, Kennedy as president in the 1960s decided that the United States needed to stand up militarily to the Communists in Southeast Asia. He believed that if any nation in that region were to be taken over by Communists, then one-by-one each other nation experiencing internal unrest would likewise come under Communism. Therefore, the threat of Communism in Vietnam had to be stopped in its tracks.

Note, however, that the painful amd embarrassing American experience in Vietnam—the fact that the United States had to withdraw its forces after extensive bombing and loss of life on both sides—has produced a Vietnam script (schema) which emphasizes the inherent dangers to a Big Power in becoming involved in far-away civil wars and nationalist anti-imperialist Third World revolutions. This Vietnam script has been reinforced by an Afghanistan script resulting from the more recent, equally embarrassing experience of the Soviet Union in attempting to control the threatening unrest in Afghanistan. The lesson (pre- 1991) for the Big Powers, as viewed by many–in part erroneously because of its oversimplication–is, mess not in small countries' civil wars, especially where guerrilla warfare can be waged effectively.

The above illustrates how a political leader's choice of a specific action may be guided or even dictated by a dominant script, or lesson of history.

4.3 Learning from Experience

How are these mental representations acquired, and, as a corollary, how can they be changed through further experience and problem solving?–questions on which psychologists have long worked. Essentially, all knowledge and all mental representations are learned. A person possesses senses and memory. From birth, one's senses are subject to experiences–and many of these experiences are recorded in memory. Moreover, the mind has the ability to form concepts which go beyond seeing, feeling, hearing, smelling, and tasting and help one to understand what he senses. For example, given a table, one sees and feels a flat, level top and four legs, which have no smell or taste and are not associated with noise. These perceptions are accompanied by the concept that the four legs hold up the flat top, and that the flat top can hold objects which will not fall to the ground. The table concept is relatively simple. Concepts of peace and war are considerably more complex. They involve abstract knowledge far beyond the knowledge derived from sensual experiences, knowledge that comes principally from language—from reading, from hearing stories (vocal communication), and so on.

I shall not enter into a lengthy discussion of learning processes (and in particular the development of an individual's mental representations). However, I do wish to make explicit two ways of learning that are pertinent for understanding negotiations and conflicts among nations, namely, *learning from experience* and *learning from search and creative problem solving*. First consider the former.

A political leader may sometimes perceive only one course of action to take, but typically he sees at least two: embark on a specific action, or do nothing; declare war or do not declare war. Often there are possible actions that he does not perceive. Or he may perceive an action that he considers feasible, but which will turn out to be technically impossible; his covert (undercover) organization may be unable to eradicate terrorism.

Naturally, what he *perceives* as possible actions depends on the number of things he can *attend* to at one time. Any individual has limited ability to absorb information, process it, store it, and then retrieve it when he needs to, and act upon it. Some leaders are more capable than others in this regard. We have only to compare Gorbachev and Reagan in the 1980s. Older people tend to have less ability to handle new information than middle-aged, although this handicap is generally offset by wisdom acquired from broader experience.

Other factors affect a political leader's perceptions at the time a decision must be made. Cues come to him from the surrounding environment. News of an opponent's aggressive act may trigger a memory of other aggressive acts of this same adversary and lead him to believe that his opponent is considering a declaration of war. The general state of the environment and conditions in his own nation are likely to influence him. If he awakens to a bright, sunny spring day he may perceive his opponent's set of actions quite differently than he would were he to wake up to a day that is cold and rainy. If he is bogged down with nonmilitary problems and crises within his own nation (strikes, racial violence, economic recession, mounting national deficits), he may have little time to *attend* to foreign policy decisions. His perception of possible actions in response to an opponent's moves in the international arena may be narrowed down to one: "do nothing to change current policy."

Given his perceptions of his own actions as well as his opponent's, and given the relatively small number of factors he can take into account, the leader must appraise the situation and decide what to do. From past experience he may believe that his opponent is going to invade his territory without a declaration of war. Or he may assign a 50-50 chance to such an invasion. Or he may think of five or six possible actions by his opponent (do nothing, bomb cities, etc.) and assign probabilities to each.

And as we have already indicated, the leader's choice of action will depend in part upon his attitude. If he is conservative and motivated to do all that he can to assure his nation's security (a "sure thing" attitude), he may choose to strengthen his nation's defenses against attack, devoting considerable resources to that effort. This decision may be based on his assigning a 50-50 probability to an invasion after news of an aggressive act. It may turn out, however, that his opponent does not invade, perhaps because of his own major internal economic problems—an additional military effort would have bankrupted his country's (the opponent's) economy and undermined its ability to maintain an effective military presence. As a consequence, the leader will have channelled additional resources to defense in vain—resources that could have gone to social welfare programs and bolstered and increased his constituency's support. The leader may thus learn to become better informed about affairs in an opponent's country, the far-sightedness of its leadership, and so forth, before taking decisions on a military budget. Of course, a script in his active memory may still tell him that dictators in developing nations often engage in warlike actions in order to shift their constituents' attention away from major internal economic problems which they have failed to solve.

That learning takes place is clear. Lessons were learned from the Soviet Union's intervention in Afghanistan, and from the United States' intervention in Vietnam, although there is no agreement on what these lessons are! Some say the domino theory is flawed. Some say never engage a small nation if it has strong leadership and is capable of effective and enduring guerrilla warfare. Still others say never under any circumstance engage a small nation capable of enduring guerrilla warfare, whether or not it has strong, effective leadership. On the other hand, the success of the U.S. and its allies in the Gulf War has undermined the Vietnam syndrome and emboldened the U.S. to put aside the Vietnam script. Now the lesson of history is that with sufficient strength, a Big Power coalition, especially when supplemented with United Nations' support and an economic embargo, can effectively subdue a small country, guerrilla warfare or no.

Notwithstanding such different views, clearly President Johnson, the Soviet leaders, their advisors, and the public in general in their respective nations learned a great deal from the Vietnam and Afghanistan experiences.

What basic processes were behind these learning experiences? Kennedy, and later Johnson (when he ordered the bombing of North Vietnam), perceived several possible actions. Each also perceived a number of possible joint actions the North Vietnamese and National Liberation Front could take concomitantly or in response. For each action Kennedy and Johnson imagined sequences of events (scenarios) that might ensue. Then after consultation with advisors, each selected that action which he expected would yield the most favorable outcome, having one or more objectives in mind. The goal may have been to contain the spread of Communism, any such spread being interpreted as a corresponding decrease in U.S. security. Or perhaps it was to both increase this security and enhance U.S. leadership in the global system.

Having chosen an action, Kennedy and later Johnson must have expected different outcomes depending on how the North Vietnamese and National Liberation Front might respond. But whatever the response, defeat of Communist forces was envisaged. Imagine the shock to President Johnson of a Communist victory and U.S. defeat–an outcome so very different from what had been expected. Johnson and others learned that bombing, use of chemicals (agent orange), possession of highly sophisticated weaponry, and so forth do not guarantee victory in unconventional warfare.

In sum, a behaving unit typically learns: when actual actions and behavior of an adversary, as perceived, are different than expected; when the realized state of the environment, as perceived, is different than expected; when his own actual outcome, as perceived, is different than expected. A learner then changes his ideas about how his opponent behaves. He changes his notions of cause-and-effect, his perception of relevant relationships–in short, his schemas, scripts, and mental representations. He also may change his goals, yielding to more realistic aspirations, and perhaps his attitude toward his opponent. This learning is then stored in his memory as processed information, to be retrieved the next time a similar type of decision is required–or, possibly, to be forgotten.

4.4 OPTIONAL: A diagrammatic presentation of the learning process

We can develop a set of figures to help us see and understand the several subprocesses that make up the process of learning. As shorthand, we use symbols to represent words and relationships.

Let a_i represent an action of an individual whom we designate i. Let A_i stand for the *set of all actions* which that individual can possibly take. However, because of his limited abilities and associated inadequacies, he may not *perceive* all of these possible actions. Letting P_i represent his "perception of," we can say that $P_i(A_i)$ is his *perceived action set*. Typically, the individual chooses an action he perceives to be possible, that is, one that lies within $P_i(A_i)$.

Now, assume individual i faces an opponent, j. He knows that j will choose among several actions. Let A_j stand for the set of j's possible actions. At the decision point of time, however, i is able to perceive only a limited number of j's actions, only $P_i(A_j)$. Furthermore, objects and happenings around them influence i and j; we shall represent these by the symbol e, designating the state of the environment (including what might be called the "state of affairs"). The individual has only a partial awareness of e, and at times an erroneous impression; the relevant factor for his decision is his perception of e, namely, $P_i(e)$.

In figure 4.1 A_i, A_j, and e are within circles, from each of which an arrow leads to an oval which combines the individual's perceptions of A_i, A_j, and e, namely, $P_i(A_i)$, $P_i(A_j)$, and $P_i(e)$, into one expression $P_i(A_i,A_j,e)$. To make explicit i's limited abilities and associated inadequacies, the symbol *Att* is added, standing for the "limited number of things i can *att*end to." This factor influences what i actively sees as relevant, hence the arrow from *Att* to $P_i(A_i,A_j,e)$.

Next, let $\hat{a}_j$ represent what individual i expects j's action will be and let $\hat{e}$ represent what i expects e to be. He may expect the environment to change as he and j execute their actions. Accordingly, given $\hat{a}_j$ and $\hat{e}$, he anticipates a certain outcome from each action in his perceived set. He chooses the action a_i whose expected outcome $\hat{o}_i$ is best, in terms of his own aspirations and objectives. Figure 4.2 illustrates how he proceeds from his perceptions and expectations, designated *Exp*, to $\hat{a}_j$, $\hat{e}$, a_i, and $\hat{o}_i$.

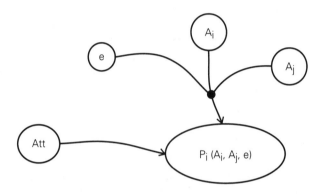

Figure 4.1 *Perception of Key Elements*

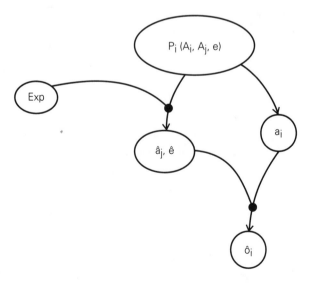

Figure 4.2 *Factors leading to Expected Outcome*

Recall that expectations derive from memory–in the form of schema, scripts, etc, that an individual retrieves. With *Mem* denoting memory, figure 4.3 shows the path from *Mem* to *Exp*. The same figure shows that the limited number of things an individual can attend to, namely, *Att*, is governed by *Cues* received from the environment *e* acting upon memory *Mem*.

We have indicated that *i* chooses action a_i. We know also that his opponent *j* chooses some action a_j (possibly "do nothing") from his own action set A_j. Also, there will be an actual state of the environment *e*, and all three of these, a_i, a_j, and *e*, determine the outcome *o*. This relationship is depicted in figure 4.4.

Given the outcome, individual i is in a position to learn. He compares the action a_j (or his perception of it, $P_i(a_j)$) with his earlier expectation of *j*'s action $\hat{a}_j$. He compares *e* (or his perception of it, $P_i(e)$) with his expected $\hat{e}$ and he compares *o* (or his perception of that outcome, $P_i(o)$) with his expected outcome $\hat{o}$. Things may or may not have turned out as expected. Or perhaps some of his expectations have come true. Whichever, he will have learned from this experience; that is, he will have acquired knowledge. This learning may be designated *L*. See figure 4.5.

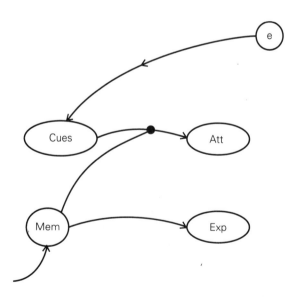

Figure 4.3 *Memory to Expectations, Cues to Things one Attends to*

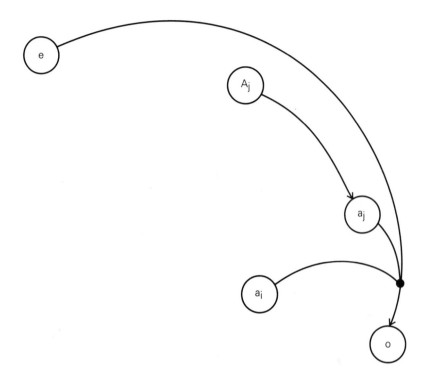

Figure 4.4 *Factors Affecting Outcome*

Knowledge from learning enters memory and is available for use the next time around. Meanwhile, of course, the individual may forget some of the stored information. Let α be the rate of his forgetting. Thus learning (L) and memory from the current period less forgetting (*Mem* - α *Mem*) together yield memory available for use in the next time period. See figure 4.6.

Finally, figure 4.7 is a composite of figures 4.1 through 4.6 which indicates in oversimplified form the process of learning. A process such as this took place between the day Chamberlain chose to pursue an appeasement policy toward Hitler and months later after Hitler had taken over the rest of Czechoslovakia and had invaded Poland; between the day ex-President Johnson ordered the bombing of North Vietnam and months later when a U.S. defeat was recognized; between the day the Soviet leadership decided to invade Afghanistan and months later when a similar outcome there became apparent. Learning experiences of past political leaders, often taught as lessons from history, critically influence leaders' decisions today.

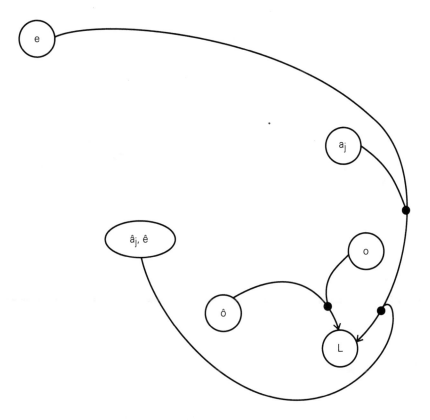

Figure 4.5 *Learning From Experience*

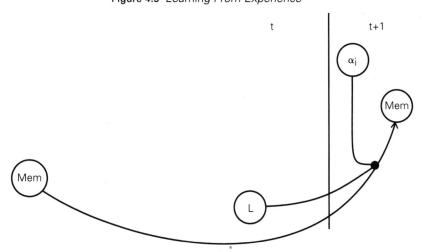

Figure 4.6 *Learning As Addition to Memory*

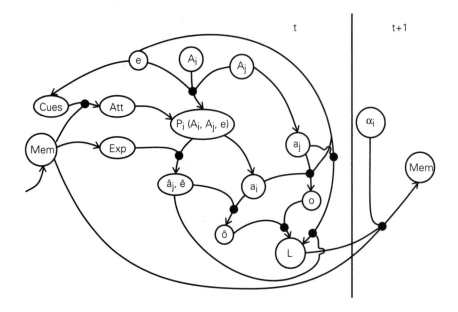

Figure 4.7 *The Process of Decision Making and Learning*

4.5   Learning from search and creative problem solving

A second kind of learning is creative problem solving. This learning comes from solving a problem that has never arisen before, where there is no experience to draw upon, and no information, or at best only a negligible amount to retrieve from memory. We are not talking here about solving a problem when one knows what steps to take–as is the case with algebra learned at school. Rather, we are referring to problem solving without benefit of experience or known procedures. A typical new problem was the one faced by Gorbachev and the rest of the Soviet leadership in the early 1990s, namely, how to transform a huge, inefficient Communist-planned economy into a Socialist market economy. Gorbachev was unsuccessful despite his having set up a team of the best Soviet economists (including mathematical model builders). Yeltsin and leaders of the independent nations and republics formerly under the Soviet Union umbrella face similar problems of major transition with no experience to draw upon. For less complicated problems, useful techniques are being developed in the field of *Artificial Intelligence,* considered by some to belong to the discipline of Cognitive Science.

One of its methods of problem solving is to develop a series of steps each designed to reduce the difference between the current (initial) state of affairs and the desired state (goal), it being impossible to identify a single action for reaching the final position. This is called a *difference reduction method.* Often, in a violent conflict the first step urged is a "cease-fire," perhaps accompanied by the presence of a United Nations police force. Such a step is designed to reduce the emotional intensity among warring parties, to calm things down in anticipation of a second step of a conciliatory nature where perhaps a compromise can be reached, or where a highly respected and experienced third party tries to help the warring parties settle some, if not all, of their differences through mediation. One does not know beforehand what this second step should be; one can only speculate. Chapter 7 presents principles of negotiation and mediation and a variety of possible steps. Since there is no scientific basis for selecting a best step, negotiation or mediation is usually called for. Needless to say, in many situations a first step, such as a cease-fire, has not been followed by an effective second step. Oftentimes this has been so with Middle East conflicts, and the recent Serbian/Croatian fighting.

Note that this approach involves setting up subgoals, the first being to stop the fighting, the second, say, to have parties agree to work with a trusted mediator, the third to reach a compromise on conflictual issues.

Another approach is the *working-backward method.* An effective compromise among warring parties requires building up a great deal of trust among them, so that they can come to the bargaining table ready to engage in unemotional, rational discussion and to see each other's point of view–ready, that is, to conduct a *successful* give-and-take negotiation–the last step. Thus, the next-to-last step must focus on trust building–in fact, several trust-building steps may be needed prior to final negotiation. And even before these trust-building steps can be taken, some direct or indirect (through a third party) communication among warring leaders or their negotiators may be necessary.

The above speaks of general steps. Often steps need to be stated in precise terms if they are to succeed. One approach involving precise steps is the *Single Negotiations Text,* a method one can use after going through the theoretical steps of working backward. Here, the first step may be a cease-fire. The next may be to bring together negotiators from all sides, perhaps at first involving the parties in social and/or recreational activities, for example, sampling wines and waltzing at the Grundzing heurigers (outskirts of Vienna).

Following such introductory informalities, a third party presents the text of a treaty, agreement, or some other document, merely for initial reaction. This text must be carefully designed–it must make overall sense but contain a number of holes (inadequacies). These holes are to allow for small changes in the text, any of which will significantly improve one party's position without harming the other's. It is the third party's job to ask each rival party to submit such a small textual change, and to encourage both to agree to these first revisions. The revised text represents definite improvement for each, and thus tends to build trust. The process can continue, each party suggesting a second, third, and perhaps further small change leading to an improved situation for himself and at most very little harm to the other. In this cumulative way, the third party may be effective in guiding negotiations through the later, more difficult give-and-take stage, in which concessions must be made. See the further discussion in section 8.5.

Use of *analogy* is still another way of solving new problems. In any specific field of knowledge, be it political science, economics, regional science, or other, one may lack the tools to solve a given problem. Theoretical findings, mental representations, and knowledge in general may be inadequate. One may need to turn to another domain for a good analogy. In attacking transportation problems regional scientists have found Isaac Newton's gravity model to be useful. Peace scientists are beginning to use this model from physics to better understand conflicts among nations and ethnic populations in Africa and Asia, thus to be prepared to propose more effective ways to curb their spread. In designing peace treaties during conflict mediation, political scientists have used the balance-of-power concept–borrowed from the physicist's concept of equilibrium of forces. Models of decision making on the level of defense expenditures have been based on equilibrium concepts from both physics and economics.

Still other approaches, such as the *General Problem Solver,* have been developed in the field of Artificial Intelligence. Some depend on the enormous computational capacities of modern-day computers to carry through simulations of arms races, chess matches, and so forth. These approaches are being used increasingly by military establishments, university research scholars, and business and political analysts to help solve extremely complicated problems, for example, how to effect the transition from a heavily militarized economy to one with significantly less arms production without causing a major recession or severe depression.

Learning from solving new problems is, of course, essential for attaining a peaceful and orderly society. The world is constantly changing. New problems constantly arise. In recent decades, for example, population growth and technological advances have given rise to major new environmental problems. A negotiator wanting to reach an acceptable agreement with an opposite party over a brand new kind of conflict may discover that old negotiation methods no longer work. He must find new techniques. Or a third party serving as mediator may need to initiate new approaches. In 1978, for example, when President Carter brought together at Camp David President Sadat of Egypt and Prime Minister Begin of Israel, he had to develop new procedures for reconciling differences between these two leaders. By using a unique variant of the Single Negotiations Text approach, he was able to score significant progress.

In short, any negotiator, mediator, or applied peace scientist called in to analyze a new type of conflict often will find it necessary to modify developed techniques or to devise entirely new ones.

4.6 Behavior and learning of a group, its members and leader

Thus far this chapter has treated the behavior of a single individual, acting independently in his own self-interest. However, individuals, especially political leaders, are influenced by the goals and attributes of groups to which they belong. It is therefore important to consider group behavior as well. Political leaders, by definition, are members of the groups they lead. The influence of a group's goals and attributes on its leader's and its other members' goals must therefore also be considered.

Although each individual is unique, and no one, least of all a leader, is 100 percent representative of his group, as indicated in chapter 2, group members have much in common. They share beliefs, myths, scripts, schemata, and mental representations. The group, too, has its ways of collecting, processing, and storing information. Whenever the group votes or decides on an action, it draws upon perceptions (and misperceptions) of its action set, those of other behaving units, and of the current state of affairs. It has social and cultural sensitivities for evaluating an outcome. Like the individual, during the time available for a decision, the group can collect and process only a limited amount of information and can retrieve only a fraction of the information stored in written materials or in its members' memories. Moreover, it may be receptive to, or perceive, certain cues and not others. It has expectations of how other groups and behaving units will act, what the state of the environment is, what outcome will ensue. It has certain attitudes and objectives and chooses the action (policy) that is expected to yield an outcome closest to its goal (or weighted sum of objectives), or to maximize the probability that its goal will be realized. Its learning process parallels that of the single individual. It compares: (a) actions of other behaving units, as perceived, with what it had expected them to be; (b) the realized state of the environment (or its perception thereof) with its expectation; and (c) the actual outcome (or its perception thereof) with the expected outcome. The resulting learning is then stored in memory, and is likely to influence future behavior.

Like the single individual behaving unit, the group also learns through creative problem solving when new problems arise. It may conduct or support research by collecting and processing new data, look for analogies, and so forth, often using Artificial Intelligence procedures and the mounting capabilities of ever more sophisticated computers.

Learning, of course, leads to changes–changes in knowledge, perceptions, sensitivities, attitudes, expectations, and objectives. Compared to the individual, the group is less likely to experience sudden change since the group is a weighted average of individuals. Group goals, too, are likely to change less often and by smaller amounts than individual goals, even when there is a dominating personality. This is so since changes in individual members' goals usually are not all in the same direction; they offset each other at least to some extent. Moreover, individuals can move from one group to another. Those whose goals have changed significantly are more likely to move out of one group into another, leaving behind those whose individual goal changes are of smaller magnitude and who thus exert less pressure to change the group's goals.

The parallel between group and individual behavior and learning, however, should not be carried too far. There are other factors to consider.

4.7   The role of political subcultures

We have spoken of the group as an average of individuals who may have different weights in deciding upon an action. Often it is more realistic to think of groups as comprising two or more subgroups–especially when examining the influence of group attributes and behavior upon a political leader's decisions. A U.S. president, a British prime minister, or a German chancellor is not much influenced by his national constituency. He is affected much more by the attributes and behavior of the subgroup (or subculture) to which he belongs or subscribes. It may be a political party, religious organization, lobbying group, or other entity, all of which comprise a nation's political subcultures.

Gamson, a noted sociologist, researched the mental representations of the Arab–Israel conflict held in the early 1980s by different *political subcultures* in the United States (1981). He reported six clusters of well-organized ideas, each of which he called an *interpretive package* (a package of interpretations). Four of the six appear in table 4.1. They are listed in column 1: Strategic interest, David and Goliath, Feuding neighbors, and Dual liberation. Column 2 lists the basic issue for each of the four political subgroups. For the strategic interest package, it is how best to pursue America's *strategic interests* in the Middle East in the context of its larger conflict with the Soviet Union. For the David and Goliath package, it is the unwillingness of the Arab world to accept Israel's right to exist.

The third column lists the position each subculture believes the U.S. should take. The strategic interest subgroup holds that the United States should support and encourage countries that share its opposition to Soviet penetration of the Middle East and will help secure the free world's oil lifeline.

Column 4 assigns appropriate metaphors that help to size up or understand the basic issue. For the strategic interest package, a relevant metaphor is a board game in which Middle East countries are the pieces to be moved and captured and the U.S. and the Soviet Union are the competing players.

The fifth column records illustrative events and situations (current and past) and lessons from history. For the strategic interest package, relevant events are the attempted Soviet takeover of Iran in 1946, and the Soviet invasion of Afghanistan. A relevant situation is Soviet military aid and advisors in various Arab countries. The lesson here is that the Soviet Union is actively seeking to expand its influence in the Middle East.

The sixth column lists relevant catchphrases. For the David and Goliath package, Arab emnity is revealed in: "Only a sword in their side" and "Push the Jews into the sea."

Table 4.1 *Interpretive packages of the Arab–Israeli conflict, 1981*

Label (1)	What basic issue is (2)	What U.S. position should be (3)	Appropriate metaphors (4)	Illustrative events, situations, and lessons (5)	Catchphrases (6)
Strategic interest	The issue is how to best pursue America's strategic interests in the Middle East in the context of our larger conflict with the Soviet Union.	The United States should support and encourage countries that share our opposition to Soviet penetration of the Middle East and will help to secure the free world's oil lifeline.	A board game in which the countries of the Middle East are pieces that can change hands, and the United States and the Soviet Union are the competing players.	Attempted Soviet takeover of Iran in 1946; Soviet invasion of Afghanistan; Soviet military aid and advisors in various Arab countries; *Lesson,* the Soviet Union is actively seeking to expand its influence in the Middle East.	—
David and Goliath	The issue is the unwilling-ness of the Arab world to accept Israel's right to exist.	The United States has a moral obliga-tion to help Israel to survive in a hostile environ-ment and to encourage the Arab countries to accept Israel's right to exist.	David against Goliath.	The Holocaust: *Lesson,* the vulnerability of a stateless people, unable to organize their own means of self-defense. Hitler's pronouncements against the Jews: *Lesson,* one cannot ignore or treat as mere rhetoric verbal threats of annihilation.	Illustrating Arab enmity: "Only a sword in their side." "Push the Jews into the sea."
Feuding neighbors	The issue is whether the fight that is going on over there will end up engulfing all of us in another world war.	The United States should try to mediate the dispute as best it can but should not take major risks that would involve America directly in the fighting in the Middle East.	The Hatfields and the McCoys.	The beginning of World War I: *Lesson,* a local conflict can spread into a world war.	A plague on both your houses.
Dual liberation	The issue is a conflict between two national liberation movements both of which have a legitimate historical claim to the same piece of land.	The United States should support a compromise in which Israel's right to exist in secure, recog-nized borders is accepted and some sort of Palestinian state is created.	—	The Benelux countries: *Lesson,* Belgium and the Netherlands did not work as a unitary state, but the two peoples, living in separate states, maintain good stable relations and close economic ties.	Israel *and* Palestine. A new partition.

Table 4.1　*Interpretive packages of the Arab–Israeli conflict, 1981 (cont.)*

Depictions (7)	*Visual images (8)*	*Basic causes (roots) of conflict (9)*	*Consequences (10)*	*Appeals to principle (11)*
Russia as having imperial designs on the region. The Middle East as a major cold war arena. Israel or pro-Western Arab countries as buffers against Soviet influence.	A grizzly bear with a hammer and sickle hovering over the Middle East.	Indigenous conflict exacerbated greatly by Soviet exploitation of the conflict for its own imperial aims.	Effect on American security and access to resources is emphasized.	Defense of the free world.
Israel as one small country against 20 Arab countries with a popu-lation more than 20 times its size. Arabs as fanatics and zealots, unwilling to make peace with Israel.	Arabs as violence-prone, fanatic extremists.	Arab unwillingness to recognize Israel's right to exist.	Effect on Israel's security is emphasized.	The right of any people to to live in peace and security, especially a people that has been the victim of a long history of oppression.
Both sides as unreasonable, fanatic. Innocent bystanders (the world) as the real victim.	Middle East as a tinderbox or time bomb ready to go off.	A destructive cycle of hostile acts that stimulate hostile responses. An unwillingness by both sides to forget the injuries of the past and make peace.	Effects on the probability of a larger war emphasized.	Live and let live; let bygones be bygones.
The Palestinian issue as more than a refugee problem since a legitimate Palestinian national movement exists.	—	Two people and two national movements each with a valid historical claim to the same land.	Effects on the legitimate rights of both sides emphasized.	Self-determination for all people.

Column 7 lists depictions. For the David and Goliath package, two are: "Israel as one small country against 20 Arab countries with a population more than 20 times its size"; "Arabs as fanatics and zealots, unwilling to make peace with Israel."

Visual images comprise column 8. For the strategic interest package, a cartoon: the Soviet Union as a grizzly bear with a hammer and sickle hovering over the Middle East (1981). For the feuding neighbors package, a cartoon portraying the Middle East as a tinder box or a time bomb ready to go off.

In column 9, basic causes (roots) of conflict are given. For dual liberation: "two people and two national movements each with a valid historical claim to the same land."

Column 10 lists consequences of the conflict. For the strategic interest package these emphasize effects on American security and access to resources.

Finally, column 11 lists appeals to principle: "defense of the free world" in the strategic interest package; "self-determination for all people" in the dual liberation package.

The above sociologic framework for analyzing a society points up the need to pay attention to the political subculture to which a political leader or other individual belongs and which he represents if we are to understand his behavior. Consider ex-President Reagan. He came from a relatively conservative, anti-Communist, big-money, powerful Republican subculture. He was nominated as president (and previously as governor of California) because he was a representative member of that subculture; he shared its beliefs and goals. As president he took actions in keeping with the "strategic interest" interpretive package of his subculture. He lobbied successfully for major increases in the arms budget to equal and even surpass the military might of the Soviets, his last effort being to mount a Strategic Defense Initiative (a Star Wars program). Indirectly he supported Afghan guerrillas in their struggle against the puppet regime installed by the Soviets. He characterized the Soviet Union as the "evil empire" and constantly appealed to the principle, "defense of the free world."

Nonetheless, his own aspirations influenced his actions as well. Toward the end of his second term, he became a much less bitter and vigorous opponent of the Soviet Union and expressed a willingness to compromise, in the hope that history would mark him favorably as a leader who took significant strides toward defusing the Cold War and promoting peace.

Now that the Soviet Union has disintegrated into a set of independent republics, each preoccupied with major internal economic and political problems, and is no longer seen as a threat in the Middle East, the "strategic interest" interpretive package *re* the Arab–Israeli conflict is being discarded. Instead, President Bush, springing from the same political subculture as Reagan, supports the "dual liberation" interpretive package, as do many others in his subculture. The last development also illustrates the dynamics of war and peace, of conflict and cooperation.

4.8   Decision-making behavior under major psychological stress and crisis conditions

Thus far, we have examined individual and group behavior, routine and creative, in situations where, by and large, the problem does not require *immediate* solution. We have assumed nonstressful situations wherein a behaving unit has limited information, perhaps many misperceptions, and responds to stimuli in accordance with scripts, schemata, interpretive packages, and other mental representations accumulated from experience. The behaving unit may even respond mechanically according to rules established through experience or dictated by culture. We have assumed the unit to have at least (1) some rough knowledge of its set of possible actions, (2) some crudely derived probabilities attached to possible states of the environment and actions of others, and (3) some ideas about outcomes that could result from different actions. The unit's behavior may be somewhat rational, somewhat oriented to precedents and customs, somewhat impulsive (playing hunches without any real reason), and perhaps partially unexplainable.

Especially in the international arena, however, decision making often takes place under major pyschological stress and crisis conditions. In this situation the process can be very different from a situation in which there is plenty of time to examine possible consequences of different actions.

Social psychologists Janis and Mann [1977] and others look upon humans and groups as reluctant decision makers. Individually or as members of a group, people are emotional beings beset by doubts and uncertainties. Moreover, they have incongruous desires, antipathies, and loyalties which give rise to conflict and psychological stress.

As reluctant decision makers, they continue along some chosen course of action until a stress-producing threat to their important goals causes them to (1) seek a better solution through vigilance and diligent search, (2) rationalize their present course, particularly if they have too little time to search for alternatives, or (3) panic.

These scholars fully recognize that (1) limited cognitive ability to digest information and (2) restrictions imposed by powerful persons or groups do stand in the way of "vigilant information processing." But so also does the anxiety caused by psychological stress.

What is "vigilant information processing"? According to social psychologists, and following the thinking of Janis and Mann, it is a standard which is met when the decision maker

1. looks carefully at a broad range of possible actions;
2. examines the set of objectives to be met and the values to be attained;
3. carefully weighs both positive effects (gains) and negative effects (costs and risks) of each possible action, as far as he is aware of them;
4. spends considerable time, effort, and other resources acquiring new information for evaluating the positive and negative effects of each possible action;
5. reexamines these effects, giving weight to information and the judgment of experts that do not support the action he initially prefers; and
6. spells out in detail the steps necessary to implement the action he chooses, including contingency plans should a recognized risk materialize.

Rarely does a decision maker under stress engage in vigilant information processing when making "consequential" decisions. This is so because such decisions cause him some anxiety and uncertainty. Will he be able to achieve his objectives? Will he incur costs (money, time, effort, emotional involvement, reputation) greater than he can afford? Will he be able to cope? Will he have sufficient time to identify a best decision and put it into effect? As a consequence, important decision making usually falls short of vigilant information processing.

There are a number of ways of coping with stress in a crisis situation where there is a clear threat to one's security, that is, where there are warnings of impending danger. The behaving unit may ask: are the risks serious if I do not change my current action, given my expectation of the outcome of this action under the new situation? This is equivalent to his asking is there a non-negligible probability of finding another action that would significantly reduce the threat to my security and welfare? He may already know this other possible action, or he may need to spend time and effort identifying it. If the answer to his question is *no*, the risks are not serious, the behaving unit probably will continue to make decisions the same old way, and in any case will stay with the current action. This strategy has been designated *unconflicted adherence*. He goes along with a limited weighing of alternatives.

However, if the answer to this first question is *maybe* or *yes*, then he needs to pose a second question, namely, is the search for an alternative action desirable? This is equivalent to asking whether expected gains would be greater than expected costs in time and effort required to reevaluate existing information and gather new. Obviously, there are two possible answers: If *no*, then the unit does not search for an alternative action. He adopts the stance of *unconflicted adherence* and proceeds with limited weighing of alternatives. This stance may also be taken simply because the behaving unit realizes that there is no time to search; an immediate decision is required, as when there was a serious nuclear plant breakdown at Chernobyl, or when a major earthquake took place in San Francisco.

If the answer to the second question is *yes*, and there is time, the behaving unit proceeds with search and reevaluation and may succeed in identifying another option. Upon evaluation of expected gains and costs, this new possible action may be judged no better than the one initially proposed. Again, the behaving unit would not be motivated to change his plan. At this point, there may be no time left for further search. He adopts the stance of *unconflicted adherence*, with somewhat less limited weighing of alternatives.

If he does find a better alternative, he can reduce his risk by choosing the new action, and he should do so if there is no time left for further search. In this case, his stance is one of *unconflicted change*. Even though there may be sufficient time for further search, he may be satisfied that this new action will overcome his risk sufficiently–in which case he can be designated a *satisficer*.

On the other hand, if there is time for further search and he is not satisfied, the behaving unit will continue the process, assuming that expected gains exceed expected costs, and try to find a still better action. Ultimately, if there are no time and resource constraints, he will achieve vigilant information processing.

In this process, however, the decision maker may search diligently and not find any action better than his initial one; or he may find a better action which still leaves the risk much too high. He may reach the conclusion that no good action is possible–that there is no solution. In this case, he will adopt a stance of *defensive avoidance.* He may *procrastinate* and do nothing–leave things alone. (This was the case, some claim, when the Nixon administration failed to do anything about the oil shortage crisis of December, 1973, despite a large number of warning signs.) He may *pass the buck*–that is, assign responsibility for taking appropriate action to another party. (Ex-President Truman displayed on his desk a plaque inscribed: "The buck stops here.") Or he may resort to *bolstering,* that is, he may select the least objectionable action and rationalize his choice, exaggerating its favorable consequences and playing down the unfavorable, while doing the opposite for the possible actions he turned down.

The decision maker may be forced into still another stance. Having identified no acceptable action, he may still believe that one can be found. However, he has run out of time. He stays on the alert, experiencing extreme anxiety and stress and emotional ups and downs. This stance is designated *hypervigilance.* (This may be said to have characterized the state of decision making of more than one political leader immediately prior to the outbreak of World War I.) In fact, when a deadline is reached, he may *panic,* search frantically for a solution, and latch onto any action that seems to promise some immediate relief from anxiety, even onto the very first that comes to mind.

It must be emphasized that in a crisis situation involving a series of actions and reactions, wherein time available for searching for an appropriate response to an opponent's move becomes shorter and shorter as the crisis mounts, constriction of one's cognitive capability becomes greater and greater. Inadequacies in decision making, sometimes designated *decision-making pathologies,* play an increasingly important role. As with bolstering, there occurs

1. overvaluation of past performance as against present reality, that is, perception of outcome values significantly different from those the best objective analysis (models) would establish from looking at past performance (higher when outcomes are advantageous, lower when disadvantageous);
2. overconfidence in policies to which the decision maker is committed; and
3. insensitivity to information critical of these policies.

These pathologies often involve the same kinds of perceptions and misperceptions discussed earlier regarding actions of other behaving units, current states of affairs, and so forth.

As a participant's set of possible actions is steadily reduced with continuous rounds of actions and reactions in a crisis situation, the behaving unit may find himself in a state of *entrapment*. Having no further time and resources for reevaluation and search, he is boxed in and perceives one and only one possible action, perhaps to carry out his threat to invade. (A leader faced with an act of mobilization by an opponent, for example, might see no alternative but to carry out his threat to invade, assuming his forces are already mobilized. Once he has acted, he may resort to rationalizations to justify his actions, especially when it has failed or proved inadequate (*post-decisional rationalization*).

Note once more that people have limited analytical capabilities and capacity to encode new information when confronted with a tremendous amount of it. Since they cannot absorb it all, and since they may have no objective criteria for differentiating among pieces of information thrown at them, it is efficient for them to absorb only that information consistent with the information they have already encoded and to be insensitive to (discard) new information inconsistent with their existing set of perceptions of, and theories about, the world. That is, they find it advantageous to use a *cognitive consistency principle*–a principle used extensively, most often not consciously, but which leads to poor decision making when significant information is discarded.

Also, poor decision making (inadequate attention to the full set of possible actions and their proper evaluation) may result from the phenomenon of *group think*. Janis (1972) has defined group think as a tendency for members of a highly cohesive group to seek concurrence–to share beliefs and judgments on best actions and other matters. Some of the symptoms of group think are:

1. a shared illusion of invulnerability leading to excessive optimism and willingness to take extreme risks;
2. collective rationalization and discounting warnings of dangers and misinformation;
3. unquestioning belief in the group's basic morality and rectitude;
4. stereotyped views of adversaries as evil, weak, stupid, or inferior;
5. pressures and sanctions against group members who deviate or dissent;
6. self-censorship of such deviation and of critical and challenging discussion;
7. a resulting shared illusion of unanimity; and

8. self-appointed "mindguards" who discourage members of the group from questioning any adverse information regarding the effectiveness and morality of their decisions.

As these symptoms imply, group think is also responsible for

1. limiting the perceived range of alternative actions in emotion-laden situations, as was indeed the case with the Johnson administration's decision to bomb North Vietnam, or which may happen when charismatic, fanatic religious leaders like Ayatollah Khomeini dominate politics; and
2. distorted estimates of outcomes, as when the Kennedy administration made such wrong assumptions and harbored such unrealistic expectations in the Bay of Pigs fiasco.

4.9   Summary

Having in mind the ideas of economists and game theorists discussed in the previous chapter, we have asked in this chapter how the hypotheses and findings of psychologists, cognitive scientists, and sociologists add to our understanding of individual and group behavior. We saw how mental images, scripts, schemas, lessons of history, and other mental representations come to influence the individual's choice of actions. We also saw how *learning from experience* takes place–a behaving unit's perceptions of actions and relationships are affected at any one time by the number of things it can attend to, how these are elicited by cues, how one's expectations are based upon memory, and how one learns from experience when the realized outcomes, state of the environment, and actions by others differ from one's expectations. Such experience is encoded in memory, available for retrieval, if not forgotten, the next time a similar or related decision must be made. Experiences of critical importance for a nation's foreign policy are often designated lessons from history and are very important to further development of foreign policy.

Learning also comes from persistent search for and development of creative solutions to problems never before confronted. Methods involving "difference reduction," "working backward," use of analogies, use of the immense capabilities of computers in such Artificial Intelligence approaches as the "General Problem Solver" and others yet to be invented can be harnessed to solve problems of the world system that are entirely new.

Next we focused on group behavior, recognizing that the earlier discussion of individual learning and behavior was relevant to groups as well. However, we cautioned against carrying the parallel too far. Though at times a group may be considered as homogeneous, an average of its individuals, at other times it must be viewed as a set of subgroups, each being a political subculture. We saw how the U.S. reacted not as a homogeneous culture, as it is so often considered, but instead as a set of political subcultures when confronted with the Arab–Israeli conflict in the early 1980s, each with a different idea of what the nation's position should be. Each subculture comes up with its own metaphors, illustrative events, catchphrases, and visual images, and differs in its interpretation of lessons from history and appeals to principle. As we illustrated, the attitudes, perceptions, expectations, memory, and other attributes of the political subculture to which a leader belongs affect the actions that leader takes.

Some critically important decisions are made under crisis conditions. Too frequently a high level of stress precludes vigilant information processing. To cope with stress, the behaving unit may adopt a stance of (a) unconflicted adherence to his current behavior; (b) unconflicted change (without further search) from a more acceptable action; (c) defensive avoidance, where the unit procrastinates, passes the buck, or resorts to bolstering; or (d) hypervigilance, where there is no further time to search for an acceptable action even though the unit believes one can be found, a situation that often leads to panic. Associated with such stress are decision-making pathologies, such as overvaluation of past performance, insensitivity to information critical of present policies, and group think leading to an uncritical sharing of beliefs by all group members.

This chapter has presented the play of key cognitive, psychological, sociological factors, having in the background the cultural, economic, and strategic (game-theoretic) factors discussed previously. Now we must move on to discuss the play of still another critical set of factors embodied by the words "politics" and "geopolitics," to which we turn in the next chapter.

References

Barash, David P. (1991) *Introduction to Peace Studies*, Belmont, CA: Wadsworth, Part II.

Brams, Steven J. (1990) *Negotiation Games: Applying Game Theory to Bargaining and Arbitration*. New York: Routledge.

Druckman, Daniel and P. Terrence Hopmann (1989) "Behavioral Aspects of Negotiations on Mutual Security," in Tetlock, Philip E., Jo L. Husbands, Robert Jervis, et al., *Behavior, Society and Nuclear War*. New York: Oxford University Press, pp. 85–173.

Gamson, W. (1981) "The Political Culture of the Arab–Israeli Conflict," *Conflict Management and Peace Science*. 5(2):79–84.

Holsti, Ole R. (1989) "Crisis Decision Making," in Tetlock, Philip E., Jo L. Husbands, Robert Jervis, et al., *Behavior, Society and Nuclear War*. New York: Oxford University Press, pp. 8–84.

Isard, Walter (1988) *Arms Races, Arms Control and Conflict Analysis: Contributions from Peace Science and Peace Economics*. New York: Cambridge University Press, Chaps. 4–6.

Janis, I (1972) *Victims of Group Think*. Boston: Houghton Mifflin.

Janis, I. and L. Mann (1977) *Decision Making: A Psychological Analysis of Conflict, Choice and Commitment*. New York: Free Press.

Jervis, Robert (1976) *Perception and Misperception in International Politics*. Princeton, NJ: Princeton University Press.

Lebow, R. Ned (1981) *Between War and Peace*. Baltimore: Johns Hopkins University Press.

5 Politics (and Behavior of Key Political Figures) and Regional Conflicts: The Political Science and Geographic/Regional Science Approaches

5.1 Introduction

At the head of a nation's decision-making structure stands a single individual, a political leader. He is an organism whose biological processes (metabolism and energy level) affect his outlook, his stability, his analytical ability, his attitudes, his perceptions, the knowledge encoded in his memory, and thus his behavior. He is also affected by his community's cultural aspects (norms, values, beliefs, etc.) which he has internalized. Moreover, the culture of his own community reflects the culture of a larger region which, in turn, reflects the culture of the nation itself, and this hierarchy of cultures has influenced his mental representations. For example, a lifelong resident of Salem, Massachusetts, has, through different experiences, absorbed certain cultural aspects of his town, which, in turn, reflect the Yankee culture of New England and to some extent the national U.S. culture. In addition, as discussed in chapter 4, a leader is greatly influenced by the political subculture from which he comes.

All of these factors–his biological processes, his life experiences, his cultural heritage, and his political subculture–affect a leader's decision making.

There is another major influencing factor; namely, constituency support. For a political leader to be elected or reelected, or for a dictatorial or military figure to retain power, he must have a following. This chapter will examine the play of this factor, building step-by-step to reality from an extreme simplification. In doing so, it will draw heavily upon location theory as developed by geographers and regional scientists.

This chapter's last sections will examine how resource endowments and boundaries have shaped the size and the economic and military might of a political leader's constituency. They will also pay attention to forces that lead to loss of his nation's sovereignty as well as the spatial disintegration of his constituency arising from regional demands and aspirations.

5.2   Policy and platform selection with two clusters of voters

Start with a leader whose only concern is with his election or reelection. Say he functions in a democracy where 51 percent of the vote is required to win. Further assume that there are only two relevant issues at stake: level of military expenditures, and level of expenditures on social welfare. Measure these along the horizontal and vertical axes of figure 5.1, respectively. For the moment, assume the political figure has his eye on two clusters of voters. One cluster, concentrated at point K, most prefers low military expenditures and high social welfare expenditures. A second cluster, concentrated at point L, most prefers modest amounts of both types of expenditures. Say each cluster constitutes 25.5 percent of the vote, so that if the political figure can gain the full support of each group, he will have the 51 percent necessary to win.

How to gain the support of both clusters, when each has a different most-preferred position? If the leader sets forth a platform of low military expenditures and high social welfare expenditures, and offers a normal set of promises to bring voters to the polls, he may expect to obtain the full support of the constituents in cluster K. But with such a platform, quite different from the preferences of constituents in cluster L, he cannot expect support from this second group unless he does something in addition.

The leader can commit himself to offering jobs and other patronage to his constituents at L if he is elected, or he can obligate himself to them in other ways, or make promises above the normal, or incur various media publicity expenditures to convince them to vote for him, and/or even buy their vote with money. In effect, he may offer them a "price" for their vote (in both monetary and nonmonetary terms), which may be designated *support cost;* and if this price is high enough, he may be able to obtain their full support and be elected.

On the other hand, the political leader may consider adopting the platform most preferred by the constituents at L: modest amounts of both types of expenditures. If he does this and complements this platform with normal promises, he can, of course, expect full support from cluster L, but then he must offer to the members of cluster K a

Figure 5.1 *Clusters in a two-dimensional policy space*

"price" (his support cost) sufficiently high to gain their full support. Obviously, he has other options such as a "middle-of-the-road" position.

Figure 5.2 makes explicit his set of platform choices. On the horizontal axis point K and point L are placed the same distance apart as in figure 5.1. Let the line **KL** represent possible positions the leader may take. Point K represents the platform most preferred by K, point L the one most preferred by L. A middle-of-the-road position is represented by point M. Adopting a platform more and more like the one most preferred by L is equivalent to moving closer and closer to L. Likewise in the other direction toward K. Any point along the stretch **KL** indicates how close the platform represented is to both K's most-preferred and L's most-preferred position. Support costs to the leader are measured along the vertical axis. (These are costs above and beyond those normal costs required to get out the vote, that is, to keep the average voter from abstaining.)

If the leader adopts the platform most preferred by cluster K, represented by point K, his support costs to gain this vote is zero. However, to hold on to the vote of his constituency at L, he must pay a price, that is, he must incur support costs, say, of **KR**. If instead the

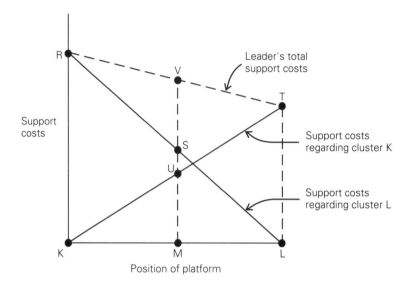

Figure 5.2 *Support costs for different positions of leader's platform*

leader chooses a middle-of-the-road platform, represented by the halfway point M, he need not pay as high a price for L's vote. Let **MS** represent this price. If his platform is even closer to L, the price will be still lower. In fact, one can construct a line–*a support cost line*–from R to L to indicate how the price for L's vote falls as the leader's position moves away from K and comes closer and closer to L. It reaches zero when his platform coincides with the most-preferred position of constituents at L.

However, if the leader does not choose a platform represented by point K, he will need to pay a price to hold on to the vote at K, and this price will rise as his platform moves farther and farther away from K. This is represented by line **KT**, the support costs of K's vote being greatest for a platform at point L.

Thus, two costs are involved whenever a political leader selects a platform, the cost to hold on to the vote at L, and the cost to hold on to the vote at K–where it is possible for one and only one of these costs to be zero. For example, for platform M his total cost will be **MV**, the sum of **MS** for holding on to the vote at L and **MU** for holding on to the vote at K. Likewise for any other platform, by addition he arrives at the total cost. This cost for every possible platform along the line **KL** is defined by the dashed line **RT**.

Observe now that the leader will choose the platform represented by point L where the total cost is lowest, being **LT**. The logic of such a choice is clear. The absolute slope of line **LR** is greater than that of **KT**. In other words, if the leader were to shift his platform away from L the increase in support cost to hold on to voters at L would be greater than the decrease in support costs caused by shifting toward K. This means that voters at L are less inclined to support the leader when his platform deviates from the one they most prefer than is the case for voters at K. Perhaps the leader has greater charismatic appeal to his constituents at K than to those at L.

Support cost lines used for illustrative purposes in figure 5.2 are not realistic. They show costs of shifting away from any cluster as rising proportionately with distance. Actually, support costs may rise by only a small amount with a small shift, but then increase more than proportionately with distance. (A constituency is insensitive to a small deviation in a leader's platform from the one it most prefers, but becomes increasingly sensitive to greater and greater deviations.) In this case, support cost lines will be curves, as shown in figure 5.3. The leader's total support cost line will also be a curve with a minimum point at F, an intermediate platform. And, logically, this is the one he will choose.

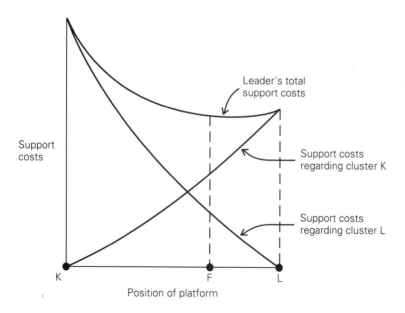

Figure 5.3 *Support costs when more than proportionate with distance*

5.3   Policy and platform selection with more than two clusters of voters

At this point we drop the simplistic assumption that there are only two clusters. In any election there will be quite a few–the Catholic vote, the Jewish vote, the Black vote, the labor vote, the women's vote, the conservative Republican, the conservative Democrat, the liberal Republican, the liberal Democrat, the peace activists. And more. To illustrate how a leader deals with more than two, another approach is needed. We will use four clusters of voters. Any number of clusters could be considered; the procedure would be the same but the accompanying figure would contain many more lines.

In figure 5.4 four clusters of voters are positioned at K,L,M, and N. For simplicity, assume that the percentage of voters at each cluster is 12.75–all told, 51 percent. Thus, to win the election, a leader must obtain full support from all four clusters. Observe that in figure 5.4 (1) voters at M most prefer military expenditures almost as low as those most preferred by K and expenditures on social welfare programs almost as low as those most preferred by L, and (2) voters at N most prefer military expenditures almost as high as those most preferred by L and expenditures on social welfare slightly higher than those most preferred by K. The leader may look at the cluster at K and ask: for a price of one million dollars (strictly speaking, the sum of money payments and monetary value of patronage and other obligations), how far can I deviate my platform from K and still fully retain the vote of cluster K? Of course, he can deviate in many directions, and in some directions he can go farther than others. Thus, in figure 5.4, all the deviations in all possible directions are connected by the oval-type line designated $1 (representing the price in millions of dollars). This line is called an *iso*line, from the Greek word "iso" meaning "the same." An isoline connects all deviations which have the same price. In the case of $1 isoline, the price is one million dollars.

The leader may also ask how far he can deviate in any direction for a price of $2 million. The answer is given by the set of points lying on the $2 oval-type isoline. Likewise for the prices $3, $4, $5, and so on. The $1, $2, $4, $6, and portions of the $10 and $14 isolines are drawn in figure 5.4 around point K.

Similarly one can construct $1, $2, $3, $4, and $5 million isolines around L,M, and N. Assume that voters at M and L have pretty much the same inclination (or disinclination) as those at K to support the

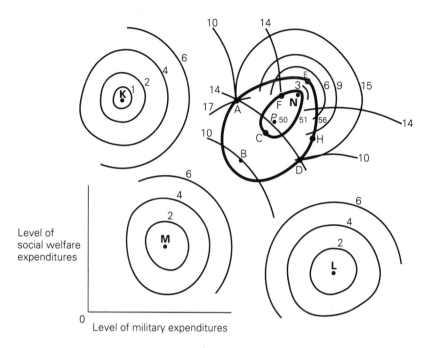

Figure 5.4 *Cost and Total Cost Isolines*

leader as his platform deviates more and more from their most-preferred position, but that voters at N are much less inclined to do so. Thus, the isolines drawn around point N are less spread out (more compact). For M and L, $2, $4, $6, and portions of $10 and $14 isolines are constructed; for N, portions of $3, $6, $9, and $15 isolines are shown.

The leader recognizes that each platform he considers involves four prices or support costs, one for each cluster, where the price at any one time can be zero for one and only one. He then asks the basic question: what will be the total cost of retaining the support of all four clusters for any position that I take? This is determined by simple addition. Take the position A in figure 5.4. That position lies on the $10 million isoline around K, the $14 million isoline around M, the $17 million isoline around L, and the $15 million isoline around N, these lines representing, respectively, the prices he needs to pay K,M,L, and N for his deviation at point A from their most-preferred positions. All told, the total price or support cost is $56 million.

He may consider other platforms, B,C,D,E, and F which total $55, $51, $56, $56, and $51 millions, respectively. Note that the platforms A,D, and E involve the same total cost, $56 million. There are probably other platforms with this $56 total cost as well. All these platforms are connected to form the bold $56 total cost isoline in figure 5.4. Likewise, platforms C and F involve the same $51 million total cost, and there are likely to be other platforms involving this same cost. All these are connected to form the $51 total cost isoline. Note that this total cost isoline lies inside the $56 million isoline. In similar manner one can construct other total cost isolines. They converge in this figure at point P, representing the platform of least total cost, namely, $50 million. This will be the platform most desired by the leader when, as is so often the case, his objective is to minimize the cost of his election.

Clearly, the foregoing analysis is still oversimplified and unrealistic. No leader constructs such figures. The underlying assumptions do not hold for any real-life situation. Typically, more than two issues are at stake, clusters differ in their emotional attachment to issues and to a leader, information on most preferred positions is cloudy, and so forth. However, the analysis does serve to point out a basic problem facing any political leader. He must continually be concerned about constituent support, especially as an election approaches. He must continually ask what shifts in his platform policies are necessary to maintain support at election time, whether for himself, or the political party he heads. As he becomes better informed about the desires (most-preferred positions) of different groups, as these desires change, as new issues arise, as other leaders compete with him for voter support among his own constituents (in a sense invade his territory), he must continually move in one direction or another to hold onto his constituency, and do so with the limited resources (monetary and other) at his command. Whereas an unsophisticated leader relies a great deal on hunches, a carefully calculating leader is always weighing changes in policy. Should he move closer to cluster M? If he does, how much will he save in the cost of holding on to M? By how much will his costs increase if he moves away from N? How are costs of holding on to K and L affected?

These calculations, whether on paper or in the mind, are further complicated by uncertainties. Thus far, all the cost calculations have been based on the assumption of full (100 percent) support from each cluster. But typically a political leader never can be certain of receiving all the votes from any given cluster. No matter what price he pays, he can count at most on something less than 100 percent. There will always be some abstainers and dissidents. He may be able to increase percentage support by upping his price, but he never can achieve a full count. No matter what set of prices he offers, one for each cluster, he knows he will receive less than 100 percent support. Thus, to win an election, in this hypothetical case, he needs to go after the vote of more than four clusters. Moreover, he generally realizes that the price he must offer depends upon which constituencies his opponent is going after, what tactics his opponent is using, and so forth. As will be seen in section 5.5, the higher the price an opponent is offering to any cluster of concern to the political leader, the greater the price that leader must offer in response.

5.4   Impact of lobbies and interest groups

Lobbies are still another major factor affecting the political leader's behavior. Who is not familiar with the military–industrial complex whose pressures on and financial support given to legislators (primarily from defense industries) ex-President Eisenhower long ago deplored? Or who is not familiar with the pressures Congress members exert upon the president and the Department of Defense when elimination of an army base or cutback in a defense facility located in their state is attempted?

Typically, interest groups within a leader's constituency can and do provide money and other resources in return for favors and promises of support on specific legislation–for example, for support for a level of military expenditures represented by point H in figure 5.4–an increase in military expenditures over that in platform P which would be partially offset by a decrease in social welfare expenditures. The leader may use these resources for literature to persuade more voters that his offers are better than his opponent's, or to conduct a media campaign to enhance his qualifications in the eyes of the public, or even to supplement his money payments for the vote. If without the support of a particular lobby the leader would adopt platform P, a contribution of money and/or other resources might cause him to shift to H, often compromising his principles, forcing him to become "polluted." H lies on the $56 million total cost isoline, $5 million higher than P, his least total cost platform. Should the lobby group offer a contribution greater than $5 million, he may well shift to platform H.

In short, the introduction of a lobby adds another element to the problem, both for the analyst and for the political leader. Where there are many lobbies, as in the United States (oil magnates, environmentalists, urban mayors, big business), things can become exceedingly complicated. Sadly, in some societies, because running a successful campaign requires accepting contributions from special interest groups and compromising on certain basic issues in order to receive such financial support, highly principled individuals of outstanding calibre with great leadership ability often are excluded from participating in the political process.

5.5 OPTIONAL: Competition among political leaders

Another complicating factor, one that enters into the thinking of every political leader, is competition. Recognize that a significant portion of a constituency usually is not clustered at one point but is spread out. To keep the analysis as simple as possible, assume that somewhere within the policy space there is a set of voters who agree on the level of social welfare and other program expenditures, but differ on their most-preferred level of military expenditures. Assume these voters are distributed uniformly along a line from U to V in figure 5.5, where the position of each individual on this line corresponds to his most-preferred level of military expenditures. Costs to the leader of carrying out the normal promises necessary to get out the vote is called the *abstinence price.* Assume that each voter has an abstinence price below which he will withhold his support, that is, not bother to vote. In figure 5.5 the vertical stretch **AP** represents abstinence price. Thus, when the leader's chosen position is not the individual's most-preferred position, in order to be certain of support, the leader must offer that person a support price equal to his abstinence price plus the price of overcoming the difference between the two positions.

Focus on point A in figure 5.5. Let the point represent level of military expenditures proposed in political leader A's platform, to which for purposes of this analysis he is taken to be committed. Level of support price offered by the political leader is measured along the vertical axis. As noted, **AP** is the abstinence price for all voters

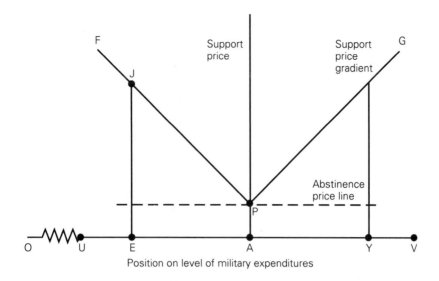

Figure 5.5 *The support price gradient*

regardless of a constituent's position in policy space. The V-shaped line **FPG**, designated the *support price gradient*, is then constructed. For any given voter, say, a voter at point E, it measures the support price which the leader must pay him (here, **EJ**) to obtain his vote. It also shows how this support price increases as the distance between a constituent's most-preferred position and the leader's position at A increases. In figure 5.5 the support price gradient is constructed as a straight line. This is appropriate only under circumstances where support price varies at a rate proportional to distance in policy space. In reality the support price gradient can be concave (reflecting a rate structure less than proportional to distance) or convex (reflecting a rate structure more than proportional to distance).

To maximize his vote in this situation a typical leader with limited resources will then be motivated to maximize his support area. This area cannot extend beyond the points, one in each direction, where the leader's resources become exhausted. In figure 5.5 these points are posited to be E and Y, and the leader's support area is **EY**. The leader is not interested in going after the vote of any individual beyond E or Y as a substitute for the vote of an individual within the stretch **EY**, since the support price of the former exceeds the support price of the latter.

Again, note that each voter receives a support price which, when reduced by the amount necessary to compensate him for being willing to vote for a leader whose position is some distance from his own most-preferred position, leaves him with a *net* price, in this case an amount just necessary to overcome his reluctance to vote, namely, the abstinence price **AP**.

Consider figure 5.6. There the right-hand side of figure 5.5 is reproduced. A second political figure, B, is introduced, who proposes a different level of military expenditures conveniently represented by point B. B's position on other issues is taken to be the same as A's. Assume that A and B each has adequate political resources to meet the abstinence price of all individuals distributed uniformly along line **AB** plus support costs necessary to offset the effect of distance separating each one's most-preferred position from the leader's chosen position. Both leaders are taken to be spatially immobile, that is, committed, at least for the time being, to their initial positions represented by A and B.

As already noted, leader A offers to all constituents the *net price* **AP**, his corresponding support price gradient in figure 5.6 being **PG**. If B

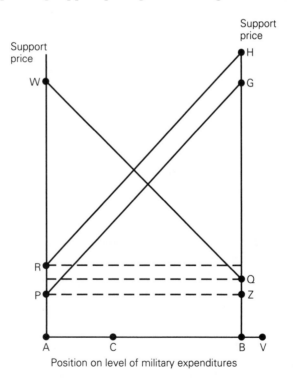

Figure 5.6 *Two competing political figures*

is to bid support of individuals away from A, he must offer them a higher net price, say, **BQ**,–one which covers not only the constituent's abstinence price (**AP** = **BZ**), but also something greater, namely, **BQ**. If he does, then his corresponding support price gradient will be **QW**. And, accordingly, he captures the support of all individuals. In turn, A may be expected to respond by offering a still higher net price, say, **AR**, the associated support price gradient being **RH**. And so, a price escalation takes place analogous to a price-cutting war among economic firms.

There is an absolute limit to this process. Eventually one of the political leaders will reach the end of his resources (face bankruptcy) and be forced to withdraw from the arena. However, it can be expected that before this limit is reached, perhaps well before, one of the leaders will voluntarily temper his attempt to capture the entire set of supporters. He will recognize that for the same resource expenditure he can relinquish his most distant potential constituent to his competitor and raise the net price offered to all others. In turn, the second leader may do the same with regard to his most distant potential constituent. The nature of the competitive process then becomes more complicated. In general, however, individuals whose most-preferred positions lie close to either political leader receive a net price only a little above their abstinence price, whereas intense competition ensues for the support of individuals whose most-preferred positions are near the center of line **AB**.

At this point, drop the assumption of continuous distribution of political constituents along line **UV** in figure 5.5, and along line **AB** in figure 5.6. Constituents in actuality are discretely distributed in a nonuniform pattern. To obtain any constituent's support, a leader still must offer a price at least as high as the constituent's abstinence price; and, if a competitor exists, at least as high as the net price offered by the competitor. To tie the analysis of this section to that of the previous, suppose there is a cluster of voters at C (say, "the urban underprivileged") whose support is essential for leader A to obtain 51 percent of the vote (assuming A has full support from other clusters like those in figure 5.4). Clearly, if B also wants cluster C's support and offers a higher net price than A, then A must offer still more. Moreover, if an election involves only two parties, with A and B the leaders, then each knows that whoever receives that vote will win. Hence, each is willing to engage in an escalation of campaign promises and of net prices.

It is possible, now, to generalize the analysis. What holds for voters at cluster C holds for voters at other clusters; and holds for any constituent who is positioned alone in policy space and not in a cluster. The political leader who can offer a constituent the highest net price, whether or not the constituent is in a cluster, receives that vote. And this statement holds when a single issue, such as level of military expenditures, is considered, or two issues such as levels of military expenditures and social welfare expenditures (as in the previous section), or many, in which case one must think in terms of a policy space of more than two dimensions.

5.6   Coalition formation and disruption

The simple diagrams already presented, and the simple assumptions upon which they are based, also provide insight into the problem of coalition formation which frequently confronts political leaders in many nations and many different situations. This is illustrated in figure 5.7. Presented here on a reduced scale are some of the total cost isolines for the political leader of figure 5.4, now taken to be $\bar{A}$. But assume that the percentages of voters at clusters K,L,M, and N do not add up to 51, but less. Suppose there are 12, 10, 6, and 8 percent of voters at these clusters, respectively. No matter what the political leader does with respect to these clusters, he cannot gain enough support to ensure an election victory. To be in a winning situation he must combine his efforts and resources with those of another leader by forming a coalition that seeks at least 51 percent of the voters' support.

Figure 5.7 also includes the most preferred positions of other clusters. In addition to opponent $\bar{B}$, assume there is one other leader $\bar{D}$ who has the support of clusters at H and J, which comprise 9 and 15 percent of the voters, respectively. For leader $\bar{D}$ a set of total cost isolines is constructed around his least total cost point Q.

Now suppose leader $\bar{A}$'s total gains from being in a winning situation (advantages in equivalent dollars) are $20 mm. $\bar{A}$'s isoline which connects positions where total cost exceeds the total cost at P (his lowest total cost point) by $20 mm is designated $\bar{A}$'s *critical isoline* and is represented in bold. Any position inside of this isoline will involve total cost less than $20 mm above the cost at position P. If $\bar{A}$ shifted his platform from P to any position within this total cost isoline and thereby realized a winning coalition, his gross gain would be $20 mm, his added costs of holding on to constituents at K, L, M,

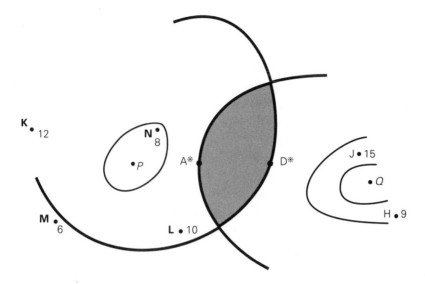

Figure 5.7 *A process of coalition formation*

and N would be less than $20 mm, and he would realize a net gain. Of course, the closer the position to P at which a coalition can form, the lower the increase in total cost and the greater Ā's net gain.

However, for a winning coalition to form, all participants must desire it. In our particular case, for example, the new leader D̄ must also foresee a *net* gain. Say his gross gain (advantages expressed in dollars) from being a winning coalition member is $25 mm. His critical total cost isoline is the one connecting positions that incur total costs greater by $25 mm than those at location Q, which is the lowest total cost position for him as independent actor. Any position inside of his critical isoline will involve an increase in total cost of less than $25 mm and will allow him a net gain were a winning coalition formed with a platform represented by that position. Again, the closer the position to Q, the greater the net gain.

It is clear that leaders Ā and D̄ must both find it desirable to form a winning coalition, and that only positions lying inside the critical isoline of each leader will assure this outcome. These positions are in the shaded area of figure 5.7.

But which specific position will it be? No theory provides an answer to this question despite many hours devoted to it by mathematicians, game theorists, economists, and regional scientists. Political leader Ā would most like the coalition's platform to be represented by point

A*. Political leader $\bar{D}$'s preference is represented by point D*. What happens will depend on the two leaders' negotiating skills, their relative aggressiveness, their ability to cooperate, their friendliness or hostility, and so forth.

The coalition problem presented above is relatively simple. Only two participants are involved. Frequently there are more than two, and the complexity of the problem mounts exponentially with the increase in number. To illustrate the complexity, assume there is a third leader $\bar{E}$ who controls the portion of the vote that $\bar{A}$ and $\bar{D}$ do not. Assume he is not passive and is himself willing to form a coalition. To illustrate, refer to figure 5.8. Percentages of constituents at K, L, M, and N are here taken to be 16, 13, 8, and 10, respectively, altogether 47 which leader $\bar{A}$ controls. Percentages at H and J are 18 and 30, respectively, altogether 48 which $\bar{D}$ controls. Leader $\bar{E}$ controls 5 percent at cluster R, his minimum total cost platform (his isolines are omitted). Clearly, leader $\bar{A}$ can form a winning coalition with $\bar{E}$ by adopting the latter's most-preferred platform at R and $\bar{E}$ will realize a net gain (assume it is $10 mm) from being a member of a winning coalition. $\bar{A}$ might even persuade $\bar{E}$ to form a coalition at some other position closer to P, in the spirit of a more fair sharing of gains from being part of a winning coalition. However, $\bar{A}$ cannot induce $\bar{E}$ to shift his platform to a location outside $\bar{E}$'s critical total cost isoline (not depicted in Figure 5.8, but which would be the locus of platforms involving $10 mm additional cost to $\bar{E}$ for holding on to his constituency's vote).

However if $\bar{A}$ and $\bar{E}$ form a winning coalition, leader $\bar{D}$ at Q is excluded. Since $\bar{D}$ does not desire this outcome, he may try to persuade $\bar{E}$ to join him in a winning coalition, not only by agreeing to adopt platform R, but also by offering $\bar{E}$ on the side a small monetary payment or the equivalent–a payment which will still leave $\bar{D}$ with some *net* gain. A winning coalition formed by $\bar{D}$ and $\bar{E}$ will exclude $\bar{A}$ (at P)–an undesirable outcome for him. He will offer $\bar{E}$ a side payment higher than that offered by $\bar{D}$. And so on. Offers to $\bar{E}$ will escalate until the net gain to $\bar{A}$ or $\bar{D}$ is reduced to zero, and even becomes negative from further bidding.

This simple example illustrates the competitive nature of coalition formation, a process which can become extremely intense. In the particular figure 5.8 it might appear that leader $\bar{A}$ at P ultimately will succeed in forming a winning coalition with $\bar{E}$ at R, since he seems able to offer $\bar{E}$ more than can leader $\bar{D}$ at Q. Together $\bar{A}$ and $\bar{E}$ will control 53 percent of the vote. Point R lies farther within $\bar{A}$'s critical

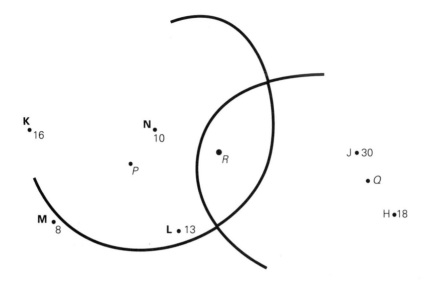

Figure 5.8 *Coalition formation and disruption*

total cost isoline than it does within $\bar{D}$'s. However, well before $\bar{D}$ at Q becomes willing to offer $\bar{E}$ at R a side payment that will reduce his ($\bar{D}$'s) own net gain to zero, he will find it desirable to form a coalition with $\bar{A}$ instead, by making it advantageous for $\bar{A}$ to team up with him instead of $\bar{E}$. Since this will result in $\bar{E}$'s exclusion, $\bar{E}$ then will be motivated to offer to join a coalition with either $\bar{A}$ or $\bar{D}$ for a smaller (even much smaller) side payment than was last discussed. If this offer is accepted, once again a leader will be excluded, who then will come up with an offer which will place him back in a winning coalition. And so the process of disrupting existing coalitions and forming new ones goes on *ad infinitum.* Formally, there exists no solution to this process. And where each leader harbors considerable uncertainty about the gains to be derived from being in a winning coalition and the exact costs of shifting to a position such as R, the outcome is even more elusive.

When more than three political leaders (parties) are active, as in Israel, France, and many other countries, coalition formation becomes still more complex. We shall not explore such situations here. It is important to note, however, that a leader who controls a small con-stituency can play a major role in determining which winning coalition survives, and thus which policies go into effect. A classic case is that of

Israel in 1990. Two major parties, the Likud and Labor, and several small parties controlled certain blocs of votes, but no single one controlled 61 or more of the 120 votes necessary to form a working government. After the Likud failed to put together a coalition controlling a majority of votes, the Labor party was given the go-ahead signal to try. On April 10, 1990, this party was about to report its success in mustering 61 votes and was formally ready to form a government. At the last moment, however, one member of the Orthodox Agadat Israel party who controlled one single vote telephoned his spiritual worldwide religious leader, the 88-year-old Grand Rabbi of the Lubavitch group, Menachem Mendel Schneerson, residing in New York. He asked the Grand Rabbi for approval of his joining the Labor party coalition, a cornerstone of whose platform was the notion of "land for peace." The Grand Rabbi, however, was standing by a religious ruling that it is against Jewish law, known as halacha, to give up religious territory, even in exchange for peace. As a consequence, this member and one other member of the potential Labor party coalition defected, leaving Labor (a party favorably disposed to the peace plan vigorously promoted by the United States) without the necessary strength. Ultimately the Likud [much more militant (hawkish) and opposed to the U.S. plan] came into power–and, as a consequence, political developments in the Middle East as they appeared at this time (February 1992), are much more warlike.

5.7   OPTIONAL: The role of political argument

As noted in a previous section, a political leader needs to present a rationale for his platform–an argument to convince constituents that his policies are best. He needs to collect evidence to support his position. This is especially necessary when he wishes to appeal to voters whose views are not those of his own subculture, and whose most-preferred platform differs significantly from the one he sets forth. Moreover, the actual needs of voters, especially their future needs, are seldom clear, and his argument must confront these uncertainties convincingly. Because of past commitments the leader may not be in a position to shift his platform in any significant way to gain support at clusters whose most-preferred position is at some distance from his own–else he might appear to others to be irresponsible and opportunistic. Instead, he must persuade these voters that his platform is best for them and not much different from the one they most prefer.

Scholars disagree on appropriate steps in developing a political argument. However, one thing is clear. A political argument cannot rely solely upon pure logic and rational objective reasoning. This is because formal logical reasoning cannot

1. handle the need to investigate, identify, and adopt a reasonable compromise position on basic public policy issues, especially when these issues are emotion laden;
2. effectively take into account practical criticisms and reactions when a leader presents his case to an audience–that is, embody such criticisms in the argument to make it more persuasive, as is so often necessary;
3. handle "what if" thinking, that is, include in the argument what the policy will be if this or that occurs; and
4. embrace thinking that is tentative or provisional, that takes uncertainties into account.

Nonetheless, formal logic can be used at certain points in an argument when there are clear-cut premises and deduction is appropriate.

One useful way to view a political argument consists of six elements: claims, grounds, justification, backing, qualifications, and possible rebuttals. (For further discussion, see Toulmin, Rieke, and Janik, 1979.)

A *claim* states a conclusion. This may be that a specific policy is best for achieving a goal, say, social welfare–perhaps specifically that a 15 percent cut in military expenditures will lead to substantial growth in Gross National Product while retaining a satisfactory level of national security. Or, the claim may be that a policy of "no first use of nuclear weapons in Europe" is desirable, a policy proposed in the U.S. in the years 1982–84 during the Cold War period, the objective being to effectively deter nuclear warfare without compromising U.S. national security.

Grounds provide the foundation for the claim. They may consist of evidence that a given policy (proposal, position, or plan) will move things toward or attain certain objectives. Such evidence may be quantitative or qualitative. In either case the evidence may be viewed as data, comprising observations, statistics, outputs of simulations with models (to be discussed in chapter 6), commonly accepted knowledge, conventions, references, previously validated claims, testimony, and the like. Grounds frequently are introduced by such words as "because" or "since."

For example, grounds for the claim that no first use of nuclear weapons in Europe by NATO is a desirable policy were the outcomes of three scenarios simulated by a group of MIT engineers and scientists. These scenarios examined

1. a large-scale preemptive invasion of the West by Warsaw Pact nations;
2. an inadvertent or spillover war; and
3. a reckless adventure by the USSR, such as the surprise capture of Hamburg or another vulnerable NATO asset.

Data on the outcomes of these three scenarios as well as the outcome of a continuing *status quo* were presented as relevant evidence (grounds) for the claim.

Justification and backing in a political argument are the underpinning for connecting the grounds and the claim or for establishing the relevance of the grounds. Justification may be a legal precedent, a universal engineering formula, a rule of thumb, a commonly accepted law (the law of supply and demand), or a scientifically established constant (the gravitational constant). But such precedents, formulae, rules, laws, and constants require *backing;* their trustworthiness or reliability must be established. In the case of the MIT study, researchers were distinguished scientists from one of the world's best engineering schools–backing enough! The proposed policy of a 15 percent cut in military expenditures may have been justified by data from an input–output analysis (about which more will be said later). Backing the input–output method would have been its successful use in many other studies, and the name of the man who created it–Wassily Leontief, son of a noted Russian economist, former Professor of Economics at Harvard University, and a most distinguished Nobel Prize winner.

Qualifications must accompany a political argument because in this highly dynamic world practically nothing can be certain. In the mid 1980s, the possibility of the Soviet Union's adopting a policy that would allow unification of West and East Germany was never imagined by any of the world's outstanding scholars, laymen, and political leaders. No matter how widespread a belief, no matter how predictable an outcome, no matter how infallible a theory may be deemed, no matter how often a method of analysis may have worked in the past, probabilities must be attached to any such elements when they are used in a political argument. In other words, most arguments can be refuted for exceptional circumstances. A good argument should include *qualifiers* (probabilities) which make explicit the force, dependability, or likelihood of a claim in a particular situation; or the particular situations to which the claim does not apply. For example, if the law of supply and demand is used to support an argument, one needs to point out that it only works for achievement-oriented societies. If an argument depends on a successful space launch, one needs a caveat which takes into account the unpredictability of weather. An argument based on a 1987 public opinion poll–say the argument by a key Democrat figure that less than half the U.S. constituency supports the Reagan Star Wars program–needs to state the probability of error in the poll results.

Possible *rebuttals* should be prepared for defending any argument. Anyone who sets forth a political argument must be ready to confront counterarguments and opposing points of view–statements that could upset the argument–even if such counterarguments are highly unlikely or not immediately apparent. Even though in certain instances they may be ignored, they should always be anticipated and usually rebutted. Rebuttals are strongest when counterarguments themselves are weak or based on clearly questionable assumptions.

For example, in estimating the number of jobs that may be lost in one industry, say, fighter aircraft manufacture, and the number of jobs directly and indirectly gained in another, say, residential construction, the input–output approach (described later on) may be used. A theoretical economist might criticize these estimates. The input–output approach typically assumes that when the residential construction industry's output expands by a given percentage, so do inputs of cement, lumber, bathtubs, labor, and every other material and service required in production. The theoretical economist might insist that this is not in accord with the best theory. Although the input–output analyst may agree, he can challenge his critic to identify a better way of arriving at estimates of jobs lost and gained–estimates needed by political leaders engaged in disarmament negotiations. At this time (March 1992), no better way is known.

Many problems are inherent in the development of a good political argument–the problems of

1. obtaining data, often complex–of selecting among existing sources of data and collecting and processing more;
2. identifying the aims of different interest groups and developing a consistent set of objectives which will have wide appeal;

3. deciding which assumptions to make as to what people know and do not know, what must be explained and what taken for granted;
4. identifying lessons of history;
5. indicating how to get *there* (the desired state of affairs) from *here*; and
6. deciding what rebuttals to prepare.

Sound argument should be set forth to support any policy (platform). It is the job of conflict analysts and peace scientists to explain the relative merits of different arguments and to expose bad ones. Arguments often are based on data, sometimes very complex. Bad arguments can be avoided by careful collection, processing, and generation of accurate data. For this purpose models are extremely valuable tools for generating (projecting) data on the outcomes of policies and scenarios. The role of models is taken up in the following chapter.

5.8   Resource endowments, boundaries, and city–state and nation might

Sections 5.2–5.6 spoke about clusters of voters in a leader's constituency. No mention was made of the absolute size of these clusters, nor their characteristics. Was their population 100 or one million? Was per capita income $200 or $2,000? Surely, population size and national income are basic to military might and capability of fomenting conflict and war. We need to address these questions, to examine certain geographic factors and concepts of regional science, starting with the impact of geographic attributes of place upon early development.

Chapter 1 discussed the interplay of competition and cooperation, and in particular how cooperation resulted from mankind's need to perform certain tasks which the individual alone could not handle. One example given was moving a boulder blocking the entrance of an ideal cave. Later, tasks emerged which the single family alone could not perform adequately–for example, defending against carnivorous beasts or against another family whose leader was stronger and more aggressive. So a group of families or clan formed,–and as the clan became larger and stronger, other families formed similar groups for defensive purposes. Moreover, early on the advantages of specialization, realizable with increase in population, began to be appreciated, and so still larger groups, clans, tribes, and clusters of tribes evolved.

While these developments were taking place, it became necessary to work out ways (rules, methods, practices) to meet the needs and demands of competitive individuals while retaining cooperative activities. Nature's gender specialization alone was inadequate. Undoubtedly, many ways tried proved unsuccessful, and those who tried them may not have survived. Other ways, and at least some of the groups practicing them, did survive. Those ways then became embedded in the developing culture of these groups. In effect, these were early efforts at government. They represented the beginning of law (the legislative process) prescribing how output, windfalls, and spoils should be distributed among individuals or allocated for use as inputs into certain activities. When a conflict arose in interpreting the ways, an old wise man, experienced and knowledgeable, may have been asked to mediate, to provide a correct interpretation or a needed reinterpretation. Such mediation represented the beginnings of the judicial process. In time, most of the wise man's hours may have been spent on judicial activities and fulfilling the need to pass down to others his own and his tribe's accumulated knowledge (rules, practices, and customs).

Food and other consumption items had then to be provided to him and his family. A simple tax system had to be devised and later put into place, perhaps only by informal common law. Such a tax system represented the beginnings of administration–tax collectors, or other civil servants whose responsibility it was to see that individual members made proper contributions. Perhaps in the beginning the wise man served as administrator also and took on diverse leadership functions.

One thing is clear. The manner in which government arose for clans, tribes, or other groups inhabiting a particular area was greatly influenced by the attributes of that area–by its geographic features. Imagine how vastly different a tax system for a nomadic tribe roaming the Arabian desert had to be from that for a tribe settled in a highly fertile river valley. How different the laws, formal and informal, regarding the use of water resources!

The forerunners of the Kurds of mountainous Iraq, and of the Iraqi farmers who till the fertile land of the Tigris and Euphrates valleys, must have developed cultures–laws, educational processes, religious practices, concern for civil rights, economic activities–each greatly different from the other, each strongly influenced by the geography of its area. No wonder their sharp conflicts through the centuries, persisting to this day.

The play of geographic features, however, has been even more significant in the development of the world system. This has been so in large part because of technology–of man's curiosity and his propensity to develop tools–and today, of advanced production and control processes. Technology has and always will revalue resources, the significance of the geographic features of place, and ties among regions. Major advance has constantly occurred in transport technology–the wheel, the boat, the road, the canal, the railway, the automobile, the airplane (and in the future, the spaceship). Each in turn reduced the time and effort for people to move and to move goods. Trade developed, along with geographic specialization among localities and regions. Major trading centers arose at ports surrounded by abundant fertile agriculture land, for such land could support not only the population cultivating it but also the population engaged in trade and crafts. Emergence of the city–state of Venice within the Po Valley region during the Middle Ages is a case in point. Additionally, the land could support the families of those engaged in developing and producing weaponry and forming an army. This geographical advantage permitted an aggressive power-aggrandizing political leader to conquer other settlements less able to support non-agricultural populations and armies. Or such may have encouraged an insecure leader, apprehensive of a surprise attack by an unfriendly neighbor, to strike first and conquer that neighbor.

Advancing technology caused continual reevaluation of resources and geographic features. Italian port cities lost their strategic position in the world system. Nation–states arose as a consequence of any number of factors: kings consolidating power; rise of the middle class; rebirth of the rule of law; the Renaissance and its impact; the need for small states and other political units to unite (form abiding coalitions) for defensive purposes against threatening powers or to attain certain civil rights; the coming of the printing press and other inventions and practices facilitating administrative control and possibilities for scale economies in diverse economic, political, social, and cultural activities; increasing urbanization and interregional trade; and so forth. Geographic resources and features were always present conditioning the growth and power of nation–states. Clearly, the relative economic and military might of nations at the close of the 19th century and first decades of the 20th was related to their deposits of coal and iron ore.

The first successful use of coal as a substitute for charcoal (from timber) took place in England in the early 18th century. This stimulated tremendous development of the iron and steel industry. Based on activity locationally oriented to excellent deposits of coal and iron ore in Durham, Northumberland, Yorkshire, Cumberland, Lancashire, and South Wales, England became the world's leading iron and steel producer. The continental European counterpart to the British experience was associated with the combination of geographically close Westphalian coal and Lorraine ore. Such led to Germany's major iron and steel development by the beginning of the 20th century. Without question, these geographic endowments of ore and coal were absolutely essential for the emergence of England and Germany as the major military powers at the dawn of World War I, and prior to that for their engagement in a critical dreadnought (battleship) race so profligate in the consumption of iron and steel. (For a preteenager in the 1920s, budding appreciation of the indispensability of iron production for military might was tied to his perception of the huge Big Bertha cannon pounding away at Paris.)

Time and technology march on. The strategic significance of uneven geographic endowment of coal and ore deposits and associated iron and steel production has disappeared. The experience of the Gulf War with its successful use of electronic-oriented weaponry has made clear to political geographers, regional scientists, and others that the uneven spatial distribution of high technology–human resources capability is now the strategic element that governs military attack and deterrence potentials of nations, and the ability of an aggressive subculture and its leaders to engage in warfare.

Another major line of geopolitical thought centers around boundaries. Boundaries have always been a source of conflict and always will be, given mankind's insatiable desire for territory, wealth, and power. The significance of boundaries, too, is subject to change with technology and socio-politico-economic development. At one point in time, a broad, deep river, a natural geographic boundary separating two cultural groups, may be of little economic or military significance; at a later time, it may be a highly valuable resource for shipping, recreation, and water supply, giving rise to conflict among bordering political units regarding its utilization and control.

Treaties or other agreements among nations have often imposed *artificial* boundaries which sooner or later generate major conflict. A classic case is the partition of British India in 1947 into India and Pakistan as independent nations within the British Commonwealth. Essentially, the boundary between the two was drawn so as to separate Muslim and non-Muslim areas. Perhaps this criterion was all-important in the highly emotional context of that time. Clearly, however, that boundary, placing East and West Pakistan more than 1,000 miles apart, yet forming a single nation, flew in the face of reality. There was no geographical basis for it–and one could easily have predicted the physical violence and warfare that resulted. Eventually, Pakistan was divided into two separate countries: Pakistan (formerly West Pakistan) and Bangladesh (formerly East Pakistan).

In recent decades, mounting pollutant-emitting activities (industrial, household, and government) have generated conflicts and will continue to do so. Spatial diffusion of air pollutants, progenitor of the acid rain problem, for example, brings into question the relevance of many present administrative areas, regional divisions, and national boundaries. Likewise do uses of common bodies such as the Mediterranean and Baltic seas. Global warming, rising ocean levels, and other predicted greenhouse effects necessitate, in the opinion of many, a redefinition of the concept of boundary and consequently new thinking about national sovereignty–ideas that are certain to meet with resistance.

In attacking urban problems geographers and regional scientists have recently developed the concept of a central place network–a hierarchically ordered system of central places. Consistent with this concept in this world of global pollution and increasing and intricate interdependence of financial markets and economic activities, is the reality, already implied, that a nation no longer has a single boundary. It has a set of hierarchically oriented boundaries and administrative areas. These boundaries are related to the different spatial extents of the problems it confronts–in the environmental area ranging from control of local solid waste disposal, metropolitan air quality, regional spread of air and water pollutants, use of air and watersheds and bodies of water common to the nation and its neighbors, all the way to use of the common global environment.

Need for redefinition of the concept of boundary, and the emerging notion of an hierarchically ordered set of boundaries and administrative areas, is apparent from the many regional (intranational) conflicts which are mushrooming in all parts of the globe.

5.9   National disunity and regional resurgence

Historically, forces of unification reached their peak in the establishment of Colonial empires–for example, the British, Spanish, Portuguese, French and German empires of the 19th and 20th centuries. Such unification, primarily by military conquest, was motivated by a power-acquisitive drive as well as high expectations of profits from control of valuable raw materials and markets. In time, administration of these empires became too costly and problem-ridden. Expectations of economic gains turned out to be grossly exaggerated. Empires gradually crumbled; a process of disunification ensued.

Disunification within nations is taking place today. Many nations have in effect been coalitions–either voluntarily entered into by small states to achieve security and economic gain or forced via conquest and subsequent imposition of military control over various territories. Today, some of these coalitions are stable and more solidified than ever–witness the United States, originally a coalition of 13 colonies. Others are breaking up. Yugoslavia (June 1991)–an imposed illogical collection of six republics and two autonomous areas, three religions, two alphabets, and five languages–is a case in point. Two ethnic groups, the Slovenes and Croats, have successfully fought for independence. Likewise the Soviet Union (1991). Ethnic and national groups dwelling in areas conquered prior to World War I and officially acquired via the World War II Yalta treaty, have by now achieved independence. In Canada, Czechoslovakia, Spain, Sri Lanka, India, and elsewhere regional conflicts are raging.

Why the rising tide of demands for independence? Why is coalition disruption gaining strength in a number of countries? Many different hypotheses can be advanced. One may argue that higher levels of education and dissemination of knowledge within these nations have made ethnic, language, and religious populations more aware of and sensitive to suffered discrimination, economic, social, and political. Or, one may contend that developments in weapon technology have made possible more effective guerrilla warfare, terrorist tactics, and resistance capability (violent and nonviolent). Or, that advance in media and communications technology has called attention to, and led to debate over the question of human rights, and consequently stimulated increased demands for rights. Or one may point to the increasing role of multinationals in regional development, freeing regional economies from dependence on national support; or to the fact that affluence in some nations has allowed minorities to devote time and effort to resistance and independence movements. Or one may focus on the decrease in market size required by a number of economic areas for efficient operation, thus permitting greater economic self-sufficiency of regions and enabling them to function independent of national authority and assistance.

There are other factors as well. All together, and in various combinations, they spur regional drives for independence–the disruption or weakening of previously formed political coalitions.

At the same time, diametrically opposite forces are at work. This is evident in the partial unification of nations into a European community without tariff barriers and with a common currency and banking systems, all of which represents a coalition to achieve economic progress and to obtain protection against competitive trading blocs. These nations are also eliminating passport requirements for travel and developing a common military mission. Concomitantly, more legitimacy is being given to world organizations: the United Nations in its peace-keeping activities, GATT (General Agreement on Trade and Tariffs), and perhaps in time the International Court. One may venture to predict that nations will yield some sovereignty, form some kind of worldwide coalition, to attack global environmental problems.

Some of the discussion in this section smacks of geographic determinism, aspects of geopolitics. It speaks of geographic features as by-and-large governing political phenomena. However, with deeper thought, the fallacy of any doctrine of geographic determinism becomes clear. As pointed out, technology constantly revalues resources and the significance of the attributes of place. Technology is the result of man's social, political, and economic drives. Although resources and attributes of place are always basic factors in development and in a number of major conflicts, they must take their place side-by-side with non-geographic factors.

It is interesting and enlightening to note here some geopolitical doctrines of the past in order to avoid pitfalls in analysis. Friedrick Ratzel, father of political geography, developed an *organic* theory of state evolution. All states are like living organisms that grow and decay; in order to maintain vigor and continue to thrive, a state requires an increasing amount of space. Nevertheless, Admiral Mahan, pointing to Russian domination of the core area of Asia, maintained that seapower would be able to contain Russian expansionism and would be *the* dominant world power force. Later, the British geographer Mackinder, defining a Eurasian Pivot Area (later named the Heartland) as consisting of Eastern Europe together with a very large core area of Asia, set forth what has become a famous hypothesis:

> Who rules East Europe commands the Heartland
>
> Who rules the Heartland commands the World-Island
>
> Who rules the World-Island commands the World. (de Blij, 1967, p. 106)

where World-Island comprises Eurasia and Africa.

The extreme oversimplification of the hypothesis has become crystal clear in the present era of mounting stocks of electronic weaponry capable of penetrating any land mass. Yet recall how Hitler in his *Lebensraum* doctrine paid close attention to Ratzel's and Mackinder's thinking as interpreted by the German geographer Haushofer, and how until recently British and U.S. foreign policy makers' fears of the tremendous land masses controlled by the USSR were unconsciously exaggerated as a result of previous exposure to the highly oversimplified Mackinder doctrine. This is understandable. Extreme oversimplification of a major conflict situation such as the Cold War can be resorted to by political leaders who, as pointed out in chapter 4, are subject to cognitive constriction and decision making pathologies–especially when their analytical capability is limited and they are overwhelmed by the number of decisions they must make. After all, it is not the actual significance of spatial factors but the perceived significance of these factors that govern policy making and efforts at conflict management. And returning to the mounting number of regional conflicts throughout the world, it is important to understand that it is not actual costs and gains that might be associated with struggles for unification and disunification, centralization and decentralization, concentration and deconcentration, but the perceived costs and gains.

5.10 Summary and conclusion

One main theme in this chapter has been decision making by political leaders, and how the political process and short-run considerations govern their behavior. A leader needs to incur expenses to maximize his probability of winning an election and/or staying in power. To minimize these costs, he constantly considers shifting, and often does shift his platform and set of policies. Given that the voting population is distributed nonuniformly, often in clusters, a leader with limited resources constantly searches for a location in policy space–some combination of policies–which will maximize his support.

Lobbies can change the cost-benefit thinking of political leaders and change the platforms and policies they espouse. Competition from other leaders for constituents' votes can cause them to escalate their promises and commitments to constituents, reflected in the "net price" they offer. During the process of coalition formation a political leader undertakes a cost-benefit analysis to judge whether he should join in forming a winning coalition. When there are more than two leaders (and none controls enough votes to win by himself), competition for inclusion in a winning coalition leads to an unending sequence of coalition formation and disruption. There exists no solution to the political game involved.

When international conflicts arise, what clout does a national leader have? This depends, among other things, on the basic factor of economic and military strength. Here, resource endowments, geographic attributes of place, relative levels among regions and nations of technology and know-how, have been and will continue to be important. These factors, too, affect regional conflicts and the emergence of drives for autonomy by regions within his nation that a political leader must face.

Finally, political leaders frequently need to set forth arguments to advance and defend their platforms and policies. These political arguments consist of basic elements. Developing political arguments involves a number of problems.

Although a leader may have a deep-seated desire to advance the welfare of his region, nation, or the world, his short-run desire to be in power frequently injects itself forcefully into the interplay of factors governing his behavior and causes him to act inconsistently with, or without reference to, his basic, long-run objectives and aspirations for his people and others. How many times have leaders been "politically forced" to advocate increased levels of arms production, physical violence, and warfare, when such a policy was not in their hearts, and not an outcome of rational thinking!

References

de Blij, Harm J. (1967) *Systematic Political Geography*. New York: Wiley.

Isard, Walter (1988) *Arms Races, Arms Control and Conflict Analysis: Contributions from Peace Science and Peace Economics*. New York: Cambridge University Press, Chaps. 7 and 8.

Prescott, J. R. V. (1987) *Political Frontiers and Boundaries*. London: Allen and Unwin.

Toulmin, S. E., R. Rieke, and A. Janik (1979) *An Introduction to Reasoning*. New York: Macmillan.

6   *Models to Generate Data and Test Policies*

6.1   Introduction

Most political leaders need to issue policy proposals as part of an election platform or to clarify their leadership position. As indicated in the previous chapter, they require data and other evidence to substantiate their claims pertaining to the outcomes of policies. Obviously, outcomes cannot be observed at the time a proposal is made. They occur after a policy has been put into effect. Therefore, leaders need models, simple or complex, to generate data on these outcomes–that is, models that forecast or project data on the results of these policies. These data help them judge whether a policy is good or bad. If several policies are being considered, the data generated can help them judge which are acceptable, or which one is best. This chapter examines how several simple models generate data.

6.2   Factors affecting arms production in Third World countries: multiple regression and correlation analysis and econometric models

One set of models relates to the increasing concern about arms production in Third World countries. There has been considerable research attempting to understand the forces underlying such production. A number of hypotheses have been advanced. One is that a Third World country's arms production increases as its GNP rises–the reasoning being that the wealthier a country, the more resources it can afford to devote to making weapons. This relationship can be represented algebraically by a simple straight-line equation:

$$X = a + b_1 W_1 \qquad\qquad 6.1$$

where X = arms production in dollars (the dependent variable), W_1 = GNP (the independent variable), a = a constant, and b_1 = the slope of the straight line. If b_1 were equal to 0.1, the equation would state that every time GNP increases by \$1.00, the dollar value of arms production rises by 10 cents.

This hypothesis is too simple. Some scholars add another factor, saying that arms production also increases as a Third World country develops skills, acquires know-how and advanced technology, and moves forward from primary economic activities to production of fully assembled and highly processed manufactured goods, this development being measured by some index designated W_2, a second independent variable. The reasoning here is that the more advanced a country's industrial technology, the more capable it is of producing sophisticated products such as weapons. Here, the equation becomes:

$$X = a + b_1W_1 + b_2W_2 \qquad\qquad 6.2$$

where b_2 is the slope of the straight line that would result if W_1 were held constant–indicating by how much arms production (in cents) would rise from an increase of one in the index W_2, when the value of W_1 does not change.

Still other factors have been introduced in explanation. Arms production increases as a country's military burden, its ratio of military expenditures to GNP, (W_3), increases–the reasoning being that the higher this ratio, the greater the demand for arms, and thus the greater the incentive for arms producers to supply more.

A Third World country's arms production increases as its general dependence on arms imports (W_4) increases–the reasoning here being that the greater a country's arms imports, the more likely that it will adopt a strategy of developing indigenous production to substitute for imports, especially when these imports are supplied expensively (use up foreign exchange earnings) and possibly unreliably.

Finally, a country's arms production is higher or lower depending upon whether it has been subjected to an arms embargo (represented by a variable W_5, which equals unity when the country has been subjected to an embargo, and zero when not). The reasoning is that any embargo encourages domestic production of critically important commodities.

Taking into account all the above factors, the equation becomes:

$$X = a + b_1W_1 + b_2W_2 + b_3W_3 + b_4W_4 + b_5W_5 \qquad\qquad 6.3$$

A recent study (Rosh, 1990) examined such hypotheses (in terms of data on these variables [dependent and independent]) for 72 Third World countries, using 1982 data for arms production and 1978 and

1980 data for the independent variables. Some findings of the study's standard *multiple regression analysis* (where an error term is added to the above equation) are

1. an increase of one percent in a country's GNP will result, on average, in a 0.46 percent increase in its arms production stated in dollar terms;
2. an increase of one percent in a country's index in skill and know-how realized in manufacturing will result in a 1.29 percent increase in its arms production; and
3. countries which have suffered an arms embargo typically start off producing more arms than those that have not.

Many problems arise in conducting this type of study and interpreting the findings. One concerns the quality, let alone quantity, of available data. Another concerns the validity of a study that considers arms production for one year only, uses data on independent variables for one year only, and has a time lag between these years (in the Rosh study of 4 to 2 years). Still another concerns the fact that the independent variables, the factors with which the dependent variable is correlated, are themselves correlated and interdependent. These problems are covered in the standard literature on multiple regression; we need not discuss them here. The point is, however, that despite the many problems, this kind of study can be useful. A political leader considering an arms embargo of a Third World country as a way of trying to reduce military violence there needs to be aware that such an embargo may have the undesirable effect of increasing that nation's arms production capacity. Or a leader in an advanced industrialized nation considering foreign aid and technical assistance to a Third World country will want to know whether or not such aid will directly or indirectly lead to an increase in the recipient's arms production; and if that is likely, as the above model suggests, that leader may impose conditions on the aid to discourage such increase.

Or take a political leader considering the pros and cons of an alliance. He may, of course, be concerned with immediate (short-run) effects on security and current costs (budget allocations). But he may also be concerned with long-run effects or with the need to counter arguments of those interest groups that are forcefully calling attention to long-run effects. Here the exceedingly careful empirical work of Singer and his colleagues in painstakingly gathering data and pursuing correlation analysis can be very useful. They find, for example, that

1. the hypothesis that while *"the greater the number of alliance commitments in the system, the more war the system will experience"* was borne out for the 20th century, the opposite hypothesis was found to hold for the 19th century; and
2. the hypothesis that *the closer to pure bipolarity the system is, the more war it will experience* seems to hold for the 20th century, but was not the case for the 19th century.

Another of Singer's many empirical findings suggests that the general profile of a state successful in a war is "one that, when compared with its rival, has a relatively heavy industrial base, moderately high military expenditures, relatively low military personnel preparedness (both absolute and relative to population), and a relatively low military expenditure allocation" (Singer, 1990, pp. 217–18).

Or consider trade policy, often examined because of short-run fiscal problems. Yet in the minds of some far-sighted political leaders, the mitigating impact of trade upon political conflict may be of marked importance, especially given the recent problem of incorporating Eastern European economies into the world system. Here the exploratory work of Polachek (1992) and Gasiorowski and Polachek (1982) suggests that trade lessens conflict and promotes cooperation, while on the other hand Pollins (1989) posits that trade follows conflict (cooperation).

Or coming closer to immediate day issues, a political leader concerned with Middle East policy and how to confront existing and potential crises emerging from the Gulf War, may find very useful the results of regression analysis and related studies on the spatial spread of conflict. Siverson and Starr (1989), for example, find a greater likelihood that conflict will spread from one nation to another when they have a common border, presumably because of more interaction opportunities, and they examine the relative importance of the "common border" factor in the spatial diffusion of conflict.

Econometric-type studies are much more complex. They may be concerned with how the level of military expenditures affects the rate of inflation, interest rates, unemployment, government spending, GNP, and so forth. The LINK model developed by Nobel Laureate Lawrence R. Klein and his associates links together models of 79 countries. It also captures basic aspects of the arms race. One LINK study conducted in the mid 1980s found that a 10 percent increase in military expenditures by both the United States and the Soviet Union in 1986 and each subsequent year, by 1989 would have:

1. directly and indirectly caused the inflation rate to be higher than otherwise would have been the case by
    0.4 percent in West Germany,
    0.7 percent in Japan,
    1.1 percent in the United Kingdom, and
    0.2 percent in the United States;
2. directly and indirectly caused the interest rate to be higher than would otherwise have been the case by
    0.04 percent in West Germany,
    0.03 percent in Japan,
    0.21 percent in the United Kingdom, and
    0.35 percent in the United States; and
3. directly and indirectly caused the unemployment rate to be lower than would otherwise have been the case by
    0.3 percent in West Germany,
    0.06 percent in Japan,
    1.7 percent in Great Britain, and
    0.2 percent in the United States.

The above findings and many others which sophisticated econometric models generate can be useful for policy formulation by political leaders who are savvy about the strengths and weaknesses of such models. But the typical legislator (say, a U.S. representative or senator), although concerned with the effect of changing military expenditures on *national* employment, usually is much more interested in the effect on jobs (employment) in the area he represents, and in specific industries of that area. To study this effect, an input–output model is very useful and is, in fact, the best available tool.

6.3 Employment and other impacts of armament and disarmament: a simple input–output approach

This section presents two different perspectives on the input–output approach.

6.3.1   Direct and indirect requirements approach

Begin with a simple notion. Given a particular technology, to produce
one kwh (kilowatt hour) of electric power (output), an enterprise
may need one pound of coal (input). It is reasonable then to assume
that to produce two kwh of electric power, the enterprise will need
two pounds of coal; to produce 100 kwh of electric power, 100 pounds
of coal, and so on. If x_1 = output of power (in kwh) in an economy
and y = pounds of coal required, then

$$y = x_1 \qquad\qquad\qquad 6.4$$

However, the electric power industry is not the only industry using
coal. A second industry may need three-quarters of a pound of coal
per unit output. If the total level (number of units) of output of the
second industry is x_2, then the coal it requires is $0.75x_2$. So the total
amount of coal required by the two industries is

$$y = x_1 + 0.75x_2 \qquad\qquad\qquad 6.5$$

Introduce a third industry, whose output level is x_3 and which requires
one-tenth of a pound of coal per unit output, then

$$y = x_1 + 0.75x_2 + 0.1x_3 \qquad\qquad\qquad 6.6$$

And so on, when we consider the level of output of the fourth, fifth, . . .
and last coal-using activity in an economy.

  If coal were manna from heaven, available in any amount at any
place, our analysis could stop there. Unfortunately, this is not the case.
Coal must be mined, and coal mining itself requires electric power–to
run drilling machinery, provide lighting, and so forth. Thus,
producing the above x_1 quantity of electric power requires not only
(directly) an amount of coal equal to y, but (indirectly) an additional
amount, since in order to mine that coal a certain amount of electric
power, say, z, is needed. But to produce z amount of electric power
one needs another quantity of coal, which then requires some more
electric power, which then requires more coal, and so on. That is, coal
is required not only to meet the direct input needs of each industry in
the economy, but also to meet indirect input needs, since coal production itself depends on commodities whose production, in turn,
requires coal. Thus, the output of the coal-mining industry is the sum
of the direct and indirect input requirements of coal by all industries,
plus the consumption of coal by households and other non-producing
sectors. In the same way, the output of the electric power, steel, or any
other industry is the sum of direct and indirect requirements of its
own output for use as inputs into all producing sectors plus consumption by households and other non-producing sectors.

At first glance, one may throw up his hands in dismay at this maze of interdependencies. But input–output analysis can sort it out very quickly and easily with modern computers, and calculate all the direct and indirect input requirements, and thus the outputs of and the number of jobs to be filled in an economy. To develop this point, it is useful to examine input–output modelling from a quite different stance–namely, as a linear system–always having in mind the direct and indirect requirements just discussed.

6.3.2 OPTIONAL: Input–output as a linear system

Consider a simplified version of an economy. It has three producing sectors: agriculture (including mining), manufacturing, and services. In that order, they are the headings (abbreviated) for the first three rows and columns of table 6.1. It also has a household–nonmilitary government sector and a military sector (army, navy, air force) designated Hds + Gov't and Mil., respectively. See headings of columns 4 and 5.

Table 6.1
An input–output table
(in billions of dollars)

	Agri. (1)	Manu. (2)	Serv. (3)	Hds + Gov't (4)	Mil. (5)	Totals (6)
(1) Agri.	1	3	2	5	1	12
(2) Manu.	4	6	4	6	4	24
(3) Serv.	2	3	5	8	0	18
(4) Hds + Gov't	5	12	7			24
(5) Totals	12	24	18			

The first three rows indicate how the dollar value of the total output of each of the three producing sectors is distributed among all sectors (including itself). Each cell shows the dollar value (in billions) of (1) sales of the producing sector of its row to the sector heading the column of that cell (or the value of the row sector's output received by the column sector), or (2) purchases by the column sector from the row sector (or payments by the column sector to the row sector).

To illustrate, along the first row the table indicates that the agriculture sector sold $1 billion of output to itself, $3 billion to manufacturing, $2 billion to the services trade, $5 billion to households and nonmilitary government programs, and $1 billion to the military sector. All told its sales were $12 billion as shown in column 6 (the totals column). Total sales (output) of the manufacturing and services sectors were $24 and $18 billion, respectively.

We have also included in table 6.1 a Households and Government row (row 4) and a Totals row (row 5). The first three cells of row 4 record the sum of (1) wages and salaries paid to households; (2) interest, rent, dividends, and profits that were distributed; and (3) taxes paid to government, for each column's producing sector. The total of these items for each producing sector is shown in the last cell of that row.

Each of the first three columns of table 6.1 lists that sector's expenditures, including payments for household and government services, the total for each column being recorded at the foot. Thus column 1 shows that the agriculture sector purchased $1 billion of output from itself to be used as inputs in agriculture production, $4 billion of output from the manufacturing sector, $2 billion from the services sector, $5 billion from households and government (corresponding to wages and salaries, rent, interest, dividends, and profits and taxes). All told its costs were $12 billion.

Turn briefly to table 6.2. The first row records the output of each of the three producing sectors. Assume that output per worker in these three sectors is $20,000, $30,000, and $40,000, respectively. Dividing these outputs per worker into the total output of their corresponding sectors yields the number of jobs in each sector, as recorded in the second row of table 6.2. For the moment, postpone discussion of rows 3–5.

Table 6.2
Output and jobs by sector

	Agri.	Manu.	Serv.
(1) Output	$12mmm	$24mmm	$18mmm
(2) Jobs	600,000	800,000	450,000
(3) Output	11.5mmm	22mmm	21mmm
(4) Jobs	575,000	713,000	525,000
(5) Change in number of jobs	-25,000	-87,000	+75,000

Now, return to table 6.1. Note the purchase of manufactures by the agriculture sector recorded in the first cell of the second row. It is $4 billion. Note also the total at the foot of the first column which is the total costs of the agriculture sector. It is $12 billion, which is also equal to the total value of output of the agriculture sector, as recorded in column 6. Divide the $4 billion by the $12 billion to obtain $0.3333, or

33 1/3 cents. This is the cents worth of inputs of manufactures per dollar output of agriculture. This figure is called an input–output coefficient. Dividing the first cells in the first and third rows by the same total output yields inputs of agriculture, and of services, respectively, per dollar output of agriculture, these being the input–output coefficients $0.0833, and $0.1667, respectively, or 8 1/3, and 16 2/3 cents. These coefficients are entered in column 1 of table 6.3.

Table 6.3
Input–output coefficients

	Agri. (1)	Manu. (2)	Serv. (3)
(1) Agri.	0.0833	0.1250	0.1111
(2) Manu.	0.3333	0.2500	0.2222
(3) Serv.	0.1667	0.1250	0.2778

Input–output coefficients for manufacturing and service sectors are derived in similar manner and recorded in columns 2 and 3 of table 6.3. Each column records the inputs required to produce $1.00 of output of that column's sector.

Now move on to exploit these input–output coefficients. Suppose a U.S. political leader in 1992 is developing a disarmament proposal as a result of drastic reorganization within the Soviet system. Should there be a 20 percent reduction in military expenditures, a 40 percent reduction, or some other percentage? This leader's basic concern is jobs–the number that may be lost as a result of a cutback.

He knows that if the military sector is slashed, outputs of all industries will be affected. But because of indirect input requirements of any production sector, he is unable to say by how much. As a specific case, suppose a leader contemplates a 50 percent reduction in the defense sector, and plans to use the $2.5 billion savings to purchase $2.5 billion of services for social welfare programs. Columns 4 and 5 from table 6.1 become columns 4 and 5 of table 6.4.

Table 6.4
New demands of households + nonmilitary government and military sectors (in billions of dollars)

	Hds + Gov't (4)	Mil. (5)	Total
Agri.	5	0.5	5.5
Manu.	6	2	8
Serv.	10.5		10.5

So far the effect on outputs of the three producing sectors, agriculture, manufactures, and services, is not known. Let X_1, X_2, and X_3 represent these sectors' respective outcomes. It is known that the output of agriculture X_1 must be sufficient to meet

1. its own demand for agricultural products, which will be 0.0833 X_1 (cents requirement of agriculture output per dollar output of agriculture times the output [unknown] of the agriculture sector);
2. the demand of the manufacturing sector, namely, 0.1250 X_2 (cents requirement of agriculture output per dollar output of manufacturing times the manufacturing output [unknown]);
3. the demand of the services sector, namely, 0.1111 X_3; and
4. the combined demand of the household and government and military sectors, namely, $5.5 billion (see table 6.4).

Hence

$$X_1 = 0.0833 \ X_1 + 0.1250 \ X_2 + 0.1111 \ X_3 + \$5,500,000,000 \qquad 6.7$$

or, bringing all unknowns over to the right side of the equation and collecting terms:

$$(1 - 0.0833)X_1 - 0.1250 \ X_2 - 0.1111 \ X_3 = \$5,500,000,000. \qquad 6.8$$

In like manner, equations can be derived for the unknown manufacturing and services outputs:

$$-0.3333X_1 + (1 - 0.2500)X_2 - 0.2222X_3 = \$8,000,000,000 \qquad 6.9$$
$$-0.1667X_1 - 0.1250X_2 + (1 - 0.2778)X_3 = \$10,500,000,000 \qquad 6.10$$

These are three independent equations with three unknowns. By substitution or other algebraic procedure (or using a computer) these three equations can be solved for X_1, X_2, and X_3:

$$X_1 = \$11,490,000,000 = \text{new output of agriculture}$$
$$X_2 = \$21,890,000,000 = \text{new output of manufactures}$$
$$X_3 = \$21,170,000,000 = \text{new output of services}$$

Round off these numbers and enter them in the third row of table 6.2. Dividing them respectively by $20,000, $30,000, and $40,000 (outputs per laborer for the producing sectors) yields the number of jobs in each sector, as recorded in the fourth row. Comparison of numbers in rows 2 and 4 shows a loss of 25,000 and 87,000 jobs in agriculture and manufacturing, and a gain of 75,000 jobs in ser-vices–or a net loss of 37,000 jobs, given the contemplated scenario of a 50 percent reduction in military spending and the redirection of these resources to purchase services for social welfare.

6.3.3   Further remarks

The computations of the previous section and data of table 6.4 really do not answer the question raised there by the political leader– namely, how the outputs of (and employment in) all industries will be affected were the defense sector slashed by 50 percent with the released funds spent on services for social welfare programs. This is so because of the simplified version of an economy just discussed–one with three aggregated producing sectors and two "final demand" consuming sectors. It is not enough to say that there would be a loss of 25,000 and 87,000 jobs in the aggregates of agriculture and manufacturing, respectively, and a gain of 75,000 jobs in the aggre-gate of services (as indicated in table 6.4). The political leader wants more detailed information–say, change in jobs in each of the several or many agricultural (and mining) activities, manufacturing opera-tions, and service trades in his local area, state or region. Actually, such detailed information is obtainable. Modern input–output tables divide the economy into anywhere from 50 to 500 sectors, not just five. Hence, looking at any arms reduction scenario in an input– output framework enables one to determine how output and employ-ment in each of many sectors are affected. For example, one early study of the impact of a 10 percent cutback in national military expenditures indicated that loss of jobs in the transport equipment industry (primarily aircraft) of the Los Angeles–Long Beach metro-politan area would be 11,799, but gains in employment in the con-tract construction industry from an offset program of housing and business and government investment would, under one set of assump-tions, be 16,082 (Isard and Schooler, 1964).

Such data generated by input–output analysis thus can be very useful and can provide the detailed information desired by the poli-tical leader. They suggest where specific locally oriented and sector-oriented policies are needed to combat potential pockets of unem-ployment and poverty–policies which are going to be required as the

U.S. Department of Defense carries through a proposed (1991) new round of base closings in an effort to reduce its expenditures.

The outcome of an arms reduction scenario depends not only on the extent to which each of the specific military programs is reduced, but also on what offset programs are introduced: whether the government uses savings from the cutback in military expenditures to increase services to the population, reduce taxes, promote research and development projects, spur natural resource development, or for some other purpose. In some instances, net effect on total regional employment may be positive; in others, negative. In the Los Angeles–Long Beach study, a national offset program involving a reduction in personal income taxes (resulting in greater disposable income) would have reduced employment in that region, whereas a housing and business and government investment program, as mentioned above, would have increased it.

When military expenditures are cut, weaponry useless for household consumption and for industrial purposes is replaced by commodities which households wish to consume and which industries wish to use in the construction of plant and manufacture of equipment. The effect of such construction and manufacture, which comprise investment, cannot be overemphasized. A productive investment in plant and equipment (or in human capital via education and training) leads to an increase in the output of goods in future years, and thus has a strong, long-run, positive effect on a society's welfare. It is a widely accepted hypothesis that restrictions placed by World War II victors on military buildup in West Germany and Japan caused resources that might otherwise have flowed to their military sectors to be channelled into productive economic investments. These investments enhanced the cost efficiency and competitive position of these two countries in the world economy and led to their significant economic growth and to their becoming two of the three major economic powers in the late 1980s.

Anyone who argues that a high level of military expenditures is undesirable must, of course, confront the reality of politics. One can always identify public expenditures on civilian programs, which can be as stimulating to an economy as military expenditures when there is high unemployment of labor and capital. It is far more likely in the short run that legislators and government administrators will reach agreement on increased military expenditures than on increased civilian program expenditures. This is because national security is a more commonly shared objective to which interest groups can appeal. Hence, substituting civilian programs for increased military expenditures can be extremely difficult politically. Likewise, a research and development program oriented to civilian production in general has significantly greater potential for long-run national productivity and welfare than an equivalent program oriented to the military sector (whose spinoffs to the civilian sector rarely are as significant as those from knowledge gained from comparable programs directly related to civilian production). Nevertheless, when an economy urgently needs a major research and development effort to improve its overall productivity and ability to compete for world markets, legislators and government administrators are far more likely to agree on such an effort tied to the military sector than on one oriented to civilian production.

6.4 Conversion from military to civilian production and industrial restructuring

The previous section looked at both macro and micro models. The Klein-LINK macro model examines impacts of scenarios involving changes in military expenditures and diverse offset programs. It can throw light on resulting changes in the inflation rate, government deficits, interest rates, trade balance, unemployment rate, levels of investment and household consumption, GNP, and so forth. However, macro models tend to generate broad, average-type data, and fail to point up effects on particular regions and localities, industries, occupations, and incomes of socioeconomic groups. For analysis of this sort, the micro-type models of input–output and social accounting frameworks can generate valuable data.

However, conversion from military to civilian production and industrial restructuring involve problems besides those that models can attack. Workers must be retrained for new occupations, or in some instances taught new skills within an existing occupation. A highly skilled engineer turned gas station attendant is not an uncommon phenomenon–indicative of conversion failure. Tools and equipment need to be put to different use, or new machinery may be required; investment is needed for this retooling process. Industrial plants must be redesigned or in some cases completely scrapped and replaced by new ones. Moreover, serving many markets in a highly competitive system where cost-efficient production and marketing is a *sine qua non* for survival requires much different management than serving a one-consumer (government) market which places great emphasis on a product's performance capability (say, a bomber) and pays less attention to cost.

Conversion problems of the 1990s are different from those of the period following World War II. Conversion then was extremely successful; unemployment never rose above 3 percent. During the war the U.S. had switched from civilian production to military. Once the fighting ceased after over three and a half years, managers, engineers, and others in the labor force had no trouble switching back to what they had been doing before. In contrast, over the course of the last several decades, completely new production operations have evolved to serve military markets employing first-time managers, engineers, and other labor with no previous experience in the commercial marketplace upon which to fall back.

6.5 Summary

This chapter has been concerned with the role of models in examining the implications of various policy scenarios and generating data useful for policy proposals and political argument. The multiple regression approach frequently examines the effect of different factors (supposedly independent variables) on some magnitude (such as the arms production of a Third World country). The econometric model is particularly well suited for generating for a nation a set of macro magnitudes (such as GNP, investment, and consumption) and values for key variables (such as interest rates) which critically affect these magnitudes. The input–output framework is useful for examining shocks and major changes in final demand upon the output of particular industries, their employment, and income of diverse socioeconomic groups in localities, regions, and nations.

Of course, each of the models discussed here, and others that peace scientists and other social scientists may employ, must be used cautiously, with full knowledge of their shortcomings. Moreover, a model's validity depends on the quality of data and the definitions and concepts used by the analyst, and on many other factors. A model does not replace sound judgment. Rather, it provides a decision maker with information to complement his judgment and intuition.

Appendix to Chapter 6. The Mechanics of Input–Output

Take the set of equations 6.8–6.10 depicted by table 6.1. To avoid the use of the cumbersome four-decimal-place numbers of table 6.3, let

$a_{11} =$ inputs (in cents) of agriculture commodities per dollar output of the agriculture sector

$a_{12} =$ inputs (in cents) of agriculture commodities per dollar output of the manufacturing sector

$a_{13} =$ inputs (in cents) of agriculture commodities per dollar output of the services sector

$a_{21} =$ inputs (in cents) of manufactured commodities per dollar output of the agriculture sector

.

.

.

$a_{33} =$ inputs (in cents) of services per dollar output of the services sector

The constants $a_{11}, \ldots, a_{33}$ are input–output coefficients sometimes designated *production coefficients*.

Also let

$Y_1 =$ combined demand for agriculture output of the household and government and military sectors

$Y_2 =$ combined demand for manufactures of the household and government and military sectors

$Y_3 =$ combined demand for services of the household and government and military sectors.

The Y's may be designated *final demands*, and constitute sales to the *final demand sector*, namely, the aggregate demands of the household and government and military sectors.

Equations 6.8–6.10 then become

$(1 - a_{11}) X_1 - a_{12}X_2 - a_{13}X_3 = Y_1$ 6.11
$-a_{21}X_1 + (1 - a_{22}) X_2 - a_{23}X_3 = Y_2$ 6.12
$-a_{31}X_1 - a_{32}X_2 + (1 - a_{33})X_3 = Y_3$ 6.13

Following standard algebraic procedures, one can solve these three equations for the three unknown outputs, X_1, X_2, and X_3. For example, multiply each term of the first of the set of equations 6.11–6.13 by a_{23} and the second by a_{13} and subtract the resulting second equation from the first. This yields an equation in two unknowns:

$$(a_{23} - a_{23}a_{11} + a_{13}a_{21})X_1 + (a_{13}a_{22} - a_{13} - a_{23}a_{12})X_2 =$$
$$a_{23}Y_1 - a_{13}Y_2 \qquad\qquad 6.14$$

The variable X_3 has been eliminated.

In similar fashion, multiply the second of equations 6.11–6.13 by $(1-a_{33})$ and the third by $-a_{23}$; subtract one of the resulting equations from the other, and derive a second equation in two unknowns (X_1 and X_2); X_3 has been eliminated. There are now two equations in two unknowns. Following the same procedure, multiply each of these two equations by an appropriate term, subtract, and obtain an equation which expresses X_1 in terms of the constant a's. Do the same to derive X_2. Multiplying by different constants and repeating the entire set of steps, one solves for X_3. Accordingly,

$$X_1 = A_{11}Y_1 + A_{12}Y_2 + A_{13}Y_3 \qquad\qquad 6.15$$
$$X_2 = A_{21}Y_1 + A_{22}Y_2 + A_{23}Y_3 \qquad\qquad 6.16$$
$$X_3 = A_{31}Y_1 + A_{32}Y_2 + A_{33}Y_3 \qquad\qquad 6.17$$

where A_{11} equals
$$[(1-a_{22})(1-a_{33})-a_{23}a_{32}] \text{ divided by}$$
$$[(1-a_{11})(1-a_{22})(1-a_{33})-a_{12}a_{23}a_{31}-a_{13}a_{21}a_{32}-a_{13}a_{31}(1-a_{22})$$
$$-a_{12}a_{21}(1-a_{33})-a_{23}a_{32}(1-a_{11})] \qquad\qquad 6.18$$

and where every other A coefficient in equations 6.15–6.17 is a *constant* derived from the "a" coefficients of equations 6.11–6.13 and consisting of as many terms as A_{11}.

It is important to emphasize that these A coefficients are constants. They are derived by standard operations upon constant production coefficients (the a's) which are given at the start. The A coefficients are independent of the magnitude and composition of final demand, that is, of Y_1, Y_2, and Y_3. No matter how Y_1, Y_2, and Y_3 vary, they are multiplied, respectively, by the same A's to derive the unknown sector outputs X_1, X_2, and X_3. In essence, the A's combine direct and indirect requirements. For example, in equation 6.16, A_{21} represents the cents' worth of the output of sector 2 (manufactures) required both directly and indirectly to produce one dollar of output of sector 1 (agriculture) for final demand, and $A_{21}Y_1$ represents the *total* of direct and indirect requirements of output of sector 2 that the system requires to deliver Y_1 quantity of the output of sector 1 to the final demand sector; A_{22} represents direct and indirect requirements by sector 2 of its own product to produce one dollar of its output for final demand, and $A_{22}Y_2$ represents *total* direct and indirect requirements of this product that the system requires to deliver Y_2 quantity of sector 2's product to the final demand sector. And so forth. Thus, $A_{21}Y_1 + A_{22}Y_2 + A_{23}Y_3$ equals total direct and indirect requirements of sector 2's product needed to produce all the outputs to be delivered to the final demand sector. In the input–output framework, this must equal total output of sector 2, that is, X_2.

These A's provide a general solution to the problem. When arranged in the following way

$$
\begin{array}{ccc}
A_{11}, & A_{12}, & A_{13} \\
A_{21}, & A_{22}, & A_{23} \\
A_{31}, & A_{32}, & A_{33}
\end{array}
$$

they form a matrix, and in particular a matrix that is the inverse of a second matrix:

$$
\begin{array}{ccc}
(1 - a_{11}), & - a_{12}, & - a_{13} \\
- a_{21}, & (1 - a_{22}), & - a_{23} \\
- a_{31}, & - a_{32}, & (1 - a_{33})
\end{array}
$$

where the a's are the constant production coefficients of equations 6.11–6.13 and where each A is defined in terms of the a's. Taking values for the a's from equations 6.8–6.10, the A values are found to be

$$
\begin{array}{ccc}
A_{11} = 1.2264 & A_{12} = 0.2493 & A_{13} = 0.2623 \\
A_{21} = 0.6570 & A_{22} = 1.5398 & A_{23} = 0.5677 \\
A_{31} = 0.4003 & A_{32} = 0.3412 & A_{33} = 1.5465
\end{array}
$$

These values are the constants by which Y_1, Y_2 and Y_3 are to be multiplied to derive estimates of X_1, X_2 and X_3. Hence, we can quickly estimate the implications for output, employment, income, etc., for many, different, scenarios. One might consider the effects of a 10 percent reduction in the military sector with an offset program of business tax reduction, or personal income tax reduction, or both. Or one might look at a 50 percent cutback in the military sector, combined with an offset government program of low-income housing construction, or environmental pollution control, or foreign aid, or industrial research and development, or some combination of these.

The above equations hold for a simple hypothetical economy with three producing sectors. One may consider an actual economy with many, say, n, producing sectors. There are many n equations:

$$
\begin{aligned}
X_1 - a_{11}X_1 - a_{12}X_2 - a_{13}X_3 - \ldots - a_{1n}X_n &= Y_1 \\
X_2 - a_{21}X_1 - a_{22}X_2 - a_{23}X_3 - \ldots - a_{2n}X_n &= Y_2 \\
X_3 - a_{31}X_1 - a_{32}X_2 - a_{33}X_3 - \ldots - a_{3n}X_n &= Y_3 \\
\ldots\ldots\ldots\ldots\ldots\ldots \\
X_n - a_{n1}X_1 - a_{n2}X_2 - a_{n3}X_3 - \ldots - a_{nn}X_n &= Y_n
\end{aligned}
$$

6.19

Again, each equation indicates how the total output of any industrial sector is allocated to each industrial sector (including itself) and to final demand. The a's stand for the cents' worth of inputs produced by the industry indicated by the first subscript required to produce one dollar of output in the industry indicated by the second subscript.

The set of n equations 6.19 in n unknowns are independent, and, therefore, may be solved. One finds that

$$X_1 = A_{11}Y_1 + A_{12}Y_2 + A_{13}Y_3 + \ldots + A_{1n}Y_n$$
$$X_2 = A_{21}Y_1 + A_{22}Y_2 + A_{23}Y_3 + \ldots + A_{2n}Y_n$$
$$X_3 = A_{31}Y_1 + A_{32}Y_2 + A_{33}Y_3 + \ldots + A_{3n}Y_n \qquad \text{6.20}$$
$$\text{................................}$$
$$X_n = A_{n1}Y_1 + A_{n2}Y_2 + A_{n3}Y_3 + \ldots + A_{nn}Y_n$$

In each row of 6.19 there are n number of a's and there are n rows. None of the a's are the same. Hence, there are n^2 coefficients. Each of the A's in equations 6.20 is related to all the n^2 constant production coefficients in equations 6.19 in much the same way as A_{11} in equation 6.18 is related to each of the nine (3^2) constant production coefficients of equations 6.11–6.13 that relate to an economy of three producing sectors. If, for example, one were to consider a 500-sector breakdown of an economy, the denominator of each A in equations 6.20 would contain 1,000 (2n) terms, each term being the product of 500 constants; and the numerator of each A would contain 998 terms, each term being the product of 499 constants. These A's can be arranged in matrix form:

$$
\begin{array}{cccc}
A_{11}, & A_{12}, & \ldots, & A_{1n} \\
A_{21}, & A_{22}, & \ldots, & A_{2n} \\
\multicolumn{4}{c}{\text{................................}} \\
A_{n1}, & A_{n2}, & \ldots, & A_{nn}
\end{array}
$$

which is the inverse of

$$
\begin{array}{cccc}
(1 - a_{11}), & -a_{12}, & \ldots, & -a_{1n} \\
-a_{21}, & (1 - a_{22}), & \ldots, & -a_{2n} \\
\multicolumn{4}{c}{\text{................................}} \\
-a_{n1}, & -a_{n2}, & \ldots, & (1 - a_{nn})
\end{array}
$$

The matrix of A's provides the constants by which final demands (Y_1, Y_2, . . ., Y_n) for any given scenario are to be multiplied to obtain estimates of sector outputs (X_1, X_2, . . ., X_n).

Immediately apparent is the tremendous saving in time and effort which a general solution based on calculating the set of A's provides.

And all the operations can be performed quickly and easily on a high-speed computer. Thus, using input–output analysis a political leader can examine many different policy scenarios to help him develop sound policies.

References

Dumas, Lloyd J. and Marek Thee (1989) *Making Peace Possible: The Promise of Economic Conversion.* New York: Pergamon Press.

Gasiorowski, Mark and Sol Polachek (1982) "Conflict and Interdependence: East–West Trade and Linkages in the Era of Detente," *Journal of Conflict Resolution* 26 (4): 709–29.

Isard, Walter (1988) *Arms Races, Arms Control and Conflict Analysis: Contributions from Peace Science and Peace Economics.* New York: Cambridge University Press, Chap. 9.

Isard, Walter and Eugene W. Schooler (1964) "An Economic Analysis of Local and Regional Impacts of Reduction of Military Expenditures," *Papers,* Peace Research Society (International), 1:15–42.

Leontief, Wassily and Faye Duchin (1983) *Military Spending: Facts and Figures, Worldwide Implications and Future Outlook.* New York: Oxford University Press.

Polachek, Sol W. (1992) "Economic Trade and Political Interactions Among Nations," in Isard, Walter and Charles H. Anderton *Economics of Arms Reduction and the Peace Process.* Amsterdam: North Holland.

Pollins, B. (1989) "Does Trade Still Follow the Flag?" *American Political Science Review,* Vol. 83: 465–80.

Rosh, Robert M. (1990) "Third World Arms Production and the Evolving Interstate System," *Journal of Conflict Resolution* 34, (1, March): 57–73.

Singer, J. David (1990) *Models, Methods, and Progress in World Politics.* Boulder, CO: Westview Press.

Siverson, Randolph M. and Harvey Starr (1989) "Alliance and Border Effects on the War Behavior of States: Refining the Interaction Opportunity Model," *Conflict Management and Peace Science,* 10, (2, Spring): 21–46.

7   *Principles of Negotiation and Mediation and Qualitative Conflict Management Procedures*

7.1   Introduction

The last chapter examined models, the kinds of data they produce, and the validity of such data. When a policy scenario is inputted into a model, the data generated represent outcomes of that scenario.

Imagine now that two political leaders are in conflict. As behaving units, they want to reach a compromise or agreement on a joint action or policy. How do they proceed? Bear in mind previous discussion of the following:

1. effects on decision making of a behaving unit's attitudes, perceptions, goals (aspirations), motivations, expectations, limited abilities, and so on (chapters 3 and 4);
2. impact of stress and crisis on a participant's behavior and his perception of outcomes, given his behavioral pathologies (chapter 4);
3. how a behaving unit's mental representations influence his actions, and the way he uses artificial intelligence or other approaches to solve problems (chapter 4);
4. the way he uses his labor and resources to acquire new information and to learn more about a situation to help him decide, perhaps with other members of his group, what policy is best (chapter 4);
5. how he conducts policy analysis (if he is a political leader who does so) (chapter 5); and
6. the way he develops a political argument, utilizing data generated by models (chapters 5 and 6).

Each political leader perhaps has set forth an effective argument that has led to his successful election. They are in major conflict on an arms control policy. On the basis of expected outcomes or some other evidence or hunch, each has determined the policy scenario he most prefers. As negotiators, they or their representatives face the question of what *principles of negotiation* to use to try to reach an acceptable compromise or agreement. If a mediator or other third party is brought into the picture, he faces the question of what *principles of mediation* to use. Furthermore, each leader and third party (if any) may find that the one or more negotiation principles or the one or more mediation principles he tried did not resolve the conflict and thus may confront a second question: what quantitative conflict management procedure (CMP) to use to reach an acceptable compromise (agreement).

This chapter and the following develop one of many possible approaches to achieving a compromise joint action or partial or complete resolution of a conflict. This approach is first to identify *key characteristics* of a conflict situation and then to select one or more *negotiation or mediation principles* constituting a qualitative conflict management procedure relevant for these characteristics, to use in striving for compromise, and finally, if no agreement is reached, to use a *quantitative conflict management procedure*, first having evaluated various quantitative CMPs for political and economic feasibility. In this regard models (world models in the case of some international conflicts) may prove useful. These models can provide additional information to help parties assess the "acceptability-desirability" of each of the quantitative CMPs proposed. At this point, basic concepts should be defined.

7.2   Definitions of basic concepts

Negotiation is the interaction through verbal exchange between one party and his opponent(s) for the purpose of coming to terms or reaching a mutually acceptable agreement or resolution of a conflict.

Mediation is the process whereby a third party attempts to help conflicting parties reach a voluntary agreement. It is to be distinguished from arbitration where the third party is empowered to make a binding decision to settle a dispute.

A *principle of negotiation* is a rule of thumb adjudged to be an appropriate basis for guiding the behavior of a negotiator.

A *principle of mediation* is a rule of thumb adjudged to be an appropriate basis for guiding the behavior of a mediator.

A *qualitative CMP* is a set of compatible (noncontradictory) principles of negotiation, mediation, or other third-party intervention to be used in seeking a mutually acceptable or imposed resolution (partial or complete) of a conflict.

A quantitative CMP is a technique or combination of techniques for processing data or quantitative information as inputs–a procedure to be used, often in conjunction with a qualitative CMP, in seeking a mutually acceptable or imposed resolution (partial or complete) of a conflict.

7.3 Conflict situation characteristics: identification of key characteristics for a given situation

The first step here is to list possible characteristics of conflict situations so that a negotiator, mediator, analyst, or any other interested party can better identify the relevant key characteristics of a particular situation. Tables 7.1–7.3 present only a partial listing. Parties in conflict often are two or more nations, regions, or ethnic groups, or a region and a nation, or two or more other meaningful communities, where each community may be regarded as a system. Characteristics of these systems may play a major role in any attempt at conflict resolution. As indicated by the headings of table 7.1 on *Systemic structural characteristics,* characteristics pertain to: culture, social psychology, the set of social groups and organizations, economic system, political system and subcultures, and other.

For example, a nation as a system may have a strong need to exercise power, and/or to have security, be governed by a Roman legal system, be conservative, bureaucratic, and precedent-oriented in solving problems. It may be a rapidly growing democracy whose economy is dominated by large-scale enterprise and may have developed a high level of information and extensive experience with major wars. For a negotiator or mediator any one of these characteristics may be key for understanding and trying to resolve a conflict. Table 7.1 constitutes a useful checklist of possible key systemic characteristics.

Table 7.1 *Systemic structural characteristics*

I. Culture

    1. Need to have (exercise) power
    2. Need to have identity
    3. Need to achieve
    4. Need to have security
    5. Type of legal system (e.g., Roman, Common, Islamic, Old Testament)

Table 7.1 *Systemic structural characteristics (cont.)*

II. Social psychology
  10. Degree of conservativeness (boldness)
  11. Solutions sought via
  – group (bureaucratic) means
  – individualistic action
  – individualistic action subject to group approval
  12. Approach to problem solving
  – calculating (methodical)
  – abstract (logical)
  – intuitive (religiomystic)
  – experimental
  – precedent (tradition) oriented
  .
  .
  .

III. The set of social groups and organizations
  20. Degree of division within society
  – regarding public purpose
  – among socioeconomic classes regarding wealth and consumption
  – among political groups regarding influence and power
  21. Status of division within society
  – recently emergent
  – protracted
  – rate of change (trend) in
  – potential for revolution
  .
  .
  .

IV. Economic system
  30. Level and stage of development (developed, developing; stable or about to take off)
  31. Growth/decline (stagnation) pattern
  32. Degree of dependence on external relations (trade, foreign aid and investment, military assistance, etc.)
  33. Industrial structure and organization (small business, large domestic corporations, multinationals, etc.)
  34. Magnitude and type of structural change
  .
  .
  .

V. Political system and subcultures
  40. Degree and type of democracy
  – Western style
  – military style
  – Soviet bloc style
  41. Position along big power–small power continuum
  42. Stability of incumbent political leaders and political system (party structure)
  43. Internal decision-making structure
  – centralized
  – decentralized
  – hierarchical
  .
  .
  .

VI. Other
  50. System information (low, medium, high)
  51. Experience with major conflict

A second useful checklist consists of those characteristics that are *nonsystemic*, but which also relate to the *structure* of the conflict. As indicated by the headings of table 7.2, these include: nature of disagreement (issues and stakes), participants involved, coalition-related characteristics, reference position and magnitudes, time-related characteristics, policy options (joint actions) available, fractionation/logrolling possibilities, information-related characteristics, and communication channels available.

Table 7.2 *Nonsystemic structural characteristics*

I.   Nature of disagreement: issues and stakes
    100. Qualitative, quantitative, or mixed
    101. Intensity of (major, minor)

         .
         .
         .

II. Participants involved
    110. Number
    111. Presence or absence of
       – negotiators acting on behalf of a constituency
       – technical support team
       – third party
       – coalitions among participants
    112. Relations among
       – degree of hostility (friendliness)
       – degree of trust (and mutual respect)

         .
         .
         .

III. Coalition-related characteristics
    120. Type and size of
    121. Stability

         .
         .
         .

IV. Reference position and magnitudes
    130. Current situation
    131. Ideal situation
    132. Reservation/fallback position
    133. Worst scenario position
    134. Nature of credible threats, promises
    135. Nature of current demands/offers
    136. Inherent constraints (on actions, outcomes, etc.)
    137. Nonnegotiable issues

         .
         .
         .

V.   Time-related characteristics
    140. Historical factors
    141. Presence of deadline(s)
    142. Time path of conflict

Table 7.2 *Nonsystemic structural characteristics (cont.)*

      – unchanging (static), slowly changing, explosive
      – sharply discontinuous
      – widely fluctuating

                                               .
                                               .
                                               .

VI. Policy options (joint actions) available
      150. Number
            – small, many
      151. Component elements
            – one, few, many
      152. Scale of measurement
            – discrete or continuous
            – nominal, ordinal, relative, cardinal
      153. Agenda (sequence of consideration)

                                               .
                                               .
                                               .

VII. Fractionation/logrolling possibilities
      160. Regarding issues
      161. Regarding participants (groupings of)
      162. Regarding actions (or elements of actions)
      163. Regarding outcomes (or elements of outcomes)

                                               .
                                               .
                                               .

VIII. Information-related characteristics
      170. Quality and quantity regarding structural conflict situation characteristics
            – much or little
            – degree of "accuracy"
            – extent of uncertainty
      171. Quality and quantity regarding participant characteristics
            – as in 170
      172. Quality and quantity regarding CMPs
            – as in 170
      173. Models/tools available
            – number, quality, type

                                               .
                                               .
                                               .

IX. Communication channels available
      180. Few, many
      181. Formal, informal
      182. Congested, noncongested

For example, a dispute may revolve around territory each of two nations claims. The number of participants may be four (say, a negotiator from each of the nations in conflict, a United Nations observer, and a highly regarded diplomat from another country); intense hostility may prevail, and one of the negotiators may be highly distrustful of the others' proposals. The possibility for coalitions does not exist since the U.N. observer and outside diplomat are completely neutral, but the suspicious negotiator may not be fully convinced that this is the case. The worst scenario would be the invasion of one country by the other if no agreement is reached, the latter having first made a credible threat in a situation where the conflict has become explosive and there is only limited time to consider policy options. One such option which perhaps could forestall an invasion might be to introduce several minor, unrelated issues on which there can be give-and-take in a logrolling manner to build trust between the two nations. Considerable information about the conflict may be available since the territory has passed from one nation's hands to the other's several times in the past, but the two countries may only be able to communicate via respected, neutral third parties.

A third set of characteristics of a conflict situation consists of those that pertain to the parties themselves. As indicated by the headings of table 7.3, they relate to participants' psychology, pathologies in crisis situations, levels of education and knowledge, control of resources, perceptive capabilities, receptive capabilities regarding information, learning potentials and preference structure and ability to state preferences. For example, one participant may be bold and aggressive, the other conservative and nonmyopic. Each may be overconfident in the "rightness" of his proposal. Each may have little knowledge of analytical tools and models. One may control sizeable economic resources and the other considerable political resources. Each may have limited ability to perceive the other's characteristics. One, a conservative, may be highly receptive to all kinds of new information and the other bold and not receptive. Whereas each may have considerable learning capability, one may be able to attach precise values to outcomes and the other only relative values (that is, for example, to be only able to say that this outcome is twice as good as that).

Table 7.3 Participants' characteristics

I. Their psychology
    200. Position along various continua
        – conservative to bold
        – pessimist to optimist
        – risk averse to risk lover
        – competitive to cooperative
        – passive to aggressive
        – myopic to nonmyopic
        – self-interested to altruistic
        – tradition bound to creative
    201. Pathologies in crisis situations
        – overconfidence in "rightness" of one's proposal

Table 7.3 *Participants' characteristics (cont.)*

- insensitivity to objective information questioning "rightness" of one's proposal
- overvaluation of "rightness" of past proposals that were successful

.
.
.

II. Their level of education (sophistication) and knowledge
    230. General (low, medium, high)
    231. Regarding conflict situations (low, medium, high)
    232. Regarding analytical tools and models (low, medium, high)
    233. Regarding conflict management (low, medium, high)
    234. Nature and extent of their misperceptions

.
.
.

III. Their control of resources
    240. General (economic, political, social, etc.)
    241. Specific to (relevant for) the conflict

.
.

IV. Their perceptive capabilities
    250. Limited or extensive—in noncrisis situations
        - regarding interdependence
        - regarding structural conflict situation characteristics
        - regarding other participants' characteristics
        - regarding new options and creative approaches
    251. Limited or extensive—in crisis situations
        - as in 250

.
.
.

V. Their receptive capabilities regarding information
    260. Limited or much (abundant)—in noncrisis situations
        - on interdependence
        - on structural conflict situation characteristics
        - on other participants' characteristics
        - on new options and creative ideas
    261. Limited or abundant—in crisis situations
        - as in 260

.
.
.

VI. Their learning potentials
    270. Capability (little, much)
    271. Willingness (little, much)

.
.
.

VII. Their preference structure and statement capabilities
    280. Can only order their preferences for outcomes
    281. Can state relative preference for outcomes
    282. Can give precise values to outcomes

.
.

A negotiator or mediator who has these checklists to help him identify key characteristics of a conflict situation may be able to understand the situation better, to avoid failing to consider some basic factor, and to make more effective proposals.

How does a participant identify key characteristics of a given conflict situation? The lists of possible characteristics in tables 7.1–7.3 can be useful; but clearly each participant must also answer this question on the basis of his own current stock of knowledge, experience, perceptions, and learning acquired in workshops and other discussion arenas.

What if the negotiators select as key characteristics certain ones that are incompatible? For example, in a conflict over what should be the level of a nation's military expenditures one negotiator may insist that the key issue is the perpetuation of a basic religious doctrine (a qualitative non-negotiable element) that denies any concern for material welfare, whereas the second may insist that assurance of economic growth (through control of resources) is the key issue. Such incompatibility (which is different from conflict over the level of military expenditures *per se*) may be viewed as a subconflict within the primary conflict and may need to be resolved first. One of the procedures available for use in managing primary conflicts may also be employed to lead to a settlement (compromise) that eliminates such a subconflict. Of course, incompatibilities may persist, yet a conflict may be partially or fully resolved if these are minor and do not bring the settlement process to a halt.

7.4 Principles of negotiation (for a two-party conflict)

Remarks here are confined to two-party conflicts. As indicated in section 5.6 of chapter 5, when more than two parties are involved, coalitions become possible. Unfortunately, coalition analysis has little to say so far about the outcome of coalition formation and disruption processes in real-life situations, and thus one cannot suggest any negotiation or mediation principles relevant for situations where coalitions may form.

Once negotiators and any third party construct their own mental representations of the conflict and its key characteristics, they must decide what stance to take and what to propose. They need some rules of thumb, cultural norms, ethical standards, or other guidelines.

These are referred to as principles of negotiation and mediation. A partial summary of such principles follows. It is important that the reader *constantly keep in mind two caveats*:

1. This summary covers only a small fraction of principles advanced by numerous and diverse practitioners over the years.
2. Corresponding to any principle advanced, in some conflict situations an opposite principle may be claimed to be effective. The principles listed are generally useful, but certainly not for every occasion.

Table 7.4 lists selected principles of negotiation in four sections. Each section corresponds to a phase in the negotiations process; these phases are ordered in time. (For certain situations there need not be as many as four phases; other situations call for more.) The first section lists principles negotiators may use in preparing themselves for exchanging proposals and in conducting analysis prior to making proposals. Next come principles for the second, proposal-making phase. After proposals have been made, there is an interaction phase for which are listed principles that negotiators may use in trying to reach agreement on a mutually acceptable "solution" to the conflict. Finally, there is a list of principles for the last phase, namely, trying to ensure implementation of, and compliance with, the agreed-upon solution. These principles of negotiation are discussed in sections 7.4.1–7.4.4 in the order in which they are listed in the table. (Some of these principles will appear again in later phases.) Keep in mind that in any real-life negotiations this order may be reversed and/or modified. Feedback loops and retracing of steps may be expected in any negotiations process. And, as will be seen from the brief sketches of actual negotiations, in any given situation combinations of these principles are almost always used.

7.4.1 Principles for the preparation and analysis phase

(a) Understanding enhancement: A negotiator should analyze and come to understand the give-and-take and the interdependent aspects of negotiations, and, further,

the key issues for himself and his opponent;

possible assumptions he may be making about his own and this opponent's behavior, and vice versa, in setting forth and responding to proposals, and later during the interaction phase;

Table 7.4   *Selected principles of negotiation*

1. Preparation and analysis phase
   a. Understanding enhancement
   b. Monolithicity attainment
   c. Third-party intervention
   d. Misinformation spread

2. Proposal-making phase
   a. Interdependence appreciation
   b. Opponent sensitivity
   c. Pathology awareness
   d. Unilateral–reward action
   e. Long run–short run trade-off
   f. Stance-issues separation
   g. Approximate cost-benefit balance sheet
   h. Deterrent threat
   i. Time exploitation
   j. Monolithicity attainment

3. Interaction phase
   a. Continuous evaluation
   b. Strategic element highlighting and questioning
   c. Trust/respect/knowledge building
   d. Time exploitation
   e. Third-party intervention
   f. Realism in the face of failure

4. Final packaging phase
   a. Enhancement of implementability

possible proposals he and his opponent may set forth, and/or
possible negotiation stances each may take and their points of
conflict; and

the logistics of the situation (time and place of interaction,
sequence of proposals, negotiating conventions, etc.).

In conducting an analysis the negotiator should, when feasible,

use tools and models, capable of exploiting sets of relevant data,
such as simple regression and input–output, and proceed to the
level at which expected costs of further analysis begin to
outweigh expected benefits.

This principle was applied in the Panama Canal negotiations of
1975–76. The situation was exceedingly complex, let alone highly
emotional. On both sides, United States and Panama, many different
interest groups were involved, each seeking its own set of objectives.
With pressure, both public and private, coming from all directions,
Ambassador-at-Large Ellsworth Bunker spent considerable time at *self
understanding enhancement*. He participated in seminars with various
interest groups in the United States to learn more about their desires
and fears.

(b)   Monolithicity attainment: A negotiator representing an organization, nation, or other heterogeneous body should prepare that body for the negotiations he is about to undertake, and whenever possible see that it is committed to implementing whatever agreement he and his opponent may reach. This requires an analysis of the body's own internal conflicts for understanding how various interest groups view the situation and thereby determining how best to help them reach agreement on priorities. Whenever it is in his interest, he should suggest to (urge) his opponent to come so positioned.

Ambassador Bunker surmised that although attaining monolithicity was not possible at the early negotiation stages it was very necessary if a treaty was to be approved by the U.S. Congress. The seminars with various interest groups provided insights into the kinds of proposals that would minimize differences in their reactions and pressures they would subsequently put upon their representatives.

(c)   Third-party intervention principle: In light of his analysis of the conflict situation a negotiator should determine whether third-party intervention (say, mediation) is desirable, especially if the parties are deadlocked or cannot communicate directly.

This principle was applied in the 1965 Indo–Pakistani conflict over Kashmir. After a period during which hostilities had escalated, both Prime Minister Shastri of India and President Ayub of Pakistan came under great pressure from the United Nations and all outside powers (except China) to enter into negotiations. Recognizing the brink on which they were teetering and the unattractive uncertainties of stepping back, they accepted the invitation from Premier Kosygin of the Soviet Union to meet at Tashkent. Each saw the need for outside efforts to restore some form of peace.

This principle was also applied in the conflict situation relating to U.S. hostages in Iran during 1979–80. At that time the central purpose of the political movement of Iranian revolutionary leaders was rejection of the West, and they particularly portrayed the U.S. as the "Great Satan," the ultimate corruptor of Iranian spiritual values. Clearly, it was impossible for Iranian leaders to deal with the United States directly, and ultimately an Algerian mediation team was called in.

(d)   Misinformation spread principle: At times a negotiator may perceive the situation to be closer to a zero-sum game (where what one party gains from a joint action the other always loses) than to a variable-sum game (where both gain). Sad but true, if he is self-interested, as is most often the case, the negotiator should spread

misinformation (including bluffing, suppression of information, etc.) when, after analysis, he thinks it will be distinctly to his advantage. This would be so if expected benefits of such a move exceeded expected costs by more than for any other action. Note that this principle, although consistent with the competitive aspect of natural selection, runs counter to the cooperative spirit of conflict resolution.

7.4.2   Principles for the proposal-making phase

(a)   *Interdependence appreciation:* A negotiator should recognize and appreciate the interdependence of the diverse elements in the negotiations process, being particularly alert to the existence (possibility) of common goals.

(b)   *Opponent sensitivity:* In selecting and/or presenting his proposals, a negotiator should recognize and be responsive to his opponent's needs and/or problems. There may be a need for identity, for legitimacy, or for feeling competent and effective.

(c)   *Pathology awareness:* A negotiator should recognize that he and his opponent may be suffering from certain decision-making pathologies. Such pathologies may relate to

1. overconfidence in the "rightness" of one's proposal and its probability of being adopted;
2. insensitivity to information critical of the "rightness" of one's proposal; and/or
3. overvaluation of the "rightness" of proposals that were successfully set forth and/or accepted in the past and that led to advantageous outcomes.

Application of the above three principles of negotiations occurred when President Sadat of Egypt undertook his historic visit to Jerusalem in November 1977. This visit reflected his keen recognition of the complex interrelationships that had to be considered in any negotiation between Israel and any of the Arab states, and clearly indicated his willingness to address directly the most deep-seated fear and longing of the Israeli people for genuine acceptance by their neighbors–application of the principles of *interdependence appreciation* and *opponent sensitivity*. In his speech before the Israeli Knesset he referred to the barriers of suspicion, rejection, fear, deception, and hallucination–to the barrier of distorted and eroded interpretation of every event and statement–an application of the principle of *pathology awareness*.

(*d*) *Unilateral-reward action:* In designing a proposal, the negotiator should consider the possibility of a unilateral action that will reward his opponent at little cost to himself, the negotiator, thereby to

1. change his opponent's image of him,
2. lead to tension reduction,
3. reduce his opponent's cost of conceding,
4. generate an unstated obligation on the part of his opponent to reiprocate, and
5. help reinforce any tendency toward concession from any or other "good" behavior on his opponent's part.

(*e*) *Long run–short run trade-off:* In setting forth his proposal, a negotiator should be aware of trade-offs between immediate short-run gains and possible longer run gains. Such longer run gains may come from

1. not precluding future concessions or other changes including fractionating the conflict into smaller parts (subconflicts);
2. not precluding future extension of one's alternatives (e.g., via logrolling or expanding the total pie to be shared);
3. not discouraging or precluding inventiveness by himself, his opponent, or a potential third-party intervenor; and
4. not antagonizing his opponent or casting aspersions on him, thereby foregoing future "good" relationships.

Clearly, President Sadat's visit (a step in the direction of recognizing the legitimacy of Israel) was a unilateral action aimed at facilitating future negotiations, an application of the principle of *unilateral–reward action.* Although he was fully aware of major short-run costs (the negative reactions of other Arab leaders that would ensue), he surely had in mind the long-run gains that could eventuate–an application of the principle of *long run–short run trade-off.*

(*f*) *Stance-issues separation.* A negotiator should evaluate his first proposal in terms of his underlying basic interests (his net benefits) and those of his opponent and avoid taking any firm stance. In his subsequent proposals and in viewing those of his opponent he should continue to separate stances from underlying basic interests.

(*g*) *Approximate cost-benefit balance sheet:* A negotiator should consider making a proposal consistent with a problem-solving approach, basing it, where possible and appropriate, on a logical, step-by-step analysis and the construction of a balance sheet of expected benefits and costs, both to negotiator and opponent. He should recognize that intangible elements may be present and that not everything is negotiable.

Ambassador Bunker applied the above two principles in the Panama Canal conflict situation. Early on, he and Panama's foreign minister identified ten basic issues consistent with the principle of *stance–issues separation* For further *understanding enhancement,* Bunker, with the help of a team of consultants and staff, gave importance weights to each issue for *both* the United States and Panama; some of these issues and their corresponding importance weights are listed in table 7.5. This table reflects a crude *approximation of a cost-benefit balance sheet.* Once these issues and weights were identified as the core of the conflict, Bunker assigned roles to members of his team and conducted brainstorming-type bargaining sessions to develop a feel for the negotiations coming up. These steps also reflect the use of the principles of *interdependence appreciation* and *opponent sensitivity* as well as the potential of analytical frameworks (models), however simple.

Table 7.5 *Some hypothetical importance weights for the United States and Panama[a]*

			Importance weights	
Issue	*Units*	*Range*	*United States*	*Panama[b]*
U.S. defense rights	Percentage to be given up	10–25	0.22	0.09
U.S. use rights	Number of rights	20–30	0.22	0.15
Land and water	Percentage U.S. to give up	20–70	0.15	0.15
Duration of treaty	Years	20–50	0.11	0.15
Compensation by U.S.	Millions of dollars	30–75	0.04	0.11
U.S. military rights	Percentage to be given up	10–25	0.02	0.07
Defense role of Panama	Percentage to be given up	10–25	0.02	0.13
Other			0.22	0.15
Total			1.00	1.00

[a]Based upon Raiffa (1982, Table 10, p. 177).
[b]Importance weights for Panama are as perceived by the United States negotiator.

(h) Deterrent threat: If a negotiator deems it desirable to incorporate threats in a proposal, in general these should be designed to deter, that is, to keep one's opponent from doing something (for example, a threat to invade *if* the opponent kills any hostage) rather than to compel one's opponent to do something (say, a threat to invade *unless* he releases hostages).

(i)   Time exploitation: Where possible, a negotiator should exploit the role that time can play in achieving an "advantageous" settlement. He should recognize that not all issues need to be resolved at the start. Actions on some can be deferred and made contingent upon learning from experience, especially in view of uncertainties that no analysis can handle. Time often has a way of solving inscrutable problems. Hence, the negotiator should limit his proposal to those issues that can and need to be addressed at the start.

(j)   Monolithicity attainment: As in the earlier phase, a negotiator should ensure support for his proposals from the body he represents.

7.4.3   Principles for the interaction phase (to reach agreement)

(a)   Continuous evaluation: Once initial proposal(s) have been made, a negotiator should continuously reevaluate the costs and benefits expected to accrue from each subsequent proposal that he may contemplate. He should carry out this evaluation in a manner consistent with principles outlined in section 7.4.2, using analytical tools and models wherever possible and relevant.

(b)   Strategic element highlighting and questioning: After each round of proposal making, a negotiator should both highlight and raise doubts about various elements of the current proposals in an attempt to identify avenues for inventive thinking, concessionary behavior, fractionation, logrolling, and so on, in subsequent rounds.

(c)   Trust/respect/knowledge building: A negotiator should respond to the emerging dynamics of the conflict resolution process and take actions (including making a proposal) in such a way as to encourage a buildup of mutual understanding, trust, and respect.

Ambassador Bunker used the above three principles. Once ten basic issues were highlighted (some of which are noted in table 7.5), he, along with his counterpart from Panama, constantly reevaluated their importance and shifted priorities as negotiations proceeded– (*continuous evaluation* and *strategic element highlighting* and *questioning*). Both negotiators decided to focus initially on those issues easiest to resolve, thereby reaching threshold agreements that would build up confidence among Panamanians that the U.S. was seriously interested in reaching a fair treaty and that would thus ease the way to final agreement on other issues *(trust/respect/knowledge building)*.

(d)   Time exploitation: In the interaction stage, also, a negotiator should exploit the role of time. He should postpone action on issues too difficult for current resolution, particularly when accumulation of

relevant information can be expected. Where possible and appropriate, he should attempt to agree with his opponent on what future joint actions regarding these issues should be adopted if and when certain events occur (contingency planning).

(e)   *Third-party intervention:* Periodically a negotiator should consider (in terms of expected costs and benefits) whether third-party intervention might prove desirable–perhaps for breaking stalemates, suggesting creative alternatives, and so on.

(f)   *Realism in the face of failure:* A negotiator should recognize that at times inaction, withdrawal (particularly when loss-of-face can be avoided), a rigid/inflexible stand–and, alas, misrepresentation and dishonesty, reneging on commitments (gracefully), or similar negative behavior–may be unavoidable and even desirable.

In the 1965 Indo–Pakistani conflict the protagonists and Premier Kosygin, the third party, were unable to reach agreement on basic issues (objectives): (1) Prime Minister Shastri's demand for a "pact of no-war" over Kashmir between Pakistan and India, and (2) President Ayub's demand for "negotiations" on the future status of Kashmir that would lead to a just and honorable settlement. The outcome (agreement) was a declaration which in effect restored the *status quo ante* with regard to territory–a declaration so carefully worded that each leader was able to claim something for his effort. Cleverly designed by Kosygin, the declaration permitted both Ayub and Shastri to save face (*realism in the face of failure*).

7.4.4   Principles for the final packaging phase: enhancement of implementability

When the negotiator represents a body not fully committed to accept an agreement he may work out, and when such an agreement has been achieved, the negotiator should

1.   develop as sound a political argument as possible (as discussed in chapter 5) and, if necessary, rephrase the agreement;
2.   hold discussions with his constituencies; and
3.   otherwise engage in activities likely to enhance acceptance and implementation of the agreement.

Kosygin's declaration not only was endorsed by the two political leaders, but also became acceptable to their countrymen since each leader was able to interpret it as a partial victory.

7.5 Principles of Mediation (for a two-party conflict)

Often in conflict situations, participants agree to use a mediator or may be required to undertake mediation. This section discusses principles of mediation for third parties who have considered the characteristics of conflict situations as discussed in section 7.3 and have identified or tried to identify key characteristics of the particular conflict they must address.

Selected principles of mediation are listed in table 7.6, categorized in three phases: preparation and analysis before mediation and negotiation start, interaction during mediation, and negotiation and final packaging after an agreement has been reached. Recall that mediation is a process whereby a third party attempts only to help conflicting parties reach a voluntary agreement. A mediator does not have the power of an arbitrator to settle a dispute. There is no agreement to abide by the outcome–parties need not give up sovereignty over the ultimate choice of a compromise solution.

These principles will be considered in the order listed in table 7.6. To a large extent they parallel the principles of negotiation already discussed. Bear in mind, however, that the nonmonolithic nature of national interests and the internal battles over national decision making frequently stymie attempts to introduce mediation or other third-party intervention.

Table 7.6 *Selected principles of mediation*

1. Preparation and analysis phase
    a. Self understanding enhancement
    b. Participant understanding enhancement
    c. Monolithicity attainment
    d. Ground rules (agenda) setting

2. Interaction phase
    a. Flexibility in approach
    b. Tread lightly in early rounds
    c. Tension releasing
    d. Encouragement of inventiveness
    e. Impartiality establishment and maintenance
    f. Minimal aim
    g. Exploitation of fractionation/logrolling/side payment potentialities
    h. Encouragement of analysis by participants
    i. Test for fairness and stability
    j. Compromise constraint
    k. Time exploitation

3. Final packaging phase
    a. Enhancement of implementability

7.5.1 Principles for the preparation and analysis phase

(a) Self understanding enhancement: A mediator should conduct an analysis to reach a better understanding of :

> critical issues and other conflict characteristics considered, both in an objective sense and as perceived by the disputant parties;

> behavioral assumptions that participants may be making when setting forth or responding to proposals;

> options (alternative actions) available to resolve the conflict both in an objective sense and as perceived by the disputant parties.

> the initial proposals and/or "negotiation" stances likely to be presented by each disputant party and how these initial proposals may differ from actual interests;

> decision-making pathologies to which each disputant party may be subject;

> objectives (targets), absolute minima, reservation prices, and other bounds likely to be set by each; and

> the evolving dynamics (logistics) of the conflict.

Moreover, in this self-preparation phase the mediator should

> when feasible, engage in discussions with each disputant in isolation from the other and use tools and models capable of handling large volumes of data and complex interrelations; and

> proceed with his analysis up to the level at which expected costs begin to outweigh expected benefits.

Henry Kissinger made use of the above principle in his mediation efforts in the Middle East after the 1973 October War (the two parties involved being at one time Israel and Egypt and at another time Israel and Syria). So did President Carter at Camp David in 1978, Israel and Egypt being the adversaries (see Stein [1985] for a succinct and penetrating analysis). Both Kissinger and Carter had become very well informed beforehand concerning the many factors in the conflict, Carter having set up a task force in preparation for his mediation effort.

(b) Participant understanding enhancement: Prior to interaction a mediator should help disputing parties understand the evolving dynamics (logistics) of the conflict, the interdependence of outcomes, and

the critical (emotional) issues and other characteristics of the situation as each perceives them–raising doubts where differences in perception are apparent or where perceptions differ from objective reality;

the behavioral assumptions they may be making–raising questions constructively when it is apparent that these assumptions are unrealistic;

the options (alternative actions) available to them–encouraging each party to discard or reconsider alternatives misperceived as available or unavailable;

the initial proposals and/or "negotiation" stances each is likely to bring to the interaction phase–attempting to "modify" these where they appear to be incompatible and unlikely to lead to resolution of the conflict within a reasonable time span;

the decision-making pathologies to which they may be subject–encouraging each party to recognize problems these pathologies may create; and

the objectives (targets), absolute minima, reservation prices, and other bounds each is likely to impose–attempting to modify these where they appear incompatible or seem to restrict the range of possible solutions.

In working with participants to enhance their understanding and awareness, the mediator should try to hold discussions with each in isolation from the other. Algeria's role in the 1980–81 U.S.–Iran confrontation is an excellent illustration of the application of this principle. Algerian mediators helped the United States perceive correctly the ideological requirements of the Iranian revolutionaries and appreciate factors motivating their behavior. These mediators subjected U.S. proposals to careful scrutiny and a stream of questions. Politely but firmly they addressed specific points that would concern the Iranians and pressed the U.S. negotiators to give clear reasons for their positions on these points and to accept rewording more consistent with Iranian perceptions and viewpoints.

In his attempts in 1981 to resolve the Northern Ireland conflict, Peter Brooke, British Secretary of State for Northern Ireland, planned long talks with each party separately before the start of roundtable discussion.

(c) *Monolithicity attainment:* Where disputant negotiators represent an organization, nation, or other body consisting of more than one interest group, the mediator should attempt to ensure that each one fully represents his parent body–that is, that each negotiator's leaders have considered differences among interest groups (as to reservation prices, constraints, priorities to be assigned to various possible outcomes, elements, etc.), have informed their negotiator of acceptable trade-offs between these interest groups' different demands, and have sufficient confidence in his capabilities to be willing to make a prior commitment to implement any agreement that may be reached.

(d)   Ground rules (agenda) setting: In arranging the interaction phase (setting the agenda, procedural rules, behavioral conventions, etc.) the mediator should attempt, implicitly or explicitly, to acquire as much control over discussions and final say as is possible without diminishing the goodwill, trust, and respect that the disputants have for him.

Both Kissinger and Carter, in their mediation efforts, carefully constructed and controlled the agenda. Kissinger's tactics were less defined than Carter's. Generally Kissinger elicited proposals from each side, but once these were set forth, he would begin with the easier issues and proceed to the more difficult, believing that once agreement was reached on less contentious ones, it would be easier to attack the more difficult. Carter, on the other hand, initially chose a more comprehensive approach, namely, to confront basic issues at the start, along with those of lesser importance.

7.5.2   Principles for the interaction phase

In most instances, a mediator will bring disputants together in a workshop or similar setting. He may find the following principles useful during these interaction sessions:

(a)   Flexibility in approach: A mediator should bear in mind that there is no CMP and/or mediation technique that is best for all conflicts. He should match his performance program (which may include one or more relevant CMPs and other mediation techniques) to his characterization of the conflict (grievance) situation, his perception of his own role, and his particular style (art).

Consistent with his incrementalist approach to conflict resolution, Kissinger, in mediating the Middle East conflicts, shifted his tactics and procedures whenever he surmised that an approach could not succeed, and whenever failure to resolve an issue was imminent. To him, failure at any point in the negotiations was dangerous; it could destroy agreements already reached, and undermine the trust already built up between protagonists and their confidence in himself as mediator.

(b)   Tread lightly in early rounds: In early rounds of interaction, a negotiator should:

1. foster activity and discussion likely to establish effective communication, building trust between disputants;
2. encourage a search for common values and noncompetitive solutions; and
3. highlight points of agreement.

(c)   Tension releasing: Where relationships among disputants are heavily strained, when tensions reach dangerous levels, or when there is an impending stalemate, a mediator should consider the merits of shifting to group activities, to live participation in recreational, social, or cultural events that will release tension and change moods.

(d)   Encouragement of inventiveness: A mediator should encourage participants' inventiveness when a solution is not apparent, being careful not to be too directive and not to place unnecessary restrictions on use (and/or exercise) of threats. He should encourage participants to examine possibilities for gains from use (and/or exercise) of rewards. He should not allow ideas to be dismissed automatically without due consideration of their merits, and, whenever possible, not allow participants to become committed to a particular option too soon.

In 1987 Roger Fisher, an internationally recognized expert on negotiations, acting in an informal "invited/assumed" role of mediator in the then South African conflict, pointed out the need to apply these last three principles. The strong and warm personal relations that Carter established with Sadat later proved invaluable in easing tension and inducing the Egyptian president to make certain final concessions to reach agreement at Camp David.

(e)   Impartiality establishment and maintenance: To maintain his effectiveness, a mediator should avoid giving judgmental advice, arguing unnecessarily, becoming enmeshed in the dispute, accepting one party's definition of the problems, perception of issues, assumptions, and so on; and should in other respects establish and maintain impartiality.

(f)   Minimal aim (acceptable outcome): Where a mutually acceptable solution proves unobtainable, a mediator should at least aim for widespread agreement on a declaration of intent or statement of general positions.

Kosygin's mediation effort in the Indo–Pakistan conflict clearly was successful because he adhered strictly to the principle of *impartiality establishment and maintenance.* Moreover, as already noted, his objective was a minimal one, namely, a tactfully worded statement of a declaration that permitted each participant to save face while reestablishing territorially the *status quo ante* in Indo–Pakistan relations.

(g)   Exploitation of fractionation/logrolling/side payments potentialities: When the going gets tough, a mediator should consider

> fractionating the problem–to stop mounting distrust or to build trust by achieving effective compromise on easier issues prior to attacking more difficult ones;
>
> encouraging logrolling as a mechanism for offsetting the effective costs of a participant's concession on one issue with gains from a reciprocal concession by the second participant on another issue; and
>
> encouraging side payments by a party having resources in exchange for a concession by the second party.

After many years of tortuous negotiations and mediation over the Rhodesian–Zimbabwe problem (1963–79), this principle was neatly applied in the 1979 Lancaster House conference. There, Lord Carrington divided into three steps the task of settling the three basic issues–dealing first with drafting a constitution for Zimbabwe, then with transitional measures (including brief British control to ensure free and fair elections), and lastly, with a cease-fire. Cumulatively, he built up vested interests in a final settlement as incremental agreements were reached.

(h)   Encouragement of analysis by participants: A mediator should encourage participants to use tools, models, data sets, cost-benefit balance sheets, and other techniques to evaluate the impact upon both themselves and their opponent of each proposal under consideration and to evaluate inventive ideas.

(i)   Test for fairness and stability: A mediator should test an evolving agreement for fairness and stability to ensure that neither party will suffer loss-of-face, identity, and/or sense of effectiveness (power) as a result of its adoption.

As already noted, in the U.S.–Iran confrontation the Algerian mediators subjected U.S. proposals to careful scrutiny and questioning. Not only did they force the U.S. to state reasons for its proposals, but in the case of some proposals they pressed for the underlying analysis. And, in the final stage, the mediators set forth a "declaration" by the government of Algeria, incorporating points of agreement between the two countries, presumably representing a fair and reasonable solution sensitive to the needs of both parties.

(*j*)   *Compromise constraint:* A mediator should recognize that not everything is subject to compromise and that some issues require more compromise than others.

(*k*)   *Time exploitation:* All issues may not need to be resolved at one and the same time. A mediator should recognize:

1. that action on difficult issues may be deferred until participants have learned from the experience of agreeing on less difficult ones; and
2. that settling issues involving future uncertainties may have more appeal to participants if they can first settle on what future joint activities they will engage in if such and such events occur.

In his mediation prior to Carter's presidency, Kissinger, as already noted, left untouched inscrutable issues in the Israeli–Arab conflict– for example, the future of the Palestinians, which he considered most intractable. Carter, although initially bent on a comprehensive solution, also had to postpone reaching a solution on a number of basic issues and remove them from his bargaining agenda. Negotiations on Palestinian autonomy and on final status of the West Bank and Gaza strip had to be put off. Via an exchange of letters, Israel and Egypt stated their positions on Jerusalem's status, agreeing to disagree.

On the other hand, time pressures may force agreement when a conflict might otherwise continue interminably. In the U.S–Iran confrontation the pending incumbency of President-elect Reagan, whose posture toward Iran was definitely menacing, proved effective in inducing Iran to come to an agreement prior to January 20, 1981.

7.5.3   Principle for the final packaging phase: enhancement of implementation

The mediator should encourage and help participants:

1. develop sound political arguments (as discussed in Chapter 5) and, if necessary, rephrase the agreement;

2. conduct discussions with their constituencies; and
3. engage in other activities and make commitments likely to enhance acceptance and implementation of the agreement.

Perhaps it was this principle that was most basic to agreements reached as a result of the Carter mediation. The United States had to

1. guarantee to both sides the *observance* of the agreement (should the United Nations' Security Council fail to establish and maintain an international police force, as required by the Camp David treaty, the United States would establish and maintain an acceptable alternative force);
2. provide *insurance against violation* (Carter committed the United States to monitoring implementation of the limitation of forces provision); and
3. furnish *substantial side payments*, (Carter pledged $3 billion aid to Israel and $2 billion to Egypt).

Given (1) the partial list of general characteristics of conflict situations in tables 7.1–7.3, (2) a particular set of key characteristics identified by a negotiator or mediator, and (3) the principles of negotiation and mediation, just discussed, how does one proceed? How does one decide what set of compatible (noncontradictory) principles to use in seeking resolution (partial or complete) of a conflict? This question is one that a negotiator or mediator must decide for himself–on the basis of his current stock of knowledge, experience, and perceptions supplemented by learning acquired in and out of discussion arenas.

Of course, a negotiator may use a fixed set of principles out of pure habit, and these principles may be partially contradictory, of which fact he may or may not be aware. A more sophisticated negotiator will behave in a way consistent with a set of principles that constitutes a meaningful qualitative conflict management procedure (as defined in section 7.2).

A mediator also may use a fixed set of principles out of pure habit, again not necessarily noncontradictory. More likely an experienced and qualified mediator will have in mind a set of principles constituting what he considers an effective qualitative conflict management procedure for the given situation. Likewise with any third party intervenor.

What if the participants adopt principles that are incompatible? Suppose principles on seating arrangements are important to them.

One may want to negotiate in an informal setting at a round table in a secluded villa while the other may insist on formal discussions, with officials seated by rank along a long, narrow table in a statehouse and on-the-record discussion governed by protocol. This inconsistency may be viewed as a subconflict within the primary conflict which needs to be resolved before face-to-face interaction takes place. Likewise with any subconflict over key characteristics.

7.6   An illustration of a qualitative CMP: the U.S.–Iran confrontation

In the U.S.–Iran confrontation in 1980–81 Algerian mediators recognized as a key characteristic the tremendous differences between Iran's Arab culture and that of the U.S.–differences in legal systems, societal values, and the role of religious beliefs in controlling economic and social development and politics in both countries. Consequently, in the preparation and analysis phase of their mediation effort, the Algerians fully understood that enhancement of participant understanding (a basic mediation principle)–in particular, of one another's culture–was absolutely essential. Also, because the Algerians' culture was itself Arabic, they had to enhance their own understanding (another basic mediation principle) of American culture, particularly of the constitutional relationship between the U.S. administrative branch and the courts, and of the basis for U.S. demands.

Another key characteristic of this conflict was the tremendous distrust and animosity between the two parties–resulting from the overthrow of the Shah regime (strongly supported by the U.S.) by revolutionary forces led by the Ayatollah Khomeini–feelings so intense that the parties could not communicate directly. Thus, in the *interaction phase,* the Algerians not only had to tread lightly in early rounds and attempt to reduce tension, but also had to establish and maintain complete impartiality (another basic mediation principle) and in the beginning simply translate and transmit messages from one party to the other. As already noted, they had to encourage, and at times even insist, that the Americans provide the analysis behind their demands (another basic mediation principle). And when they finally issued a declaration, incorporating points of agreement between the protagonists–set forth as promises to Algeria and not to each other–they had to word this document very carefully and apply to it a test for fairness and stability (one more principle).

Although the *time exploitation* principle was not followed in the manner discussed in the previous section, the Algerian mediators did continually remind the Iranians of a deadline, namely, January 20, 1981, when President-elect Reagan would take office. They pointed out that he already had exhibited a menacing posture toward Iran and that as a consequence their country was unlikely to obtain in the near future, if ever, any of the funds they sorely needed in their war with Iraq.

Undoubtedly, other scholars analyzing the U.S.–Iran confrontation will note other principles of critical importance. In any case, the Algerian mediators were skillful indeed, and in one way or another used a conflict management procedure comprising a number of the principles discussed above.

In the Algerian mediation effort little if any quantitative analysis was undertaken. The conflict management procedure used was primarily qualitative. In contrast, in the Panama Canal negotiations Ambassador Bunker did conduct some quantitative analysis. Together with his Panamanian counterpart, he listed key issues and attempted to assign to each a weight of importance. He thus used the principle of constructing an approximate cost-benefit balance sheet. This was in addition to using the principles of understanding enhancement and monolithicity attainment in the initial preparation and analysis phase, and the principles of interdependence appreciation, opponent sensitivity, stance—issues separation, and others in the proposal-making and interaction phases. One can wonder, however, whether Ambassador Bunker did use quantitative analysis as fully as possible and whether, had he done so, a more positive agreement might have been reached.

Certainly the Sadat–Begin Camp David talks mediated by President Carter did not resolve as many issues as Carter had hoped for initially. As already noted, Carter failed to reach agreement on the Jerusalem issue, Palestinian autonomy, and the status of the West Bank and Gaza Strip. Today these are still extremely troublesome problems and the cause of much physical violence. Had Carter and those who followed as third-party intervenors moved beyond a qualitative CMP and used a quantitative one embodying the processing and analysis of data and other quantitative information, perhaps one or more of these issues could have been partially or fully resolved.

7.7   Summary

This chapter has examined principles of negotiation and mediation and qualitative conflict management procedures (CMPs) that may be used to reach an agreement (compromise) when there is a conflict. First, a partial list of characteristics of conflict situations was presented. These characteristics are structural, some relating to the system and some not; others relate to the participants. The list presented, albeit partial, can be extremely useful for identifying key characteristics of any given conflict and for checking that no key one has been omitted from consideration. Even the most experienced and intuitive mediator can use such a list to advantage, if only to feel more confident that he has not overlooked any significant factor.

In negotiation and mediation certain principles have been found useful for managing, coping with, or resolving conflicts. The negotiations process has four phases: preparation and analysis, proposal making, interaction, and final packaging. Negotiation principles for each phase have been listed and discussed and some actual applications cited. The mediation process has three phases: preparation and analysis, interaction, and final packaging. Here, also, principles for each phase have been considered and examples of applications given.

In the 1980–81 U.S.–Iran hostage confrontation Algerian mediators used a number of these principles. The set of principles they used in effect constituted a qualitative CMP, quantitative methods and analysis not being essential to the task. In other situations quantitative CMPs might indeed have contributed to success. One may question whether Ambassador Bunker in the Panama conflict or President Carter in the Sadat–Begin (Egypt–Israel) Camp David talks and others who subsequently have been third parties in Middle East conciliation efforts could have reached more satisfactory agreements had they used quantitative procedures.

References

Barash, David P. (1991) *Introduction to Peace Studies*. Belmont, CA: Wadsworth, Part III.

Fisher, Roger (1987) "Negotiating South Africa's Future," *Negotiation Journal* 3(3, July): 231–3.

Fisher, Roger and William Ury (1981) *Getting to Yes*. Boston: Houghton Mifflin.

Isard, Walter (1988) Arms Races, *Arms Control and Conflict Analysis: Contributions from Peace Science and Peace Economics*. New York: Cambridge University Press. Chaps. 10 and 11.

Isard, Walter and Christine Smith (1982) *Conflict Analysis and Practical Conflict Management Procedures*. Cambridge, MA: Ballinger. Reprinted (1989) Department of City and Regional Planning, Cornell University, Ithaca, NY, Chap. 10.

Raiffa, Howard (1982) *The Art and Science of Negotiation*, Cambridge, MA: Harvard University Press.

Stein, Janet G. (1985) "Structures, Strategies and Tactics of Mediation: Kissinger and Carter in the Middle East," *Negotiation Journal* 1(4, October):331—47.

Touval, Saadia and I. William Zartman (eds.) (1985) *International Mediation in Theory and Practice*. Boulder, CO: Westview Press.

8 *The Use of Quantitative Conflict Management Procedures*

8.1 Introduction

In section 7.6 a set of negotiation principles, a *qualitative* conflict management procedure (CMP), used in the Camp David talks was noted. The question was asked: could still more progress have been achieved had a supplementary *quantitative* CMP been used, a procedure that a peace scientist collaborating with a skillful and artful mediator might have proposed. Recall that the Camp David talks left completely unresolved the political and administrative control of Jerusalem, the form and substance of Palestinian autonomy, and the final status of the West Bank and Gaza Strip –issues that have contributed to the intensity of the recent Iraq–U.S. confrontation, and the current Middle East conflicts and those to follow.

This chapter explores the potential of quantitative CMPs, starting with one that has considerable appeal for future use.

8.2 The Priorities-determining procedure

The simplest of all quantitative CMPs is "split-the-difference," where each of two parties goes 50 percent of the way in conceding to the other. In effect, where each party sets forth his most preferred joint action, the procedure is to average the two. A somewhat more involved procedure is to take a weighted average, assuming that weights to be applied to each have been determined beforehand. Another procedure is to have each party rank several possible joint actions, including the current joint action (current state of affairs), from best to worst, say 1 to 6, if six joint actions are being considered. One then searches for a joint action that yields equal improvement for each party in terms of increase in rank (from lower to higher). Or if no joint action will achieve equal improvement, one selects the one that maximizes total rank improvements, or one that minimizes the difference in rank improvements.

Where each participant is focused on his most-preferred joint action, then concession-type procedures become relevant. One is to choose a joint action that involves equal concessions (in terms of ranks); or, if there is no such action, to choose the one that minimizes the concession by that party whose concession would be greater.

There are many other quantitative procedures, a number of which are listed in table 8.7. Here, necessarily in oversimplified fashion, one of the more sophisticated procedures will be illustrated—one developed by Saaty (1972, 1977) which has significant potential for assisting a mediator tackling complex international conflicts (such as the one in the Middle East), and civil conflicts with international implications (such as those in South Africa, Lebanon, Iraq, and Northern Ireland).

In many conflict situations, the parties cannot spell out objectives, outcomes, and/or policies in precise quantitative terms. Yet they may be able to make relative statements. The ability of the parties to speak in relative terms, to state relative values, is assumed in the priorities-determining procedure. In this procedure, a mediator (or other third party) sets up a scale indicating relative importance. Suppose the scale given in table 8.1 is found appropriate. In the hypothetical conflict situation to be examined the mediator asks each party to make pairwise comparisons using this scale. A party may state that one particular objective is three times more important to him than another, or that one particular policy is twice as desirable as a second for achieving a given goal, and so forth. The mediator assumes that experts whom he may call in for assistance will also be able to make pairwise comparisons using such a scale.

Consider a type of conflict that is likely to occur frequently in years ahead. There exists a nation or region in which power and economic wealth have for years been concentrated in the hands of an elite ethnic, religious, military, or other group—henceforth designated the Ingroup. Because of discrimination, inequities, and poverty conditions, the rest of the population—the Outgroup—is dissatisfied and civil unrest prevails. The Outgroup may be divided into two major subgroups—the Outgroup Moderates who are pressing for major change, and the Outgroup Radicals, a revolutionary cadre which desires to do away with the Ingroup. Dissatisfaction may be so rampant that physical violence is anticipated unless some settlement of the diverse issues is reached. A mediator respected by all parties is called in from outside. He establishes effective communication with all parties, is extremely skillful and ingenious in applying the principles we discussed in the previous chapter, yet is unable to obtain an agreement acceptable to all. He needs to involve the parties in negotiations more effectively but recognizes that he first needs a more accurate reading of their desires and feelings.

Table 8.1 *The Saaty Scale and its description*

Intensity of importance	Definition	Explanation
1[a]	Equal importance	Two policies contribute equally to the objective
3	Weak importance of one over another	Experience and judgment slightly favor one activity over another
5	Essential or strong importance	Experience and judgment strongly favor one policy over another
7	Demonstrated importance	A policy is strongly favored and its dominance is demonstrated in practice
9	Absolute importance	The evidence favoring one policy over another is of the highest possible order of affirmation
2, 4, 6, 8	Intermediate values between the two adjacent judgments	When compromise is needed
Reciprocals of above nonzero numbers	If policy i has one of the above nonzero numbers assigned to it when compared with policy j, then j has the reciprocal value when compared with i	
Rationals	Ratios arising from the scale	If consistency were to be forced by obtaining n numerical values to span the matrix

[a]On occasion in 2 by 2 problems, Saaty has used $1 + \varepsilon$, $0 < \varepsilon < 1/2$ to indicate very slight dominance between two nearly equal activities.

Source: adapted from Saaty and Khouja (1976:34).

At this point the mediator may call in experts. He may first ask them to rate the relative importance (in terms of power or other criteria) of the three groups using the scale of table 8.1. The experts may differ and may be somewhat inconsistent in their pairwise comparison; but if they do not differ significantly and are not too inconsistent, he may average their comparisons and, rounding numbers, come up with the pairwise comparisons of table 8.2. In this table the three groups are listed in the same order along the rows and columns. Across any given row, the numbers in each cell indicate how important the row group is relative to the column group. Thus, across the first row, the numbers indicate that the experts judge the Ingroup and the Outgroup Moderates to be equally important, and the Ingroup twice as important as the Outgroup Radicals (or the Outgroup Radicals only half as important as each of the other two groups). Numbers in the other rows indicate the same. The mediator calculates the normalized weights (weights that add to unity, obtained by dividing each weight in any column by the sum of the weights in that column). These weights to be used in considering the demands or needs of each group are 0.4, 0.4, and 0.2. They are listed in the last column of the table.

The mediator carries on further discussion with each group to obtain a more precise sense of their objectives and the relative importance of these objectives. Suppose he identifies three basic objectives of the Ingroup, namely, (1) *maintain its sphere of influence*, (2) *have good relations with the Outgroups*, and, as a carrot, (3) *share power* to a limited extent. He then asks the Ingroup to make pairwise comparisons, using the scale of table 8.1. (He may of course, receive different pairwise comparisons from each member of the Ingroup, and minor inconsistencies may prevail, even after discussion. After all, inconsistent comparisons, while bothersome to a person trained in the scientific tradition of the West, may not be bothersome or seem irrational to people schooled in other traditions.) Suppose, on average, he obtains the pairwise comparisons in the first three columns of table 8.3. The numbers indicate that the Ingroup considers that maintaining its sphere of influence is of *absolute importance* compared to either seeking good relations or sharing power, so its value *relative* to each of its other objectives is 9. This means that the respective weights (normalized) are 0.818, 0.091, and 0.091 as listed in column 4 of the table. (Note that because the highest value on the scale in table 8.1 is 9, and thus the lowest value

Table 8.2 *Relative importance of parties*

	Ingroup	Outgroup Moderates	Outgroup Radicals	Weights
Ingroup	1	1	2	.4
Outgroup Moderates	1	1	2	.4
Outgroup Radicals	1/2	1/2	1	.2

Table 8.3 *Pairwise comparisons by Ingroup of its objectives*

	Maintain influence	Seek good relations	Share power	Weights
Maintain influence	1	9	9	0.818
Seek good relations	1/9	1	1	0.091
Share power	1/9	1	1	0.091

obtainable is 1/9, every objective in a three-objective set will have a weight of at least 0.091. To be able to attach a lower weight to one of the objectives, say share power, one needs to set up a scale with a larger range than in Table 8.1, say 1 to 25.)

In discussions with Outgroup Moderates, the mediator finds that they have two key objectives, namely, *sharing power* and *economic well-being*. After obtaining pairwise comparisons from representative members of the group he derives weights of 0.4 for sharing power and 0.6 for economic well-being. See table 8.3a in the appendix to this chapter.

Similarly, the mediator carries on discussions with Outgroup Radicals and finds that they have two key objectives: *drive the Ingroup out of power* and *redistribute land and other wealth.* Since these objectives are judged to be equally important, he derives a weight of 0.5 and 0.5 for each.

The mediator now reasons: I know each group's key objectives and I have derived weights for these objectives from their pairwise comparisons. I have inferred that the weight the Ingroup gives to maintaining its sphere of influence is 0.818. But I have also judged that the Ingroup's relative importance is 0.4. Therefore, when considering the three groups' seven objectives I derive the relative importance or weight of the Ingroup's objective of maintaining its sphere of influence to be only 0.4 x 0.818 = 0.327. This weight is entered in row 1 of column 1 in table 8.4. Likewise, since I have inferred that the Ingroup assigns weights of 0.091 to each of its other objectives, seek good relations and share power, I derive a weight of 0.4 x 0.091 = 0.036 for each. These weights are recorded in the second and third rows of column 1 of table 8.4. One of these figures is rounded to 0.037 and the other to 0.036 in order that the weights of the Ingroup's objectives may add to unity.

In similar fashion, the mediator, taking into account the relative importance of the Outgroup Moderates, namely, 0.4, and the weights he has inferred that the Outgroup Moderates assign to their objectives (economic well-being and sharing power), namely, 0.6 and 0.4, derives the respective weights 0.4 x 0.6 = 0.24 and 0.4 x 0.4 = 0.16 when he considers the overall picture involving seven objectives. These two figures are also recorded in column 1 of table 8.4. In the same way, the mediator derives the total situation weights 0.2 x 0.5 =

Table 8.4 *Calcultation of relative importance or likelihood of policies*

		Minor reform	Major reform	Transition to democracy
Ingroup	(1)	(2)	(3)	(4)
1. Maintain sphere of influence	0.327	0.267	0.030	0.030
2. Have good relations	0.037	0.006	0.028	0.003
3. Share power	0.036	0.005	0.028	0.003
Outgroup moderates				
4. Economic well-being	0.240	0.016	0.144	0.080
5. Share power	0.160	0.010	0.090	0.060
Outgroup radicals				
6. Drive the ingroup out of power	0.100	0.008	0.017	0.075
7. Redistribute land and wealth	0.100	0.009	0.009	0.082
Total	1.00	0.321	0.346	0.333

0.1 and 0.2 x 0.5 = 0.1 for each of the two Outgroup Radicals' objectives, drive the Ingroup out of power and redistribute land and other wealth. They, too, are recorded in column 1 of table 8.4. This column now lists the weights of all seven objectives; they are normalized weights since they add to unity.

At this point, the mediator identifies several options that are in the minds of the parties in conflict and/or that he himself considers reasonable: minor reform (such as providing free primary education for all); major reform (such as freedom of entry into all occupations and professions and universal free college education); and commitment (with transition steps fully spelled out) to a democratic system ensuring civil rights, voting for all adults, and private ownership of property.

With the help of his experts the mediator's next step is to determine to what extent each of these three policy proposals meets the seven objectives listed in table 8.4. Starting with the Ingroup's objective, to maintain its sphere of influence, and using the scale of table 8.1, he arrives at the figures of table 8.5 when he makes pairwise comparisons of the relative importance of each of three policies for meeting that single objective. From these comparisons he derives normalized weights of 0.818, 0.091, and 0.091 for minor reform, major reform, and transition to democracy, respectively. He knows that the weight of this particular objective is 0.327 (recorded in row 1, column 1 of table 8.4). Hence, 0.327 x 0.818 = 0.267 yields the importance to the conflict situation of minor reform for meeting this objective of the Ingroup; and 0.327 x 0.091 = 0.030 yields the importance to the conflict situation of both major reform and transition to democracy *for meeting that same single objective of the Ingroup, namely, maintaining its sphere of influence.* These three magnitudes, 0.267, 0.030, and 0.030, are entered in row 1 of columns 2, 3, and 4 of table 8.4.

Table 8.5 *Ingroup's objective: maintain sphere of influence*

	Minor reform	Major reform	Democracy	Weights
Minor reform	1	1/9	1/9	0.818
Major reform	1/9	1	1	0.091
Democracy	1/9	1	1	0.091

Moving on to the Ingroup's objective to have good relations, the mediator conducts similar inquiries, and finds that the relative importance of the three policies, minor reform, major reform, and transition to democracy, in meeting that objective are 0.153, 0.763, and 0.084, respectively. See table 8.5a in the appendix. Given that the weight (normalized) of this particular objective of the Ingroup is 0.037 (as indicated in row 2, column 1 of table 8.4), he obtains 0.037 x 0.153 = 0.006; 0.037 x 0.763 = 0.028; and 0.037 x 0.084 = .003 as the respective overall importance to the conflict situation of these three policies for *meeting the Ingroup's second objective.* These three magnitudes are recorded along the second row of table 8.4.

Similarly, the mediator derives magnitudes to fill in the other cells of table 8.4. See tables 8.5b, c, d, e, and f in the appendix. (These tables derive the respective magnitudes which are to be multiplied by the weights in rows 3–7 of column 1 in table 8.4 to derive the magnitudes in columns 2, 3, and 4 of rows 3–7). The mediator now totals the magnitudes in each of the columns 2, 3, and 4. He obtains 0.321 for the Minor reform column, 0.346 for the Major reform column, and 0.333 for the Transition to democracy column. What do these totals mean? One may claim that these magnitudes indicate the relative capability of these three policies for meeting all seven objectives of the three parties to the conflict. After all, they do reflect the relative importance of the parties as well as the relative desirability to each party of its objectives. As a consequence, they may also be interpreted as the overall relative desirability of these policies–or as indicating priorities with regard to policies. Furthermore, they may indicate the relative probability (likelihood) that each may be adopted.

Given this interpretation of the relative magnitudes (weights), another question arises for the mediator. How does he move the parties from where they are now to the new position? How does he persuade the Ingroup to support a policy of major reform (the policy having the highest of the derived magnitudes) instead of minor reform, recognizing that the Ingroup will strongly oppose any notion of transition to democracy? If the Ingroup has been losing power gradually over the years, and thus has suffered a decrease in its relative importance, he may point out that this decline is likely to continue. He may then suggest that if the Ingroup does not opt for major reform now, it may face a future situation where its own relative importance has declined still more and where it will be forced to accept a policy of transition to democracy. He may illustrate with calculations. In the past when the relative importance of the Ingroup was 2 compared with the Outgroup Moderates and 4 compared with the Outgroup Radicals, magnitudes for the policies of minor reform, major reform, and transition to democracy, when calculated as in table 8.4, would have been 0.428, 0.258, and 0.314, respectively, other pairwise comparisons remaining the same. At that time minor reform would have best met the objectives of all parties. If the Ingroup's power were to continue to decline and its relative importance decrease to, say, 2/3 compared to Outgroup Moderates and 5/4 vis-à-vis Outgroup Radicals, then these magnitudes would be 0.260, 0.281, and 0.459, respectively. This means that postponing major reform, which the Ingroup much prefers to transition to democracy, will decrease the Ingroup's leverage when major change must ensue.

Or the mediator may suggest to the Ingroup that if the Outgroup Radicals are highly dissatisfied with minor reform policy and demonstrate against it, perhaps engaging in vandalism and bombing and thus forcing the Ingroup to use military power to keep things under control, this will likely lead the Outgroup Moderates to side with the Outgroup Radicals and be more sympathetic with the latter's objectives. This will shift the magnitudes away from major reform to transition to democracy.

Or the mediator may use both these arguments. But clearly, he must accompany quantitative findings with arguments skillfully contrived to exploit these findings. For pedagogical purposes I have used a simplified, fictitious example involving three parties, seven objectives, and three policies to illustrate the relevance of the priorities-determining procedure as a quantitative CMP. This procedure has much greater potential, however, when a real-life situation is confronted. Consider the Northern Ireland conflict, for example, which has been analyzed with this procedure (Alexander and Saaty, 1977a, 1977b). In the early 1970s five parties were involved:

British government (Britain)
Protestant community (Allegiants)
Catholic community (Moderates)
Irish Republican Army (IRA), a militant group
The government of the Republic of Ireland (Dublin)

Seventeen objectives were identified, ranging from the British desire to maintain Britain's sphere of influence, to the Protestants' aim to exclude Irish nationalists from the government, to the Catholic Moderates' demand to share power, to the IRA's objective to drive out the British, to Dublin's desire for a union of countries. Policies leading to the following six political structures were explored:

A United Ireland
A totally integrated parliament of Great Britain and Northern Ireland
A colonial assembly with a strong Council of Ireland
A colonial assembly without a strong Council of Ireland
A totally sovereign legislature (independence or Dominion status) with a strong Council of Ireland
A totally sovereign legislature (independence or Dominion status) without a strong Council of Ireland

The analysis, conducted for conditions in the mid-1970s, found for these political structures magnitudes of 0.147, 0.156, 0.135, 0.158,

0.236, and 0.170, respectively. This suggests that Dominion (independent) status best meets the parties' needs. Unfortunately, the conflict remains unresolved today (February, 1992) with bombing and other violence continuing. Had an artful mediator been present at some critical point of time in the past, armed with and skillful in the use of the priorities-determining procedure, perhaps the conflict could have been resolved, at least partially. One also may speculate that Britain's weight of importance has declined since the mid-1970s (when it was estimated to be 0.45, almost equal to the weight of the other four parties combined) and that in Britain's eyes the importance of maintaining its sphere of influence has fallen significantly, given the bombings and the high cost of rule from London. All this suggests that dominion or some equivalent independent status, now even more than in the mid-1970s, meets the needs of the various parties. Some say independence is inevitable. Nonetheless, successful mediation (or the equivalent) using both qualitative and quantitative approaches is still needed–to move from "here" to "there"–if further physical violence is to be averted. (At the time of writing [May 1991], still another major attempt at resolving this conflict was undertaken; the issues are fundamentally the same.)

In short, there are situations (such as the Northern Ireland and the Middle East conflicts) so complex that quantitative methods such as the priorities-determining procedure are needed to deal with the interplay of forces. Such a procedure introduces structure into an otherwise unstructured situation, and thus simplifies and expedites natural decision-making processes. It breaks down a situation into its component parts, arranging them in an hierarchical order, and synthesizes subjective judgments on the relative importance of variables. Studying the information in each component part, one at a time, enables an analyst to take into account a greater stock of information. In this regard the procedure tends to reduce the extent to which relevant information is disregarded. For example, it reduces the play of the cognitive consistency principle which, as previously stated, operates continuously since the total amount of available information always exceeds the mind's absorptive capacity, and which leads to discarding information not consistent with categories and relationships already stored in the mind.

The priorities-determining approach has other desirable properties. When there are inconsistencies in the set of an individual's pairwise comparisons (no one is 100 percent consistent in his evaluations), or when members of a group make different pairwise comparisons regarding what should hold for the group as a whole, this approach can eliminate these inconsistencies by determining the relative values that best reflect these inconsistent comparisons. Also, as already noted, this approach can show how changes in pairwise comparisons and weights lead to changes in the priorities and likelihood of policies. This (1) allows an analyst to experiment with diverse sets of changes to test for stability of priorities and most likely outcome, (2) provides the basis for some dynamic analysis when the analyst inputs expected changes over time, and (3) permits an analyst, negotiator, or mediator to examine changes necessary for a particular set of priorities or outcome to be realized, instead of the most likely outcome.

This approach has its shortcomings, of course. Much subjectivity enters into the choice of a scale. Also, an analyst, negotiator, or mediator must make subjective judgments in identifying the relevant parties to a conflict and their objectives, and in selecting joint actions (scenarios) to be considered. Moreover, when there is too much inconsistency in the pairwise comparisons, the approach is questionable.

Finally, two other points. This approach is only one of many possible quantitative CMPs. (Other techniques are noted in the next section.) It may be the best one for certain conflicts, but for many conflicts it is not relevant, let alone best. Second, to reiterate, the effective use of the priorities–determining approach can be achieved only when accompanied by skill and art in negotiations and/or mediation.

8.3   Possible properties of a quantitative conflict management procedure

As noted, effective use of a *qualitative* CMP by a negotiator or mediator may require a *quantitative* CMP as well. The participants may agree on objectives and be convinced that important universal values are at stake, such as national security for all countries. Nevertheless, they may need to solve a specific international problem: say, how to allocate fishing rights in a given ocean area, how to exploit efficiently and equitably a common water resource, how to determine relative amounts of funds for control of terrorism, or by what percentages stocks of different weapons are to be reduced. Hence, the question: what quantitative procedures are available and how shall one or more be selected?

One might begin to answer this question by presenting a partial listing of such procedures. But before doing this, it is desirable to consider possible properties of quantitative conflict management procedures to (1) gain insight into how to design or invent an effective quantitative CMP by putting together properties in a consistent way, or (2) find among existing quantitative CMPs one that is applicable or conceivably best, given the conflict situation and set of negotiation principles followed by participants. Table 8.6 lists desirable properties of quantitative CMPs without any implication that a given CMP has all or many of these properties. There is no claim that this list is exhaustive; many scholars may wish to add to it. Properties are recorded under the following headings: information requirements, structural properties, time-related properties, properties motivating parties, psychological properties, and solution properties. A full discussion of this table and many of the listed properties is presented in Isard and Smith (1982, chap. 9).

8.4   Matching quantitative CMP properties to key conflict situation characteristics and the choice of a proper quantitative CMP

Given this set of properties, which ones can effectively match the requirements that key characteristics of a given conflict situation impose on the process of managing or resolving a conflict? These characteristics may, of course, have been modified and refashioned (redefined) through the use of principles of negotiations, mediation, and a qualitative CMP.

Take the U.S.–Iraq confrontation as of January 1, 1991. Strictly speaking, this was a conflict between the United States and its partners (including the United Nations) and Iraq and its supporters. (It was usually referred to as the U.S.–Iraq confrontation since each of these nations was the major actor on its side.) A deep clash of cultures was involved. Although certain Arab nations were aligned with the U.S., this was not because of cultural similarities; it was the result of each having an exceedingly strong desire to maintain national security, and for the leaders of some, to hold on to their wealth. These considerations overcame these nations' reluctance to have aligned themselves with the U.S. and its urbanized-industrialized partners.

Another key characteristic of this conflict was the fact that possible outcomes could not be assigned precise values, nor clear relative values. They could only be ranked. Therefore, with respect to property A1 of table 8.6, any quantitative CMP that could be considered for use would have required no more information on preferences other than a ranking. Moreover, the culture clash was so emotion-laden that focusing on outcomes was unlikely to lead to an effective management or partial resolution of the conflict. (Since cultural changes are extremely slow, a culture clash precludes any full resolution. Like it or not, the world is currently confronted with protracted conflict!) Hence, any quantitative CMP considered had to focus on *actions*, and ignore outcomes (see property B14 of table 8.6). And since, at that time, only a few options were available, any quantitative CMP that the negotiator or mediator may have considered must have been able to deal with a limited number of options.

Table 8.7 (to be discussed later) lists various conflict management procedures. (The reader must refer to Isard and Smith [1982] for a full description of each CMP in order to mesh the two tables 8.6 and 8.7.) One will find that there is only one procedure that relates to the situation where

1. participants are only able to rank outcomes;
2. focus must be on actions–and actions that require the parties to make concessions from their current stances, perhaps with side payments; and
3. number of options is small.

This is *compromise over proposed actions*, the first CMP listed in table 8.7. At that time (January 1, 1991), however, a compromise involving a partial withdrawal (however conceived) of Iraq forces from Kuwait, and of U.S. and allied forces from Saudi Arabia, was certain to be totally rejected by each party. Thus, none of the techniques could have handled this conflict.

That situation suggests the need for invention. Looking over the set of CMPs in table 8.7, a negotiator or mediator might find GRIT (procedure 18) of interest–a sequence of reciprocated tension-reducing actions. But this technique calls for the presence of many options. It thus would have required the negotiator or mediator to redefine the conflict, particularly each participant's set of actions. He would have had to convert each participant's set of relatively few options to a set of many–one that would have approached a continuous set. Could this have been done? If so, there would have been some hope (January 1, 1991) of a process of deescalation, involving a first unilateral action, say, by President Bush or President Saddam

Table 8.6 *Selected properties of quantitative conflict management procedures (as viewed by a third party)*

A. Information requirements
1. Regarding preferences of parties for policies (joint actions)—
   - whether they can be stated in terms of specific values, or relative values, or only ordered by rank
   - whether weights are to be applied to the preferences of each party
2. Regarding constraints that may be in effect on the choice of policies or outcomes or both

B. Structural properties
10. Number of options (alternatives) possible to consider
    - small, large, continuous
11. Number of issues that can be dealt with in an option
    - one, two, ..., many
12. Nature of interaction
    - face-to-face, non–face-to-face
    - with or without third-party intervention
    - whether or not coalition formation is encouraged (or discouraged)
13. Cost involved in negotiation and mediation
    - in initial phases (high, low, etc.)
    - in later phases (high, low, etc.)
14. Behavior required (encouraged)
    - whether involving compromises on action or outcomes
    - whether involving the use of a strategy
15. Statement capability
    - in mathematical terms (or not)
    - in balance-sheet format (or not)
16. Context for use
    - when fractionation is involved
    - when logrolling is involved
    - when side payments are involved

C. Time-related properties
20. Number of rounds involved in negotiations/mediation
    - one, many, flexible
21. Size of steps involved
    - small, large, flexible
22. Nature of interactive (feedback) effects: whether or not with
    - learning by participants
    - knowledge accumulation
    - communication channel enhancement
    - misperception reduction
    - invention (creative ideas) encouragement
    - mechanisms for revealing preferences
    - bluffing possibilities
23. Nature of search processes: do they aim to find
    - efficient solutions
    - satisficing solutions?
24. Do they require a particular reference (starting) point
    - status quo
    - bottom line
    - ideal point
    - other?

Table 8.6 *Selected properties of quantitative conflict management procedures (as viewed by a third party) (cont.)*

D. Properties motivating parties
    30. Do they guarantee improvement
        – overall
        – on each round?
    31. Do they allow limited commitment on change in any round?
    32. Do they ensure fairness (weighted equity)
        - much, little, none?
    33. Do they permit reformulation of conflict
        – from zero to positive sum game
        – from action to policy oriented?
    34. Do they allow/encourage shifts from initial fixed positions?

E. Psychological properties: do they
    40. Preserve security
    41. Build confidence
    42. Build trust
    43. Induce reciprocal deescalating actions
    44. Provide incentives to think of others
    45. Allow leader-follower arrangement
    46. Recognize strategic potential?

F. Solution properties
    50. Steps involved
        – well defined (or not)
    51. Do they involve
        – inescapable sanctions (or not)
        – credible threats (or not)
        – veto power (or not)?
    Is the solution
    52. Predeterminate (or not)
    53. Unique (or not)
    54. Efficient (or not)
    55. Stable (or not)
    56. Uncertain, risky (or not)
    57. Probabilistic (or not)
    58. Consistent with international law (or not)
    59. Statable in simple, clearly understood terms (or not)
    60. Implementable, with or without new tools and mechanisms?

Hussein–perhaps some action equivalent to a Sadat-type visit. (Bush had retreated before from positions he claimed were fixed [irrevocable]–to wit, his classic stance "no increase in taxes"!) Then by very small steps, such as discussed in section 3.7 and illustrated in figure 3.3, effective negotiations might have been initiated.

Or consider the Cold War negotiations between the United States and the Soviet Union during the period from mid-1950s until mid-1980s when the dire prospect of economic bankruptcy from an escalating arms race compelled the Soviet under Gorbachev to initiate a major (revolutionary) policy shift. The history of this period relates the frustration arising from many impasses blocking agreements in arms control negotiations. (As already discussed, Gorbachev's unilateral initiatives were largely responsible for breaking the stalemate, led to major breakthroughs at the 1986 Reykjavik summit conference, and, after a series of Soviet concessions and reciprocal U.S. actions, resulted in the 1987 INF [Intermediate-range Nuclear Forces] treaty eliminating all intermediate-range [between 500 and 5,500 kilometers] nuclear delivery vehicles.) During this period of impasse, when nuclear warfare, intentional or accidental, hung like the Sword of Damocles over mankind, could not simulations of negotiation processes have been useful? (Could not simulation based on the use of a CMP have demonstrated that the two paramount interests shared by both parties were realizable, namely, reducing the probability of nuclear war and freeing up economic resources devoted to the military for spending aimed at reaching domestic civilian goals?) Might simulations have demonstrated that some of the issues leading to an impasse were trivial–that a relevant quantitative CMP could have shown that highly desirable outcomes for both parties were possible–outcomes that were relatively insensitive to which proposed solution to the impasse was adopted.

Which conflict management procedure might have worked? First, what properties were needed? With reference to property A1 of table 8.6, the U.S. and the Soviet were not in a position to be able to attach either precise or relative values to different outcomes; in general, they could only rank outcomes in terms of desirability. Second, with reference to property B10, the action space (set of possible options) of each participant was for all practical purposes continuous, since any level of reduction in armaments was possible. Third, with reference to property B14, the participants were in a position to control their emotions and so could concentrate on actions as well as outcomes. Fourth, with reference to properties D30, D31, F51, and F52, it would have been highly desirable if a procedure could be employed which, respectively: guaranteed improvement on each of a series of rounds; required limited commitment regarding change in each round, to accommodate a cautious party who preferred to proceed by small steps (often true of the U.S.); allowed the exercise of vetoes, at least a limited number, to remove any party's fear of being "screwed"; and assured preindeterminacy of outcomes. This last property helps avoid conflict among participants over which procedure to use when the outcomes of various procedures are predictable, each party, of course, preferring to adopt that procedure which will yield it the best outcome.

Someone having an in-depth knowledge of the properties of CMPs listed in table 8.7 (see Isard and Smith, 1982) would have found that procedure 19, *Incremax (maximizing in each of a series of small improvement steps) in action space,* fits this situation when the property of a party's having a limited number of vetoes is added. Could not the veto incremax procedure (or perhaps some other CMP whose properties matched those called for) have been used to simulate negotiations that would have broken the stalemate and led to desirable outcomes? If it had been used, could it have convinced both parties that the issue(s) causing the impasse was trivial, since regardless of whose proposal was adopted the effect on the outcome would have been minor? The simulation might have shown how the U.S. technological superiority in both warhead accuracy and strategic defenses (which the Soviet feared) would have been reduced to a low or negligible level of significance while simultaneously the Soviet superiority in heavy-weight, land-based intercontinental ballistic missiles (which the U.S. feared) would have been similarly reduced. By showing that desirable outcomes were possible, it might have considerably diminished pressure from strategic interest groups, extreme hawks, and inveterate pessimists, which effectively stalled the negotiations. It might have thwarted the tendency to escalate arms expenditures and stock up on bargaining chips, and have tempered the "tit for tat" arms race process. It might have eliminated misrepresentations about the opposing party's objectives and attitudes and led to more accurate perceptions of the issues. It might have revealed to each party the constraints operating on the other, and provided insights into the opponent's motivations, especially if the simulations could have been performed experimentally using role reversal where each party steps into the shoes of the other. Or the simulations might have been pursued for each of several internation states of affairs (for each of several possible major external events that might occur) and thus have helped combat and remove insecurity and build confidence in the capability of reaching a desirable outcome.

Consider, finally, the Camp David talks. The use of an SNT (Single Negotiations Text), a practical variant of the veto incremax procedure, helped score significant progress. But on the three issues that were set aside–political and administrative control over Jerusalem (city of Holy Shrines for both Israelis and Arabs), form and substance of Palestinian autonomy, and determination of the final status of the West Bank and Gaza Strip–could there not subsequently have been some advance? Could the options have been redefined in a way that would have made them less objectionable to both parties?

Specifically, in the pre–Gulf War period, could joint actions suggested by Middle East experts have been further explored, using simulations based on a priorities-determining procedure which would have involved, pending satisfactory negotiations on borders: (1) an ambiguous affirmation by Israeli leaders of the national and collective rights of the Palestinian people, or a halt to certain Israeli settlement activities, or both; and (2) an ambiguous conditional offer by Palestinian leaders to recognize Israel's legitimacy? Or could a small incremental step toward the internationalization or United Nations administration of Jerusalem have been considered as another joint action (policy), again pending satisfactory negotiations on borders?

8.5   Existing quantitative conflict management procedures

It has been suggested that, in one way or another, several quantitative procedures selected according to their properties (as listed in table 8.6) could perhaps have been used in two major international conflict situations (whose key aspects could have been identified with the help of tables such as 7.1 to 7.3). As already stated, table 8.7 presents a partial list of quantitative CMPs that are not too technical and that can be considered for practical use.

Some of the approaches discussed earlier in section 8.2 can be found in table 8.7. The "split-the-difference" approach, where each of two parties goes 50 percent of the way in conceding to the other, falls under category 13 in table 8.7. Use of a weighted average of two proposals falls under category 14. Section 8.2 also discussed a situation where each party ranked six alternatives, from best to worst, the rank of "1" being best and "6" being worst. Several useful procedures were suggested. One was to identify a joint action which yields equal increase in rank for each party. If more than one joint action meets this criterion, then that joint action which maximizes the resulting improvement should be chosen. This procedure falls under category 7 of Table 8.7. A second suggested procedure was to maximize the total of rank improvements. This falls under category 3. A third, to minimize the difference in rank improvements, falls under category 4.

Table 8.7 *A partial list of quantitative conflict management procedures**

1. Compromise over proposed actions (outcomes)
    – in one step *or* a sequence of steps

2. *Min. total of:* ranks (highest rank = 1), rank concessions, percentage concessions, percentage goal shortfalls, absolute concessions, *or* absolute goal shortfalls

3. *Max. total of:* rank improvements, percentage improvements, percentage goal achievements, absolute improvements, absolute goal achievements, *or* utility

4. *Min. the difference in:* ranks, rank improvements (concessions), percentage improvements (concessions), percentage goal achievements, absolute improvements (concessions), *or* absolute goal achievements

5. *Max. the min. in:* rank improvements, percentage improvements, *or* absolute improvements

6. *Min. the max. in:* rank concessions, percentage concessions, *or* absolute concessions

7. *Max. equal:* rank improvements, percentage improvements, absolute improvements, *or* goal achievements

8. *Min. equal:* rank concessions, percentage concessions, absolute concessions, *or* goal shortfalls

9. Changing actions to "if . . . then . . ." policies

10. Achievement of minimum requirements (satisficing)

11. Median efficient joint action

12. Concession along efficiency frontier

13. Split the difference in action space *or* outcome space
    – one step *or* a sequence of steps

14. Weighted average in action space *or* outcome space
    – one step *or* a sequence of steps

15. Alternating leader-follower
    – in action space *or* outcome space

16. Leadership principle
    – in action space *or* outcome space

17. Aggressive follower principle
    – in action space *or* outcome space

18. GRIT (reciprocated tension-reducing actions, a sequence of)
    – in action space *or* outcome space

19. Incremax (maximizing in each of a series of small improvement steps) in action space
    – with split the difference
    – with weighted average
    – with alternating leader-follower
    – with GRIT
    – with minimum information

Table 8.7 *A partial list of quantitative conflict management procedures* (cont.)*

---

20. Incremax in outcome space
    - with split the difference
    - with weighted average
    - with alternating leader-follower
    - with GRIT

21. Decremax (maximizing in each of a series of small concession steps) in action space
    - with split the difference
    - with weighted average
    - with alternating leader-follower
    - with GRIT

22. Decremax in outcome space
    - with split the difference
    - with weighted average
    - with alternating leader-follower
    - with GRIT

23. Equidistant movement in action space
    - regarding improvement
    - regarding concession

24. Last offer arbitration (with incentive to think of others)

25. Hierarchical programming (relaxed or not)

26. Zeuthen concession (least to lose goes first)

27. Method of determining group priorities (Saaty)

---

*Procedures 2–8 may or may not involve weights to be assigned to the relevant item of each participant.

Some other CMPs were mentioned in connection with actual past and current international conflicts. These, too, can be found in table 8.7: GRIT (category 18), incremax (category 19), and the method of determining group priorities (category 27). The reader is referred to Isard and Smith (1982) for a fuller discussion of table 8.7 procedures. Included there, as well, is a list and discussion of some rather technical quantitative CMPs not noted in table 8.7 which sophisticated negotiators and mediators, each accompanied by a team of experts, might find occasion to use.

Many other properties of quantitative CMPs have not been considered in this text: costs involved, stability and uniqueness of the outcome, extent to which there is trust building and avoidance of bluffing, and so forth. Discussion of these properties is available elsewhere (Isard and Smith, 1982). However, it is important to recognize that no quantitative CMP exists that has all the properties one would desire in treating any given complex conflict situation. In choosing one quantitative CMP rather than another there is a trade-off in terms of properties.

8.6   Inventing a conflict management procedure with reference to the Middle East

Having set forth a great many ideas in this and preceding chapters it behooves us to try to design or invent a procedure for an actual major conflict. A current and most difficult one is the Arab–Israeli confrontation in the Middle East, where through his shuttle diplomacy U.S. Secretary of State Baker was successful in arranging for Arab-Israeli conferences (January, 1992). Attaining more peaceful arrangements among the violent-prone bodies involved is of course considered desirable by the Bush administration for securing voter support for the Republicans and administration policies in forthcoming elections. What is involved in this U.S. effort is the use of a traditional old-line CMP where a strong power exerts pressures (subtle and indirect) upon feuding parties through promises of major financial assistance and political support. Many knowledgeable persons view the prospects for success of this U.S. effort as dim. We are motivated, therefore, to explore the development of an alternative procedure– one that *does not* depend on pressures by a major power and significant side payments.

Based on the ideas already presented, can a possible conflict management procedure be designed for this seemingly intractable situation? Without detailed information and specific expertise one can, of course, speak only in general terms.

First, recognize the new Arab regard for U.S. Next, in an attempt at invention we would use a variant of the SNT (Single Negotiations Text) approach–designed by Roger Fisher, a distinguished Harvard Professor of Law, and used in the Camp David talks. This approach, briefly touched upon in chapter 4 in section 4.5 and characterized later as a practical variant of the veto-incremax procedure, would involve presenting initially and in detail the text of an agreement (treaty or other conflict-reducing statement). This should be a reasonable (not outlandishly unacceptable) statement but one that is inefficient from the standpoint of rigorous economics. It would need to be skillfully constructed to contain several clauses (elements), for at least one of which it would be possible for each participant in a first round of negotiations to propose a revision that in his eyes would constitute a major improvement for himself and have a negligible (if any) negative effect on any other participant. This sets the stage for each party (assuming that the participants are inclined to examine the text or have been persuaded to do so) to participate in the agreement-making process by proposing a desirable revision. Perhaps the text can be designed to contain two, or even three such clauses (elements) for each party. In this way, two or three rounds of negotiations may be possible, additional trust may be built up, vested interest in reaching an agreement further enhanced, and as a consequence participants made more willing to compromise over other clauses relating to more conflictual issues. Even if they were not able to reach compromise on these other issues, progress will have already been achieved by agreement on the previous elements; and perhaps the formal acceptance of whatever agreement has been reached so far can be accompanied by a friendly statement of agreement to continue to disagree, and intent to reconsider their positions on these other issues at a later time.

The key to all of this is to construct an initial text for negotiations. Ideally, this text would be developed from a set of cost-benefit balance sheets, one for each participant. The initial balance sheet for each participant should indicate how the situation proposed by the text compares with the current situation and its projection into the future. It should be at least as good. Knowing what each participant wants most and anticipating their revisions, experts would construct a second balance sheet for each participant which would indicate how these revisions offer significant improvement for that participant. The second balance sheet for each participant would not initially be revealed; it would be available for use by the mediator to point up the revision possible for a participant should he fail to identify it himself.

Where, further, each participant is expected to propose a second revision for himself, a third balance sheet for each would be required projecting the improvement over the first revision after all the participants' second revisions were realized. And so on for the possibility of three rounds of revisions–all without significant negative effect on any other participant.

The Middle East conflict, as already indicated, is exceedingly complex, involving more than a handful of major participants and a number of minor. It is much more complex than the protracted Northern Ireland conflict, where fewer participants are involved and where points of contention are more identifiable. And even here progress is still to be scored. Exceedingly optimistic individuals have imagined a grand compromise over all the Middle East issues at once–true of both Carter and Bush (in his vision of a new world order). However, most informed analysts and informed scholars assign a miniscule probability to any such possibility. (Recall, however, that in early 1990 scholars considered the unification of East and West . Germany within the year equally unlikely.) It would seem better to propose taking a number of small steps–pursuing a Kissinger-style attack–a series of carefully developed SNTs on less conflictual issues for consideration by only two or three parties at a time.

To begin, there might be proposed an SNT for consideration by a Jordanian–Palestinian representation and an Israeli representative. The water resource problem, one which is not identified as primary at this moment (June 1991), will become more and more critical with time, particularly with continued migration into Israel from the Soviet Union. Historically significant progress was made by Jordan and Israel on the Maqaran dam project proposal (indefinitely postponed, however, because Syria and Jordan were unable to agree). Is there not an opportunity to draw up an SNT (limited to Israel, Jordan and Palestinians) setting forth an arrangement on water resource development of both the East and the West Banks built into which is the opportunity for each party to propose an improvement significant for itself, but having at most negligible negative effects on the other. More ambitiously, some agreement on this issue might be accompanied by a proposal to grant Palestinians limited autonomy with regard to the Gaza Strip *alone* combined with significant financial assistance from the U.S. and other possible donors to each party, to ease some of Jordan's internal problems and facilitate immigration absorption by Israel. Or it might be accompanied by the establishment of an international (perhaps U.N.) water authority with limited powers combined with significant financial assistance.

Some of the specific clauses of the SNT would need to be based on fundamental studies. Solid economic analyses using econometric, input–output, or other models would be essential for identifying the economic (GNP, employment, and other) gains that would ensue from one or more water resource development improvement steps that might be proposed. Second, a Saaty priorities-determining procedure (or other) involving experts on Israel, Jordan, and the Palestinians would be needed to identify items to be incorporated in the initial SNT which could lead to proposals for change by each party that would constitute major improvement for that party–that is, would have a relative importance of 7 or 9 when compared to the item as stated in the initial SNT. To illustrate, the thought has been advanced that the Gaza Strip is of considerably less strategic military importance to Israel than the West Bank. If the issue of Palestinian autonomy were skillfully disaggregated into Palestinian autonomy of the West Bank and Palestinian autonomy of the Gaza Strip, the clause "no Palestinian autonomy of the Gaza Strip....." might be a clause for which the Jordan–Palestinian representation may be expected to propose a change that would have relative importance of 9–provided the "....." altered part of the clause was so stated as to be judged by the experts to be perceived by the Israeli representation as having a small (if not negligible) negative effect on Israel.

Another place where a SNT approach(Egypt included) can be used is with regard to a less tractable issue of land exchange. Given the much smaller importance to Israel of the Gaza Strip when compared with the West Bank, and given the fact that the Negev desert is of little economic significance to Egypt, could there not be clauses in an initial SNT that state "no cession of the Gaza Strip territory to a Palestinian authority ....," "no cession of Negev desert area to Israel ....," in addition to other clauses relating to no financial assistance from U.S. or other developed country to Egypt and Israel on projects they urgently need. These clauses, along with tactful suggestions by a third party, might lead to (1) Israel's willingness to accept exchange of the Negev desert area for the Gaza Strip so that *on net* Israel would not be yielding on the issue of "land for peace" while gaining significant financial assistance for needed projects, (2) Egypt's willingness to yield infertile land for truly major financial assistance for needed projects, and (3) Palestinian willingness to be satisfied with the Gaza Strip under conditions judged by experts to be most likely to be acceptable by both Israel and the Palestinians. Supplementing the required SNT, Saaty-type analysis would be needed to identify the conditions judged to be most acceptable, as well as projections of the multiplier and income effects of the projects proposed for financial assistance.

8.7   Summary

A quantitative CMP is often needed to supplement a qualitative CMP, that is, a meaningful set of negotiation or mediation principles. In this chapter a few simple quantitative CMPs were outlined briefly, and then the priorities–determining procedure was discussed at considerable length–a procedure that requires participants to be able to state only relative values. This procedure, involving pairwise comparisons by participants, has been used to provide basic understanding of and insights into the Northern Ireland conflict.

There is a wide range of relevant properties that a quantitative CMP may possess. For each of the key characteristics of a conflict situation one may be able to identify one or more CMPs having the properties that most fully match all the requirements of these key characteristics. This process has been illustrated with regard to several actual conflict situations. However, it may be necessary to invent new CMPs when none of the known CMPs meets the requirements.

Simulations of the process of negotiations and mediation using a CMP with appropriate properties for the given situation may help parties who are at an impasse understand that desirable outcomes are obtainable. In that sense the simulations can help them recognize that the issue(s) causing an existing impasse is trivial or, if not, at least encourage them to move forward beyond the present stalemate.

Finally, we indicated how one might go about designing a conflict management procedure using a combination of the SNT and priorities-determining approaches and models, with the Middle East conflict as the case in point.

Appendix to Chapter 8: Supporting Pairwise Comparison Tables

This appendix provides the matrices of pairwise comparisons from which some of the magnitudes used in illustrating the priorities-determining procedure in section 8.2 were derived.

Table 8.3a. *Pairwise comparisons by Outgroup Moderates of their objectives*

	Share power	Economic well-being	Weights
Share power	1	2/3	0.4
Economic well-being	3/2	1	0.6

Table 8.5a. *Ingroup's objective: have good relations*

	Minor reform	Major reform	Democracy	Weights
Minor reform	1	1/5	9/5	0.153
Major reform	5	1	9	0.763
Democracy	5/9	1/9	1	0.084

Table 8.5b. *Ingroup's objective: share power*

	Minor reform	Major reform	Democracy	Weights
Minor reform	1	1/6	3/2	0.130
Major reform	6	1	9	0.783
Democracy	2/3	1/9	1	0.087

Table 8.5c. *Outgroup Moderates' objective: economic well being*

	Minor reform	Major reform	Democracy	Weights
Minor reform	1	1/6	1/8	0.067
Major reform	6	1	6/8	0.400
Democracy	8	8/6	1	0.533

Table 8.5d. *Outgroup Moderates' objective: share power*

	Minor reform	Major reform	Democracy	Weights
Minor reform	1	1/7	1/9	0.060
Major reform	7	1	7/9	0.410
Democracy	9	9/7	1	0.530

Table 8.5e. *Outgroup Radicals' objective: drive the ingroup out of power*

	Minor reform	Major reform	Democracy	Weights
Minor reform	1	1/2	1/9	0.083
Major reform	2	1	2/9	0.167
Democracy	9	9/2	1	0.750

Table 8.5f. *Outgroup Radicals' objective: redistribute land and other wealth*

	Minor reform	Major reform	Democracy	Weights
Minor reform	1	1	1/9	0.091
Major reform	1	1	1/9	0.091
Democracy	9	9	1	0.818

References

Alexander, J. and T. L. Saaty (1977a) "The Forward and Backward Processes of Conflict Analysis," *Behavioral Science* 22 (March): 87–98.

_____. (1977b) "Stability Analysis of the Forward-Backward Process," *Behavioral Science* 22 (November): 375–82.

Isard, Walter (1988) *Arms Races, Arms Control and Conflict Analysis: Contributions from Peace Science and Peace Economics.* New York: Cambridge University Press, Chaps. 10 and 11.

Isard, W. and Christine Smith (1982) *Conflict Analysis and Practical Conflict Management Procedures.* Cambridge, MA: Ballinger. Reprinted (1989) Department of City and Regional Planning, Cornell University, Ithaca, NY, Chap. 9.

Saaty, T. L. (1972) *An Eigenvalue Allocation Model for Prioritization and Planning.* Energy Management and Policy Center, University of Pennsylvania.

_____. (1977) "A Scaling Method for Priorities in Hierarchical Structures," *Journal of Mathematical Psychology* 15 (3, June): 234–81.

_____. (1988) *Decision Making for Leaders.* Pittsburgh: RWS Publications.

9   Synthesis

9.1   Introduction

At the risk of considerable repetition, it is desirable now to pull together the concepts and findings presented in this book. As one way of doing this, the next section starts with the materials of chapter 2 and then adds, in order, the materials in each succeeding chapter. An alternative fusion is attempted in section 9.3, which starts with the simple concept of rational economic man and adds on behavioral factors and qualifications set forth by various disciplines to come close to reality. Some general and concluding remarks on synthesis and its relevance will be covered in the final section.

9.2   A Synthesis by Order of Chapters

Chapter 2 deals with culture and cultural background. To obtain a handle on this subject and its relevance to conflict and conflict management, we explored several definitions of culture. We saw how religious, ideological, and other cultural differences lead to wars, how nationalism is a force that generates conflict, how the US and THEM categories develop and are associated with misperceptions and misguided emotionalism, how humankind is endowed with both competitive and cooperative drives, and how individual decisions, such as to mobilize troops or declare war, are conditioned by, and at the same time condition, culture. Figure 9.1 links cultural background, depicted by one circle: CULTURE (Religious and Ideological Differences, Nationalism, and US/THEM), to *CONFLICT ANALYSIS* and *PEACE MAKING* (pictured in a rectangle at the bottom).

In Chapter 3, individual and group behavior are examined from the perspective of an economist and a game theorist. There we dealt with the influence of attitude on a behaving unit's actions and outcomes, inquiring into decision making and strategy when two or more actors are involved in a conflict situation where each one's outcome depends not only on his own action but also on the others' actions. We illustrated with the Prisoner's Dilemma and Chicken games. Finally, we examined action–reaction processes leading to escalation and deescalation, referring to the U.S.–Soviet Cold War and its demise.

Figure 9.1

Adding an understanding of interdependent decision making from economic and game-theoretic standpoints (highlighted in a second circle in figure 9.2) to anthropological-sociological studies of culture permits improved CONFLICT ANALYSIS and PEACE MAKING (the rectangle at the bottom of figure 9.2). To see this, focus on attitude.

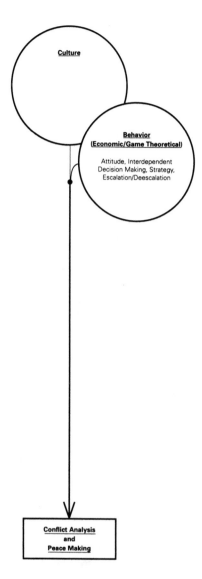

Figure 9.2

As indicated in chapter 3, an individual's or group's attitude is a key factor in any choice of action. This is so whether the behaving unit faces several possible states of the environment (say, what the weather may be tomorrow when planning an offensive move) or several possible actions on the part of a protagonist. A hesitant, submissive person will act differently than a bold, aggressive type. When it comes to the question of whether a nation pressing on its scarce resources can afford to escalate an arms race, someone who calculates expected payoff (such as Gorbachev) opts for a different policy than the 100 percent optimist (such as Ayatollah Khomeini). Thus, the timing and extent of any unilateral effort toward arms reduction is affected. But attitude itself is in large part a product of socialization, education, and other group processes within a culture as well as life experiences–factors discussed in chapter 2.

Continuing to build, chapter 4 discusses individual and group BEHAVIOR as presented in COGNITIVE SCIENCE, PSYCHO-LOGICAL, and SOCIOLOGICAL STUDIES. See figure 9.3, where a circle so headed joins the other two circles connecting to CONFLICT ANALYSIS and PEACE MAKING. We saw how scripts, schema, lessons of history, and other mental representations guide behavior. Learning takes place through experience when a behaving unit compares realized outcome with prior expectations, and via the search for solutions to new problems, with or without use of Artificial Intelligence methods. We also saw how an actor's behavior is influenced by the political subculture with which he is associated and how crisis conditions limit his perceptions of options and bring into play his decision–making pathologies.

President Kennedy's decision to become involved in Vietnam in 1961 illustrates very well the synthesis of the factors covered in chapters 2–4. Conflict had arisen between Communist forces (North Vietnam) and the non-Communists in power in South Vietnam, the latter having been supported by the French during their withdrawal. President Kennedy, a product of U.S. culture, was imbued with the spirit of democracy and was a strong proponent of civil rights. Harvard educated, he had a distinguished military record and was well informed on political and international matters. He was ener-getic and healthy and a vigorous participant in competitive sports. All these factors shaped his personality and contributed to his cautiously optimistic attitude and strong desire to make rational decisions–rational from the standpoint of preserving and promoting the U.S. cultural ideal of democracy. To help him reach wise decisions, given his definition of rationality, he surrounded himself with a team of outstanding Harvard scholars.

When Kennedy and his team faced the issue of Vietnam involve-ment, they were thinking clearly in terms of a payoff matrix, although

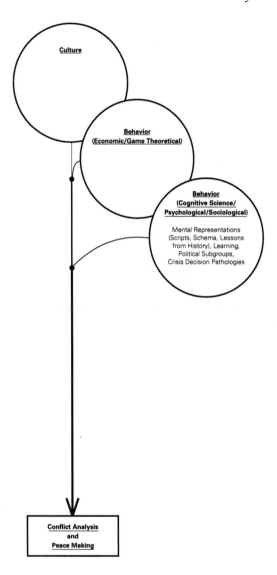

Figure 9.3

they may not have constructed one explicitly. In fact, a member of Kennedy's staff, Carl Kaysen, a young Professor of Economics at Harvard, had written some years earlier an excellent and insightful review article of the long-awaited classic tome on *Game Theory,* written by one of the world's leading mathematicians, John von Neumann, and his colleague, the Princeton University Economics Professor, Oskar Morgenstern. Doubtless, Kennedy considered several options regarding the kind and level of support to offer the South Vietnamese, one policy being "do nothing." But, despite their wisdom and knowledge, Kennedy and his team knew little about what outcomes (the numbers in the cells of the payoff matrix) to expect under different assumptions as to actions of the other involved parties. They could only make intelligent guesses. As already noted in chapter 4, the highly likely outcome of a "do nothing" (nonintervention) policy was predicted to be a takeover of South Vietnam by Communist forces which in turn would lead to a series of Communist takeovers of other Southeast Asia countries. This domino theory, based upon the consequences of the appeasement of Hitler at Munich, was for Kennedy and at least some of his advisors a lesson of history which was used to fill in an outcome cell of the payoff matrix implicit or explicit in their thinking.

Leaders have always used lessons of history, implicitly or explicitly, to enter magnitudes in outcome cells of payoff matrices where actions (along the rows) are strongly conditioned by culture and life experiences, and where attitudes determine the strategies chosen to achieve goals set by culture and personality. Lessons of history and other mental representations also often influence expectations of protagonists' actions (often headings of the columns in a payoff matrix). But learning, too, influences such expectations. People have learned from the Vietnam and Afghanistan experiences, and the domino theory is no longer in vogue. Expectations have been drastically changed regarding outcomes of a Big Power's military intervention in a little-developed, predominantly rural and small village country capable of protracted guerrilla warfare. And learning from problem solving also enters into the calculation of outcomes. Often leaders search for new ways of handling problems. They set up commissions to identify possible new strategies when no known policy can be effective. Clearly, at the time of writing (June 1991), Gorbachev and his team of economists (including fine quantitative–mathematical applied researchers) had been searching for new policies that would yield a satisfactory outcome–a transition to some kind of market economy–having in mind several possible supporting actions on the part of Germany and other industrialized nations.

Forces stemming from a leader's political subculture also inject themselves into almost every major international conflict. As already noted, in the recent (January 1, 1991) U.S.–Iraq confrontation in the Gulf, two sharply contrasting cultures were involved–the Arab and the U.S. (or highly industrialized nations in general). But aside from their basic cultural differences, the two leaders exhibited behavior typical of their political subcultures and life experiences. Influenced by the norms and goals of his conservative Republican subculture, President Bush considered it in the national interest to protect the U.S. oil supply so essential for healthy profit-making economic enterprise, in his mind the mainstay of American well-being. Thus, after the invasion of Kuwait by Iraq, he immediately sent U.S. troops to the Gulf to prevent Iraq from taking over Saudi Arabia's oil refining capacity, characterizing Saddam Hussein as another Hitler. He justified this act by appealing to the principle of liberty, to maintain political support at home and abroad. In turn, Saddam Hussein (who ironically had received considerable assistance from Bush in his war with Iran), coming from an impoverished Arab village, had been conspiring to overthrow the ruling regimes (the Ingroups) of several Arabic nations, seeking power through control of oil. Like a great many of his Arab associates, he did not view takeovers as being unprincipled nor casualties as a serious deterrent to warfare. To gain support from Arab masses in all countries Saddam Hussein coupled his actions with a call for the cessation of Israel's military administration of the Gaza Strip and the West Bank and a return of these areas to Arab rule, and pointed to the Israeli takeover of these Arab lands as being no different from his own annexation of Kuwait. He emphasized Bush's inconsistent policy of supporting Israel despite her aggression and paying only scant attention (if any) to the many other infringements of liberty elsewhere in the world.

Iraq's invasion of Kuwait was a major crisis, and to protect U.S. oil supply Bush felt the need to act. He could have waited for United Nations' discussions and recommendations, but these are known to be often long, painstaking, and indecisive. In his mind and those of his associates was the standard conservative Republican response: "send troops immediately to protect the nation's economic interests." Bush did choose that action, which immediately afterwards most of the world judged to be right. Clearly he had no time to conduct vigilant information processing. At that stage his action was accep- table to the general public. However, in his further buildup of forces and continued insistence (January 1, 1991) on "no negotiations until Iraq troops are withdrawn from Kuwait," he may be said to have been subject to the usual decision-making pathologies under stress. Unlike others, such as President Mitterand of France, he was insensitive to Islamic cultural norms and Arab nationalism and failed to recognize that he himself, like so many of his associates and the U.S. public in general, suffered from cultural blindness.

In any conflict situation, there is at least one key figure. He may be a multinational business executive, a union leader, a charismatic religious personage, a political leader. Deeper analysis of the behavior of this participant in international conflict situations is provided in chapter 5, treating elements embedded in politics.

A political leader's policies, especially in a highly urban-industrialized nation, must always be sensitive to the diverse needs and desires of his constituents, even when they comprise a relatively homogeneous population. To stay in power, he and his party need to develop a policy on each of any number of issues. His primary focus may be on matters of national security and growth of GNP, but he also needs to address other issues such as industrial productivity, crime and drug use, education, health, and quality of the environment. In effect, a leader must operate in a many-dimensional policy space. Moreover, since new problems arise and old ones change, he must constantly shift his policies to maintain voter support. His attention and perspective are thus confined to the short run–to the immediate future. Furthermore, since his election also depends on financial support from members of his own political subculture, lobbies, and certain other interest groups, he is unduly responsive to their pressures. Hence, given the typical heat of competition from others seeking election, rarely does a political leader allow his behavior to be guided by ideals and long-run goals. Given his cultural heritage, life experiences, mental representations, creative reasoning, and other factors influencing his perceptions of possible actions, almost invariably proposals which he may consider rational or best from the standpoint of achieving long-run, idealistic goals are discarded in favor of a set that is politically feasible.

Moreover, in a nation with a multi-party political system, usually a political leader cannot garner enough votes to win an election on his own. His alternative is to be in a winning coalition that forms the government. To hold together such a coalition, to prevent its dissolution or fragmentation, he must compromise still more.

Even further compromise is required when the leader joins leaders of other nations to form a set of allies concerned with military matters, such as NATO or some organization to attack critical world problems, as will undoubtedly eventuate to develop world environmental policy. In these matters, a leader's clout will often depend on his nation's military and economic strength, which in turn is ultimately influenced by the resources the nation commands, regional divisions within his nation, and other geographic factors.

And when changing technology impacts on the significance of resources, on the relevance of long-standing boundaries, on inter-regional ties, and on other geographic and economic factors, thus permitting cultural differences to come to the fore with consequent regional conflict, the leader will need to act to contain the threat to what may have been a carefully honed coalition.

Chapter 5 thus adds another dimension to our understanding of a political leader's behavior, always within a geographic and regional setting. This is incorporated in figure 9.4 where the circle headed POLITICS: GEOGRAPHY/REGIONAL SCIENCE connects three previous circles to augment the knowledge set leading to the rectangle designated CONFLICT ANALYSIS and PEACE MAKING.

Finally, a political leader usually wants to have a good political argument to support his proposals and/or his actions. As grounds for his claim of "rightness" of his policies, he often needs data. The most reliable sources of much of the data required are models that have been validated by previous experience and accumulated knowledge and that find wide acceptance in the academic community.

Chapter 6 devotes itself to models. Models can generate data on outcomes of different actions or scenarios, for example, an increase in military expenditures coupled with an increase in taxes. Outcomes may relate to Gross National Product, consumption and investment (from econometric models), or employment in specific industries (from input–output models). A leader, of course, has some latitude in what model to use in any instance; and is likely to choose the specific one which will project an outcome that best supports his policies.

Models are also useful to scholars and experts who write about and testify to the desirability and wisdom of different policies. And in many democratic societies, it is the responsibility of a political leader to project outcomes with the use of an acceptable model. These policies then must be approved by a legislative branch or some other authority. This is a further constraint. President Bush was elected on a "no increase in taxes" platform–a position he defended vehemently and declared inviolable–yet in the face of congressional opposition he

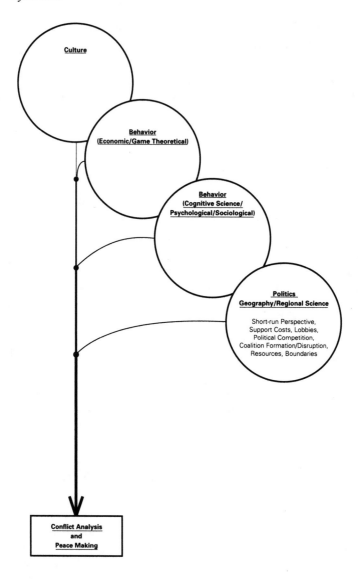

Figure 9.4

was forced to accept a budget involving a tax increase and a lower allocation of funds for Star Wars than he implicitly called for in his campaign.

In figure 9.5 the circle titled MODELS connects to the lines from the other circles, indicating that the use of models can affect a

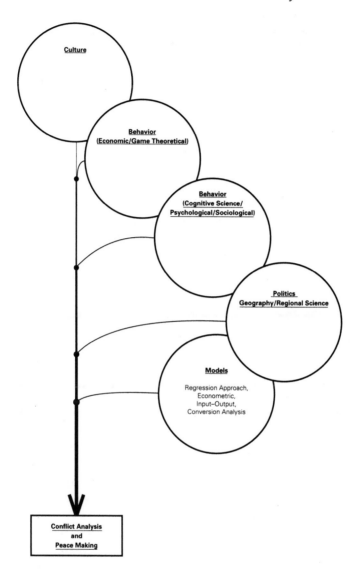

Figure 9.5

behaving unit's choice of action either by helping him to identify a most desirable (rational) one or by expanding or restricting the set of feasible policies (the rows of a payoff matrix).

Hitherto we have examined factors affecting the behavior of the individual and group, the group being, say, an ethnic community, a political subculture, or even a nation. Particular attention has been paid to the political leader. In his role as an individual *per se*, his behavior reflects such influences as his biological makeup and life experiences. In his role as a representative of a group within a society, his behavior reflects group behavior and the influence of such factors as the group's conservatism and decision-making pathologies. In his role as representative of a country, his behavior reflects such factors as its nationalism and its attitude toward civil rights.

In chapters 7 and 8 we confront the age-old problem of conflict and conflict management, and here we introduce additional factors affecting a political leader's behavior when he (or someone representing him) is in the position of a negotiator. We also are motivated to consider how he *should* behave, and how his behavior *should* or can be modified to reach a settlement.

A simple case illustrates how the subject matter of chapters 7 and 8 can be added to the synthesis of prior materials. Two political leaders are at odds over a major issue: division of a territory, possession of an oil field, fishing rights, control of environmental pollution, trade policy, or some other. Each wants to avoid war. Each also wants to avoid a deadlock (tantamount to the joint action "do nothing") since this may preclude significant economic gains from trade in products in which each specializes.

Possibly these two leaders could be persuaded to submit to arbitration, but unfortunately, an effective international arbitration mechanism does not exist. The United Nations, International Court, and other multinational organizations help solve conflicts but have no power to arbitrate. Hence, the two adversaries must try to negotiate a settlement, or call in a mediator or other third party to help them reach an agreement.

Although it is usually highly desirable that participants know the significant aspects of a conflict when seeking a settlement, often this is not the case. (This is not to deny that sometimes conflicts can be resolved in situations where participants are ill-informed and full knowledge might stand in the way.) Accordingly, we presented a list of conflict situation characteristics that may possibly be key, beginning with cultural characteristics and ending with those of individual participants. No one can cope with the entire list let alone the many other characteristics which experts in specialized fields undoubtedly would add. However, a list of this sort can be extremely useful to a negotiator for making certain that he is aware of all possible key characteristics. In accord with the discussion of previous chapters, he should check for key characteristics stemming from his opponent's culture, his political subculture, personality, mental representations, and decision-making pathologies under crisis conditions, the politics in which he is immersed (competition from others, coalition potentialities, pressures from lobbyists), and so forth.

Problems, of course, arise when participants differ as to what characteristics are key. This happens because of their own different cultural backgrounds, life experiences, personalities, and mental representations. This then makes it highly desirable for a third party to intervene–to point out these differences and suggest ways of circumventing them.

Next, each participant typically falls back on a set of guidelines, rules, standards, or other principles to follow during negotiations. Most likely he is not fully aware of all the principles that have been used in the past or that scholars may recommend. The list and discussion of principles in Chapter 7 may be useful for enlarging the set he draws upon and thus may facilitate successful negotiations.

When a mediator is brought in, he, too, should check the list of characteristics to ensure that he is recognizing all that are key, given his perspective, and to enhance his understanding of the conflict situation. He, too, will follow a set of mediation principles based on his past experience and knowledge; perhaps awareness of a broader list as presented herein will lead him to employ a more effective set and facilitate a settlement.

Chapter 7 illustrates how several principles of negotiation and mediation have been used in the past, and refers to sets of these principles as qualitative conflict management procedures. Recent decades have seen tremendous advances in collection and processing of data, in the development of new quantitative concepts, and in models that make data "talk." We explored the realm of quantitative conflict management procedures, all but the very simplest of these having been developed only recently. We discussed a priorities-determining method in some detail and illustrated its relevance to the decades-old Northern Ireland conflict. We ended with the observation that often quantitative conflict management procedures, when skillfully combined with qualitative ones, can enable greater progress in settling issues than can qualitative ones alone–and, it is hoped, will help lead to settlement of protracted regional conflicts such as those which rack the Middle East. We speculated with the invention of one.

Figure 9.6 sets the material of chapters 7 and 8 in a circle headed CONFLICT MANAGEMENT PROCEDURES, and a line connects this circle to those from the circles in previous figures.

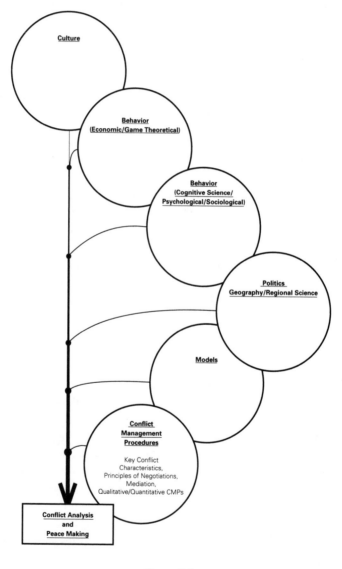

Figure 9.6

This completes a first type of synthesis of the materials covered in this book. Again, note that proper negotiation and mediation requires not only knowledge of all conflict situation characteristics that may be key; but also awareness of some of the relationships discussed.

Observe again that the discussion has focused primarily on a specific conflict situation involving two political leaders. The synthesis, however, can easily be developed further to handle any number of different conflicts involving individuals, ethnic groups, communities, regions within countries, nations, and world regions.

Finally, one should recognize that the conflict settlement itself (or failure to settle), the procedures used, the negotiations that have taken place, all feed back into the system and in turn affect the underlying cultures, political subcultures, mental representations of groups and individuals, and so forth. This is all part of the dynamics of any system and the interactions of its behaving units. In figure 9.7 feedback effects are shown as dashed lines extending from the CONFLICT ANALYSIS and PEACE MAKING rectangle to every circle.

9.3 An Alternative synthesis starting with rational man

Some may prefer an overview from a different perspective with a different core. Start with a simple entrepreneur assumed to behave as a rational economic man. He considers several input–output (production) plans for his firm. He takes as given the price of his output and the costs of his inputs (labor, raw materials, power, etc.). He has in mind selling a fixed amount of output in a particular market. For each input–output plan, he calculates the revenue from selling his output and the costs of his inputs, and chooses that plan which maximizes his profit (revenue less costs).

Suppose he is a more sophisticated profit maximizer, aware that costs (for instance, price of oil) may fluctuate widely. He then will assign probabilities, however crude, to several different sets of costs, and choose the plan that maximizes *expected* profit, (*expected* revenue less *expected* cost). Rational behavior can also be assumed for behaving units other than economic man–an archeologist who selects those digging sites that maximize the probability of a find, a medical researcher who chooses a direction that will maximize the probability of hitting upon a cure for a disease, and many others, including the

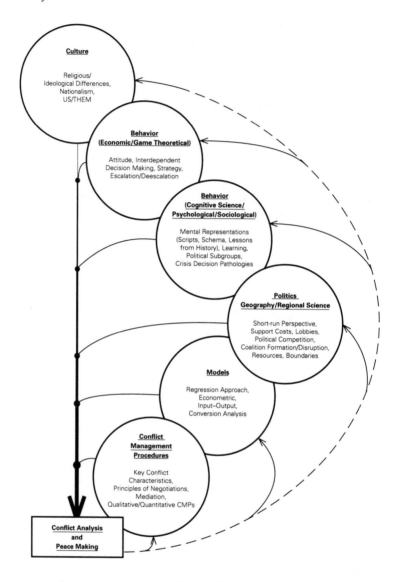

Figure 9.7

political leader who decides on a platform and associated arguments that will maximize the probability of his being elected to office.

Like that of economic man and other behaving units, political man's rationality is bounded. It is constrained by his world view, in turn influenced by his mental representations (maps, scripts, schemas, accepted lessons of history, learned behavior, and so forth), and is a product also of his biological makeup and his life experiences. He perceives neither all possible plans or actions, his own or others', nor all possible states of the environment that may materialize, nor all possible outcomes.

Bounded rationality is associated with attitude. When a man perceives that several states of affairs (including actions of others) are possible, his choice of what he views as rational action depends on the specific objective determined by his attitude. If he is conservative and risk-averse, he will choose a strategy he thinks will lead to the best outcome he can count on no matter what happens–for example, a platform and political argument (which correspond to a set of inputs by an economic entrepreneur) that will surely pull in 51 percent of the vote (corresponding to the entrepreneur's output), no matter what state of affairs materializes–rather than a strategy that will very likely result in a significant victory but also has a small chance of ending in defeat. If he is a calculating person he will assign probabilities to the various possible states of affairs that his "boundedness" allows him to perceive and opt for the strategy that maximizes the expected extent of his victory (his election plus control of Congress via election of his party's nominees for senators and representatives). (Recall that the expected extent of victory is an average of possible outcomes, including defeat, weighted by their probabilities.) However, the probabilities that he assigns to possible outcomes necessarily are subjective and may be way off the mark.

To obtain the required vote, the political leader must gear his policies and/or platform (as well as his commitments, promises, patronage, and outright money payments) to the needs and desires of voters, often clustered. Like the economic entrepreneur, to achieve any desired output (say, a 95 percent chance of victory), he is motivated to minimize the cost of inputs. As conditions change, he shifts his position in policy space to continue to minimize these costs–the cost of holding on to votes at any cluster falling as he moves closer to the set of policies most preferred by that cluster. As already indicated, he may be swayed by interest groups or lobbies offering large financial support (allowing him to use media and other means to convince the voters of the desirability of his proposed policies). Or his resources may only be sufficient for him to aspire to be a member of a winning coalition, thereby to reap expected gains that exceed expected costs of being forced to deviate from his most preferred position and to accept a compromise one–that is, if the round-by-round and often unpredictable process of coalition formation and disruption leads to an incumbency that includes himself. (Gorbachev's skillful shifts from the left to the right in early 1991 [with his former close ally Yeltsin turning into his arch enemy] and then from the right to the center in April of that year [with Yeltsin again his ally] illustrates well the highly unstable character of coalitions and the ways of compromise politics.)

As noted in the previous section, it is helpful (and sometimes required in an advanced democratic system) for a political leader to use a proven model to generate data that support the claims for his policies. This and associated points are discussed in the previous section.

Once again, we must consider still other factors already mentioned that influence the leader's behavior. Here, let us elaborate on only one that affects his choice of strategy, his world view, his perspective, and even his personality–the political subculture from which he springs. He may be a member of an Ingroup that has long been in power, complacent in its belief in manifest destiny, whose behavior is precedent-oriented, opting to maintain existing ties, and, like cybernetic man, to be guided by rules that have gradually emerged from learning experiences of generations of a dominant ruling class. Any revolutionary movement by a large subjugated class is apt to be characterized as an "Evil Insurrection," to be wiped out immediately by armed force. Any interference with ownership of wealth and its continuing acquisition by members of the Ingroup is likely to be termed "Communistic" and not to be tolerated. Such accumulation is thought to be a stimulant to investment, the backbone of a growing economy. The Ingroup's beliefs may be influenced by past geopolitical thinking and exaggerate the military capability of the hostile nation that commands the heartland. It may advocate a military buildup, a Star Wars program, among others, being not much concerned with the possible dire consequences of an arms race, perhaps arguing that arms escalation bolsters the economy and keeps people gainfully employed.

A political leader coming from this Ingroup has internalized its attitudes and has a propensity to behave in accordance with its perspective, especially when the phenomenon of group think is strong, and when self-appointed guardians monitor the thinking of group members. Ex-President Reagan and President Bush come from such an Ingroup; their attitudes and behavior have been consistent with its views.

Whereas a political subculture has its own unique views which affect the *political* behavior of its members, its social, economic, religious, and other cultural characteristics have much in common with other political subgroups in the society. In Israel, for example, members of the Likud and Labor parties have sharply differing political outlooks; yet members of both political subgroups share a common religion, a common history and language, and a yearning for a secure homeland. Such cultural characteristics also affect the attitudes and behavioral patterns of political leaders. A person reared in an Islamic culture may engage with religious fervor in what has been designated a "Holy War," fully convinced that if killed on the battlefield he will be warmly embraced in heaven. A political leader may have been taught from childhood to be tough, unrelenting, and compassionless with no conception of what it means to "turn the other cheek," indoctrinated with an eye-for-an-eye and a tooth-for-a-tooth mentality. Or he may have been raised as a Seventh-Day Adventist, believing that man is predestined to be on earth for a short time only, so why assign first priority to long-run environmental degradation problems?

Nationalism, and increasingly today regionalism, is one of the most important determinants of a political leader's behavior, a basic contributor to current-day problems. The US–THEM categorization that so frequently emerges during conflict situations may make him culturally blind, may cause him to think of his adversary as the epitome of evil–and at the same time, of course, his opponent is often just as blind.

Once in a while a leader with keener vision comes along. Though he may be impelled to wage war out of loyalty to his own people, he may well recognize that doing so will constitute disloyalty to the broader community of mankind. Recall how at the onset of the Civil War in the United States General Robert E. Lee reluctantly offered his services to the defense of his native state, Virginia, which had voted to secede over the issue of slavery–even though he was a disbeliever in slavery and secession, was devoted to the Union, had strong feelings of loyalty and duty as a citizen of the United States, and had morally rejected war as a means of resolving political conflict.

We may then find the political leaders of two nations coming together to negotiate, often through a mediator, as did President

Ayab and Prime Minister Shastri. Both wishing to arrive at a settlement, or at least save face, how do they go about this process? Or one leader, at the top of his nation, may be in conflict with a second representing a region within that nation seeking autonomy.

In any event, the two leaders will have to consider how to negotiate (or the called-in mediator may deliberate on how to mediate). Having very different outlooks and negotiating principles stemming from opposite life experiences and from different cultures and political subcultures, they may be unsuccessful in their negotiations and one of them may even declare war. Preferably, the protagonists will agree to mediation and a third party may come forth, offer his good services, and be accepted as a mediator. He may point out that a number of key issues are not being addressed. He may enlighten leaders on the nature of the conflict, broaden their perspective, explain to each protagonist the other's sensitivity, show them that some of their negotiation principles are inconsistent and stand in the way of settlement, make available to them a much broader range of principles, and relate instances where certain principles have proved effective in resolving a conflict similar to theirs.

Asymmetry with regard to principles used initially by the negotiators may not be the only factor obstructing settlement. Asymmetry in analytical ability, ability to think strategically, to envision possible states of the environment, to cope with a number of possible options, to exert influence, to issue threats, to make promises and offer contingent rewards (side payments) and punishments, may exist. Asymmetry may also exist in bargaining power due to the context of the conflict situation, in particular the extent to which heterogeneity exists among strong organizations and interest groups with different perspectives and preferences and demands in internal bargaining–to which each political leader needs to be sensitive in his negotiations.

A mediator called upon to assist in negotiations, if not already aware of these asymmetries, will need to inform himself about them. This is not to deny that an unsophisticated but warm and friendly, good-hearted person may not be the most effective mediator. He may be the one whom the protagonists come to trust, each confident that he is impartial and does not support the other's objective. This mediator's relatively simple proposals set forth in an open, good-hearted manner may generate enough confidence and goodwill to have them accepted by the protagonists who recognize that more complicated settlements involve long drawn out and costly deliberations likely to yield, at most, only negligibly better outcomes.

But returning to the typical sophisticated mediator, besides enhancing his own understanding of the conflict and what motivates each side, he needs to decide what principles of mediation to use, as well as how to approach each negotiator–whether to hold preworkshops, workshops, or roundtable discussions, very direct person-to-person exchanges of proposals, or some other form of interaction, or, for that matter, any at all. The participants, after all, may not recognize each other's legitimate existence; or they already may have created a pattern of interaction which has failed miserably, so that any further attempt at face-to-face exchange would constitute a major hurdle.

The mediator now needs to select a qualitative CMP, and, given his particular mediation skills, decide whether to complement it with a quantitative CMP. He must bear in mind the context of the conflict situation–that is, long-standing boundaries and historical background, current relations between the parties, the political world linkages of these leaders' nations, international tensions, domestic politics and regionalism in each leader's country, economic dissimilarities, and so forth, as well as the particular issues involved.

A mediator may decide not to use quantitative tools. On the other hand, he may find a quantitative CMP that suits his particular skills and fits in with the set of mediation principles (qualitative CMP) he wants to use. He may find that this combination addresses the needs imposed by the key characteristics of the conflict situation. Or he may find that no existing quantitative CMP has the properties that he can combine effectively with the qualitative CMP he has chosen.

If he considers it essential to use a quantitative CMP, he must therefore search for a satisfactory variant of an existing one or invent one–and perhaps using an econometric model or other equally sophisticated tool, enter his compromise policy as a scenario and project its outcome in order to convince the protagonists that they both will gain significantly if they adopt his proposal.

We need not repeat other materials covered in chapter 8. But we do need to point out that any mediation experience results in learning, whether or not the mediation is successful. If it is successful wholly or in part, the mediator's judgment as to the relevance of the procedure will be confirmed. If mediation is unsuccessful, the mediator will have to reevaluate the appropriateness of his approach. Each negotiator will have learned about how to approach negotiations, about negotiation principles, about the behavior of protagonists, and so forth. Likewise members of each leader's political subculture who have watched the mediation proceeding will have learned. So will a well-informed public impressed by different aspects of the unfolding series of events. A long and drawn out conflict may come to be regarded as a lesson of history, whether or not the mediation was successful. Unavoidably, this lesson will appear over-simplified in a history book for primary and secondary school children and be embedded in people's minds for generations to come. Such learning will have a feedback effect on culture. After all, a society's cultural norms and practices are based not only on its myths and actual past accomplishments and failures, but also on its present-day achievements and failures, which, of course, are soon relegated to the past. Culture changes slowly, very slowly in the case of religious practices, less so in its economic and political aspects.

As culture changes so do the goals and objectives of its political leaders, the actions they perceive as possible, the actions of leaders in other societies with whom they may come in conflict next time round or with whom they may undertake cooperative endeavors. Their bounded rationality, their mental representations, will no longer be the same. Thus, the circle of interdependence is closed and every-thing affects everything else, as a society and the world system evolve. This takes us back to figure 9.7, and the feedback there depicted.

9.4   Concluding remarks

This chapter has looked at two ways of attempting synthesis, using as a starting point culture and economic man, respectively. There are many other starting points. A sociologist viewing society as a set of social groups might begin with group and intergroup relations. Or he might start with a view of each society as composed of four sub-systems, economic, political, social, and cultural (where cultural is more narrowly defined than it is in this book). Another analyst might begin with the diverse political systems that exist, compare their structure and functioning, and after that consider the behavior of political leaders.

Or still another analyst might begin with physical environment–climate, topography, and resources–how it influences the way people eke out a living (farming, hunting, fishing), and how this in turn influences the social groups that form, the society's religious beliefs, political organization, and so forth, and thus the way its leader behaves in a conflict situation.

Selecting any one starting point automatically introduces bias. Bias comes from using the core concepts, tools, and findings of a particular discipline to treat and elaborate on variables associated with that starting point (for example, costs, revenues, profits, and payoff matrices when the economist starts with rational man and utility). That particular discipline's perspective influences which variables are included next and thus the evolving structure of the synthesis.

No one ideal synthesis incorporating the perspectives of all disciplines is possible. We favor culture and cultural background as the starting point. Cultural forces are the slowest to change, and therefore allow us to see feedback effects better and record them.

In closing, it is important to reiterate certain basic points. At any instant of time when a leader, group, or other behaving unit selects an action, all the factors and forces at play affect that choice both directly and indirectly. Further, change (dynamics) is always taking place. The physical environment (biosphere, climate, weather) is constantly changing and resource endowments are constantly being reevaluated by technological developments. Selection among species through both competition and cooperation is an ongoing process. Likewise actions, one after another, of behaving units in their diverse activities, negotiations, and mediation change the structure of the game and nature of their bargaining. A dynamic process is involved. Perceptions and mental representations change. So do attitudes, perspectives, aspirations, objectives, expectations, options, learning, and dislearning. Concomitantly, social institutions, political organizations, and economic systems are affected. Realistically speaking, the social science disciplines–economics, sociology, anthropology, political science, regional science and geography, psychology and cognitive science, and others–know very little about these dynamic processes. A highly abstract social scientist may be able to conceptualize all the variables involved and their relationships, but will have practically nothing to say about the dynamics of the real world.

But one need not give up in despair. Decisions (including "do-nothing" actions) must always be made, and it is desirable to avoid bad ones. The knowledge we do have, which I have tried to embody in previous chapters and synthesize in this one, and which may be found in the writings of others, is sufficiently comprehensive to help us avoid bad decisions. It may even lead us to right decisions in different conflict and peace-making as well as other situations. This is my hope and motivation for writing this book.

References

Isard, Walter (1988) *Arms Races, Arms Control and Conflict Analysis: Contributions from Peace Science and Peace Economics.* New York: Cambridge University Press, Chap. 12.

Index